# Tourism, Hospitality & Event Management

This book series covers all topics relevant in the tourism, hospitality and event industries. It includes destination management and related aspects of the travel and mobility industries as well as effects from developments in the information and communication technologies. "Tourism, Hospitality & Event Management" embraces books both for professionals and scholars, and explicitly includes undergraduate and advanced texts for students. In this setting the book series reflects the close connection between research, teaching and practice in tourism research and tourism management and the related fields.

More information about this series at http://www.springer.com/series/15444

Alexis Papathanassis • Stavros Katsios •
Nicoleta Ramona Dinu
Editors

# Yellow Tourism

## Crime and Corruption in the Holiday Sector

Springer

*Editors*
Alexis Papathanassis
Cruise Management and eTourism
Bremerhaven University of Applied Sciences
Bremerhaven, Germany

Stavros Katsios
International Economic Relations
Ionian University
Corfu, Greece

Nicoleta Ramona Dinu
Department of Economics
Ovidius University
Constanta, Romania

ISSN 2510-4993 ISSN 2510-5000 (electronic)
Tourism, Hospitality & Event Management
ISBN 978-3-030-06893-6 ISBN 978-3-319-94664-1 (eBook)
https://doi.org/10.1007/978-3-319-94664-1


Softcover re-print of the Hardcover 1st edition 2019


This Springer imprint is published by the registered company Springer Nature Switzerland AG
The registered company address is: Gewerbestrasse 11, 6330 Cham, Switzerland

# Preface

## Tourism Corruption Expressed as a Synthesis of Holiday-Experience Failures

Corruption is as widespread as it is elusive: in terms of defining it, as well as measuring its extent and impact. For a systemic perspective, corruption encompasses mal- and dysfunctional activity domains, preventing the corresponding political, economic or business system from fulfilling its intended purpose. Its roots may well lie in the inability of the reference system to control participant behaviour, and/or the inadequacies of the system itself, which provides incentives for corrupt behaviour (e.g. dysfunctional bureaucracy). In principle, corruption is widely regarded as an inhibitor of economic development and social equity, and as such it needs to be 'fought against'. Indeed, a number of political campaigns and fractions frequently render a 'fight against corruption' a focal part of their agenda, with transparency being the main 'weapon' against it. It is tempting to attribute corruption and its adverse effects to the devious intentions or incompetence of those in power, who either benefit from it or are not competent enough to counteract it. Yet, the systemic character of corruption and its prevalence suggest that this is a simplistic viewpoint.

> A people that elect corrupt politicians, imposters, thieves and traitors are not victims... but accomplices. (G. Orwell)[1]

Systemic corruption can be regarded as constituting a collective phenomenon, visible in daily life through a 'normalised' illegality and even criminality within a system. Although isolated criminal incidents and illegal acts do not automatically indicate widespread corruption, it is their ubiquity and high frequency within a domain that suggest a wider systemic failure. Tax evasion, nepotism, bribery and fraud can occur anywhere and at any time. And they can even remain unpunished. But it is when their occurrence and impunity become 'normality' that corruption is at

[1] Source: https://en.wikiquote.org/wiki/Talk:George_Orwell

play. Alternatively, corruption can act as a corrective mechanism for dysfunctional political and economic systems. To a certain extent, corruption is as old as humankind itself. Regardless, whether corruption can realistically (or even should) be eliminated or not, it is pertinent to understand this phenomenon's origins, nature and implications. Obviously, the first instance of examination would be to highlight recurring incidents of systemic malfunction and common participant misbehaviour in the system. Similar to a medical diagnosis, a 'corruption' disease within a system can be initially identified and observed through measuring and exploring its symptoms. This is the primary focus and ambition of this book.

In the subsequent chapters of this book, we shed light on the extent and nature of corruption in the tourism sector (or system for that matter). Tourism is a globalised business impacting the livelihood of millions of people. The intangibility, internationality and fragmentation of tourism make it susceptible to corruption and render it a highly challenging field of action for national legislators and law enforcement agencies. Novel tourist experiences, interactions with unknown environments and places and a carefree mindset all represent core elements of the holiday experience. Hence, holidays inherently entail a number of dangers for tourists, rendering them vulnerable to crime. Conversely, the anonymity that is combined with the consumerist/hedonistic mentality of many tourists may well lead to irresponsible and even criminal behaviour towards locals and others. With tourism's increasing importance as a strategy for economic development, countering corruption is increasingly becoming a priority.

This book summarises the proceedings of the 1st Yellow Tourism Conference, which took place in Corfu (Greece) from 27 to 29 April 2017. The aim of this inaugural conference was to create an interdisciplinary 'research space' for understanding tourism-related corruption whilst initiating the formation of a corresponding international network of tourism academics and practitioners. The main theme of the conference (and the title of this book) was coined 'Yellow Tourism', borrowing from Dostoevsky's novel *Crime and Punishment* the symbolism of the colour 'yellow' and its association with corruption and decay. Approximately 60 delegates, representing 19 different universities and institutions, attended the conference's three tracks, which were labelled as follows: corruption, corporate social responsibility and destination reputation; corruption and the holiday experience; and tourism corruption, crime, heritage and governance. During the conference, the following themes emerged (Papathanassis et al. 2017):

- *Multi-attribution of tourism corruption:* Corruption in the holiday domain has indeed many facets, beyond its traditional definition (i.e. tax evasion, money laundering, nepotism and bribery). In tourism, corruption is present in the daily holiday experience, and it directly affects the satisfaction, integrity and even safety of the individuals involved in it (e.g. conflict and fraud during holidays, criminal and negligence offences at the expense of tourists, exploitation and mistreatment of service workers, deterioration of heritage, cultural and natural resources and securitisation of tourism).

- *Tourism corruption 2.0:* The proliferation of the Internet and social media represents a new challenge for companies, who have a vested interest to limit the publicity of crime and corruption incidents. The line between reputation management and unethical/corruption practice is rather thin. Victims, as well as non-profit organisations, have now the means to expose malignant practices and exercise pressure on tourism companies. On the other hand, the technological possibilities of online platforms lend themselves to misinformation and public opinion manipulation.
- *Institutional weakness and the tourism system:* Digitalisation and its transparency potential can be seen as an effective, medium-term counter-measure for corruption. Yet, the digitalisation of tourism is dependent on the general level of a country's 'knowledge-based' economic development. This in turn relies on political will, on incentive/constraint structures and on the effectiveness of the overall institutional matrix. Tourism corruption can be perceived as both a symptom and a cause of arrested economic progress.
- *Corruption 'glocality':* Countering corruption in tourism requires awareness at a global level and institutionally led counter-measures at a national/local level. Raising general awareness on the scope and impact of tourism-related corruption whilst supporting and enabling national/local tourism authorities to counteract it is proposed as the most realistic way forward.

The above-mentioned themes are reflected in the contents of this piece of work. Coming to the structural logic and contents of this book, we divided it into three sections. In the first part of the book, the challenges of CSR, tourist safety and security are addressed. Arguably, meeting those challenges is the foundation of satisfying holiday experiences and the backbone of the tourism sector as a whole. Failure to adequately address threats to tourists' personal safety for short-term political and/or business rationale and omitting to responsively counteract when those risks/threats materialise can both be perceived as a form of systemic corruption, which leads to the deterioration of the tourism system as a whole. A simple safety and security incident can escalate into a media crisis, ultimately impacting on demand and arrivals for a destination and leading to its economic demise. Repeated safety and security incidents can become government travel warnings and irreparably damage the reputation and brand of a destination or a tourism segment. In the second part of the book, we look more closely on the economic side of tourism corruption, exploring service-related failures, annoyances and fraud. Whilst those types of incidents do not directly impact on the 'DNA of tourism' (like safety and security do), they are still potentially symptomatic of corruption, incompetence and failures in the governance and management of the tourism system. Over time, such incidents undermine the holiday experience and the livelihood of those depending on it. Finally, the third and last part of the book addresses the governance and management of tourism systems. Here, the role of governmental tourism institutions is examined in terms of setting up the architecture for tourism development and its evolution. To a certain degree, this determines the size and distribution of tourism-related economic impacts and externalities. Weaknesses in tourism governance and planning arguably create the space for corruption and facilitate the deterioration of sociocultural resources. Indicative of this type of deterioration is the current debate on ‘overtourism’ and the corresponding anti-tourism sentiment and demonstrations in a number of established tourism destinations (e.g. Venice, Barcelona, Dubrovnik).

At first glance, the incidents and issues covered in this volume may appear partially unrelated, leading to a fragmentation of the book’s contents. Yet, they are not, as they represent expressions/symptoms of the same cause: a ‘corrupted’ tourism system. Collecting them and classifying those ‘corruption symptoms’, under the term ‘yellow tourism’, is a first step towards defining the phenomenon (‘disease’) and understanding its mechanics. We view this piece of work as a starting point in the exploration of corruption in tourism, and we hope that it will enable and encourage other researchers to shed more light on this ‘dark’ domain of holidays.

Bremerhaven, Germany — Alexis Papathanassis
Corfu, Greece — Stavros Katsios
Constanta, Romania — Nicoleta Ramona Dinu

## Reference

Papathanassis, A., Katsios, S., & Dinu, R. N. (2017). “Yellow Tourism” – Crime & corruption in tourism. *Journal of Tourism Futures*, *3*(2), 200–202.

# Acknowledgements

This book is dedicated to the members and associates of the Yellow Tourism Consortium. It is their openness, enthusiasm and commitment that is enabling us to gradually develop an emerging knowledge base in this 'dark area' of tourism. Particular thanks to the co-authors for their contributions. Moreover, our gratitude goes to the Bremerhaven University of Applied Sciences, the Ionian University and the Ovidius University of Constanta for their support and contribution to this project. Our appreciation also goes to Christian Rauscher and Barbara Bethke from Springer (our publishers) for their patience, professional support and flexibility. Finally, we would like to explicitly mention and thank everyone who helped us, supported and sponsored the 1st Yellow Tourism Conference in Corfu (Greece).

Alexis Papathanassis
Stavros Katsios
Nicoleta Ramona Dinu

# Acknowledgements

# Contents

# Part I
# CSR, Tourist Safety and Security

# ‘Felons of the Seas’: Smoke, Mirrors and Obfuscation

Ross A. Klein

## 1 Introduction

The image projected by the international cruise industry is quite different than the reality they create in their wake. While proudly claiming environmental responsibility, vigilance to ensure passenger safety and security, and that “cruise travel is safer than virtually every other form of travel” (see cruising.org/cruise-vacationer/industry-facts/safety-at-sea), their practices reflect low standards for environmental protection, a disregard for ensuring the safety and security of its passengers (particularly safety from sexual assault and other crimes), and a tendency to blame passengers for incidents of illness outbreaks and other health problems (claiming passengers bring illness on board with them). In addition, the industry tends to misrepresent its product by claiming a cruise is all-inclusive and that the quality of dining and hospitality services are comparable to a five-star hotel or a Michelin-starred restaurant. This chapter looks at industry practices with a view toward looking beyond the smoke, mirrors and obfuscation reflected in advertising and projections in the media.

## 2 Environmental Felons

“We visit some of the most pristine areas of the world and our income depends on them staying that way, so why would we pollute?” That is a common cruise industry response to challenges of its environmental practices. Their question is disarming at first. But it can be turned back on them. Why aren’t they more conscientious in their

R. A. Klein (✉)
School of Social Work, Memorial University of Newfoundland, St. John’s, NL, Canada
e-mail: rklein@mun.ca; ross@cruisejunkie.com

 
A. Papathanassis et al. (eds.), *Yellow Tourism*, Tourism, Hospitality & Event Management, https://doi.org/10.1007/978-3-319-94664-1_1

environmental practices, especially given the increasing presence of cruise ships in environmentally delicate areas such as the Amazon, Antarctica, and the Galapagos Islands? A *London Times* reporter observes: "The more isolated the destination, the more the marketing people seem to love to send their vessels there" (Elliot 2007).

Claims of environmental responsibility contradict a pattern of serious offenses. In 5 years between 1997 and 2002, the North American cruise lines paid almost US$55 million in fines to the US Government and State of Alaska for environmental violations. The U.S. had begun stricter enforcement for pollution offences in 1993 following a number of unsuccessful attempts to have the problem addressed by the state where offending ships were registered. Between 1993 and 1998, 104 ships were charged with offences involving illegal discharges of oil, garbage, and/or hazardous wastes (U.S. GAO 2000). Almost $3 million in fines were levied between 1993 and 1997.

Fines brought unwanted and negative media attention to the cruise industry. At the height, just after U.S. Attorney general Janet Reno chastised Royal Caribbean International (RCI) for using the nation's waters as its dumping ground while promoting itself as an environmentally 'green' company, the International Council of Cruise Lines (ICCL) issued a press release affirming the cruise industry's commitment to maintaining a clean environment and to keeping the oceans clean (ICCL 1999).

Two years later in July 2001, while Carnival Corporation and Norwegian Cruise Line (NCL) were under investigation for a sustained pattern of environmental violations, and immediately after Alaska's Senate cleared the way for final vote on the Alaska Cruise Initiative (setting standards for wastewater discharges into State waters), ICCL released "Cruise Industry Waste Management Practices and Procedures." The standards effectively were the same as what already existed in U.S. law and or international conventions such as MARPOL. They represented a commitment to abide by existing laws and regulations.

Despite being mandatory, violations appeared to have no impact on a cruise line's ICCL membership or status in the organization. Carnival Corporation, for example, was back in federal court within a year of pleading guilty in 2002 to six counts of falsifying records in relation to oil discharges from five ships operated by Carnival Cruise Lines (CCL). It had been summoned in July 2003 after a probation officer reported the company failed to develop, implement and enforce the terms of an environmental compliance program stemming from its 2002 plea agreement. Holland America Line (HAL) reportedly submitted 12 audits containing false, misleading and inaccurate information (Dupont 2003). Carnival Corporation fired the three environmental compliance employees, but did not admit violating its probation. In a settlement signed August 25, 2003 Carnival agreed to hire four additional auditors and to provide additional training for staff (Perez 2003: D1).

The corporation was again under investigation in March 2004 for illegal discharges. HAL, a wholly owned subsidiary of Carnival Corporation, notified U.S. and Netherlands governmental authorities that one of its chief engineers had improperly processed oily bilge water on the *Noordam*. The improper operation began in January 2004 and continued through March 4, 2004. Several months later, in July 2004, HAL was again in the news when its former vice president for environmental compliance pleaded guilty to certifying environmental compliance audits that had never been done (Klein 2005). Despite these offenses, and the Mandatory Cruise Industry Waste Management Practices and Procedures, Carnival Corporation's and HAL's ICCL membership was not jeopardized.

The cruise industry's environmental violations continued sporadically over the years—between 2009 and 2013 the State of Alaska issued 174 Notices of Violation for cruise ships discharging in violation of Alaska Water Quality Standards. Environmental incidents became a focus again after a series of incidents between 2015 and 2017. The most visible included (see www.cruisejunkie.com/envirofines.html):

- September 2015: The Instituto Brasileiro do Meio Ambiente E Dos Recursos Naturais Renováveis (Brazilian Institute of Environment and Renewable Natural Resources—IBAMA) levied a fine of R$2.505 million (US$635,000) against MSC Cruises for dumping garbage bags during a cruise between Madeira Island and the Port of Recife.
- May 2016: *The Mercury* reports Carnival Australia was fined A$15,000 fine after a sample of the *Pacific Jewel*'s fuel showed sulphur levels nearly three times the limit.
- December 2016: *Washington Post* reports Princess Cruises agreed to plead guilty to seven felony charges and pay a $40 million penalty for polluting the ocean with waste and then trying to cover it up. Eight Carnival subsidiaries will be audited for the next 5 years by a court-supervised Environmental Compliance Program. The whistleblower engineer will be paid $1 million.
- January 2017: *Travel Weekly* reports Carnival Corporation settled with the Alaska DEC over allegations Princess Cruises and HAL violated Alaska's standards regulating visible air pollution from marine vessels.
- February 2017: *Seatrade Cruise News* reports RCI and Celebrity settled all claims related to alleged violations of the Alaska Marine Visible Emissions Standards that occurred over an earlier 5-year period on RCI and Celebrity Cruises' ships.
- February 2017: *CBC* reports *Clipper Adventurer*, which ran into a rock shelf in Nunavut, will have to pay nearly $500,000 in environmental costs to the Canadian government after a Federal Court judge ruled they were responsible for the grounding.
- March 2017: *Deeper Blue* reports the cruise ship *MV Caledonian Sky* ran aground onto a coral reef near Kri, off Raja Ampat, Indonesia. The ship freed itself not long after, but left a 20-meter-long cut through the coral reef. Loss is estimated in excess of $2 million.

## 3 Sexual Assaults and Felonious Crimes Onboard

The cruise industry not only promotes itself as safe, it says it is the safest form of commercial transportation. That is a grand claim; one which most passengers believe on its face.

The Morgans (a pseudonym) took a cruise in 2005, never thinking twice about it being unsafe for their 8-year old middle daughter to go back to the family's cabin on her own. Along the way the youngster became confused and asked a crewmember in uniform for assistance. Instead of helping, the male (wearing a cruise line name plate) allegedly took the girl to a dark end of a corridor where he masturbated in front of her. It was subsequently learned the crewmember had previously worked for a different cruise line, which had "do not rehire" marked on his personnel file. But he passed background checks and was hired. The cruise line also failed to notice that the name under which the man had applied for employment was different than the name on his passport.

Laurie Dishman also believed a cruise was safe. She and her best friend in February 2006 chose a cruise to the Mexican Riviera on an RCI ship to celebrate 30 years of friendship and to celebrate Laurie's birthday. But things quickly turned from good to bad when Laurie was raped by a security guard on day 2 of the cruise. The security guard, she learned later, was a janitor "filling in" for security in lounges to check IDs because there were not enough security personnel on board.

The cruise industry would prefer these experiences not be broadcast; when they are made public they are characterized as isolated exceptions or as statistically insignificant. But sexual assaults have been recognized since the early-1990s as a problem on cruise ships. "Cruise ships are as safe an environment as you can find," was what a Carnival Cruise Lines spokesperson said during a court case involving a 14 year old child who was raped in 1989 on Carnival's *Carnivale*. Rape, he said, "happens in houses, offices, hotels, and parking lots" (Adams 1990: 1). In this child's case, the rape occurred onboard in a cleaning closet at 5:30 AM as the ship was returning to Miami from the Bahamas. The janitor was found guilty of the charges and sentenced to 30 years in prison. This was the first time a crewmember on a foreign-flagged cruise ship had been successfully prosecuted because the assault had occurred within U.S. territorial waters.

Sexual assaults on cruise ships gained the media's attention in the late-1990s. In July 1999 CCL disclosed it had received 108 complaints of sexual assaults involving crewmembers in the 5 year period ending August 1998. RCI said it had 58 reported sexual assaults during the same 5-year period. Several months earlier an investigative journalist with the *New York Times*, Douglas Frantz, published an article entitled "On Cruise Ships, Silence Shrouds Crimes" where he describes an alarming range of passenger claims of sexual assault and discusses how they were handled by the cruise lines (see Klein (2008) for brief descriptions of a selection of cases).

With heightened media coverage and interest, four cruise corporations (Carnival, Royal Caribbean, Crystal, and Princess) representing more than 75% of the industry signed a letter of commitment in July 1999. Issued under the auspices of ICCL, they pledged a "zero tolerance policy" for crimes committed onboard ships and established an industry standard requiring allegations of onboard crime be reported to the appropriate law enforcement authorities. For vessels calling on U.S. ports, or crime involving U.S. citizens, this meant the Federal Bureau of Investigation (FBI).

Cruise lines were already expected to report to the U.S. Coast Guard all crimes involving U.S. citizens but it isn't clear this was done. The press release announcing the zero tolerance for crime policy told American passengers they were protected by U.S. laws, that cruise lines were subject to civil liabilities in U.S. courts, and that they were safer on a cruise ship than in urban or rural America—it said the number of reported shore side aggravated sexual assaults was at least 20–50 times greater than the total number of all reported shipboard assaults of any type. This claim was disputed by the industry's own expert in 2006 when he testified that the rate of sexual assault on cruise ships was half the rate of sexual assault on shoreside (see Klein 2007).

The issue took on a renewed interest in the late 2000s as Congress considered the Cruise Vessel Security and Safety Act (CVSSA), introduced in 2008 and becoming law in 2010. By then the proportion of crew-on-passenger sex-related incidents had reduced by as much as one-third while passenger-on-passenger incidents increased (more than doubled). But sexual assaults continued to be a problem, especially on mass market cruise lines. The rate of sexual assault on some lines was 50% higher than on land in Canada (see Klein and Poulston 2011; Klein et al. 2017); 34% of the victims in 1 year were under the age of 18 (Senate Commerce Committee 2013).

## *3.1 Persons Overboard*

It isn't just sexual assaults capturing the interest of the U.S. Congress. Persons overboard led to hearings in 2005 in the U.S. House of Representatives and discussed in subsequent hearings as recent as 2014. To put the problem into perspective: there have been reports of almost 300 persons overboard since 2000; an average of 23 persons annually in the 7 years between 2009 and 2015 (Cruise Junkie 2017). Men are three times more likely than women to go missing overboard; passengers are reported missing three times more often than crew members (Klein 2013). About 11% of incidents are intentional suicides; 9.5% are accidents; and at least three cases were murders (plus a fourth where a body was thrown overboard to hide a murder). There are unsuccessful attempts to dispose of a person or a body by throwing them/it overboard.

Numerous incidents remain a mystery—people who have given no sign of being suicidal, are happy and enjoying the cruise (often with family members along), but go missing. Some of these cases were presented to Congress: Merrian Carver, Annette Mizener, and Hue Pham and Hue Tram, to name a few. Each case raises to the forefront the need for better video coverage of deck areas and for real-time monitoring of video feeds.

Two other issues are raised by persons overboard. One is cost to U.S. taxpayers to search for a missing passenger. In just one case—Michelle Vilborg who went missing 70 miles southwest of Pensacola, Florida on 15 June 2009—the search cost was estimated by the Coast Guard at $813,807. Second is the need for proper detection of persons overboard. The CVSSA requires that "the vessel shall integrate technology that can be used for capturing images of passengers or detecting passengers who have fallen overboard, to the extent that such technology is available" (US Code §3507(a)(1)(D)). The cruise industry had not complied with this requirement by 2018.

### 3.2 Other Crimes

As seen in Table 1, the most common crimes reported on cruise ships are assault, sex related incidents, and theft. Also worth noting are incidents of Assault with Serious Bodily Injury (SBI) and persons overboard, however because persons overboard are not consistently reported to the FBI the actual number is higher. For example, the link from CCL's website to the website of the U.S. Department of Transportation (www.transportation.gov/mission/safety/cruise-line-incident-reports) indicates CCL has reported six persons overboard since 1 January 2010. During the same time period there were reports in the media of 23 persons going overboard from CCL ships. The same level of disparity between incidents and public reporting is found with other onboard crimes.

Table 1 shows CCL, RCI, and Celebrity Cruises with the highest number of thefts. Converting the data to standardised rates shows theft under $10,000 is highest on Celebrity Cruises (85.4 per 100,000), followed closely by Carnival (82.4 per 100,000); RCI's rate is almost half that of the others (43.8 per 100,000).

As with theft, RCI, Celebrity Cruises, and CCL report the largest number of assaults. Standardised rates show the rate of assault on RCI in 2011 was 227 per 100,000, compared to 124 on Celebrity Cruises and 11.8 on Carnival. It is difficult to know whether these differences are an artefact of the cruise line and the passengers it attracts or a reflection of a lower tolerance level for reporting incidents. However, analysis indicates a large portion of the difference between RCI, Celebrity and others lies in a high rate of domestic violence reports. Approximately half of the assaults on RCI in 2011 involved travelling companions.

### 3.3 Shipboard Security

Shipboard security is relevant given limitations in capability given the low-level of training of many security officers. Also, unlike police in a community setting who are objective and disinterested investigators, shipboard security personnel are compromised—they investigate crimes in which their colleagues or employer may be complicit, or involved. They may not be able to act in a disinterested, objective manner, placing the victim above the interests of the organisation providing their pay and continued employment.

Definition of an incident is critically important. There is no mandatory reporting of incidents labelled "unwanted sexual contact" or "sexual contact groping," even though most would be considered sexual assault by the victim and many labelled sexual assault by someone not employed by the cruise line. As an expert witness, I have seen incidents the victim views as rape or sexual assault labelled by cruise ship security as consensual sex ("he said she said") or "sexual contact—groping." Consequently, industry crime statistics are grossly misleading.

**Table 1** Crimes reported by cruise lines to the FBI, 2007/2008 versus 2011[a]

| | Year | Assault | Assault w/SBI | Death | Overboard | Sexual assault and rape | Sexual contact | Sexual-other | Theft | Theft over $10K | Other | Total |
|---|---|---|---|---|---|---|---|---|---|---|---|---|
| Azamara Cruises | 2008 | – | – | – | – | 1 | – | – | 2 | – | – | 3 |
| | 2011 | 1 | – | – | – | – | – | – | 1 | – | – | 2 |
| Carnival Cruise Lines | 2008 | 9 | 5 | 5 | 3 | 40 | 48 | 5 | 73 | 3 | 6 | 197 |
| | 2011 | 9 | 3 | 6 | 1 | 49 | 33 | 2 | 63 | 3 | – | 169 |
| Celebrity Cruises | 2008 | 5 | 1 | – | – | – | 7 | – | 2 | 3 | 1 | 19 |
| | 2011 | 35 | – | 1 | 2 | 4 | 4 | 1 | 24 | 3 | – | 74 |
| Costa Cruises | 2008 | – | – | – | 1 | 1 | – | – | – | – | – | 2 |
| | 2011 | – | – | – | 1 | – | – | – | – | – | – | 1 |
| Disney Cruise Line | 2008 | – | – | – | – | – | – | 1 | 1 | – | – | 2 |
| | 2011 | – | – | – | – | – | – | – | – | 1 | – | 1 |
| Holland America Line | 2008 | 1 | – | – | – | 8 | – | – | 4 | 3 | – | 16 |
| | 2011 | 1 | – | – | 1 | 1 | 1 | – | – | – | – | 4 |
| Norwegian Cruise Line | 2008 | 1 | 2 | 1 | – | 3 | 1 | 1 | – | – | – | 9 |
| | 2011 | 4 | – | 1 | 1 | 5 | 1 | – | – | 1 | – | 13 |
| Princess Cruises | 2008 | 2 | 1 | 1 | – | 2 | 2 | 1 | – | – | – | 9 |
| | 2011 | – | – | – | – | 2 | – | – | – | 1 | – | 3 |
| Seabourn Cruises | 2008 | – | – | – | – | 1 | – | – | – | – | – | 1 |
| | 2011 | – | – | – | – | – | – | – | – | 1 | – | 1 |
| Regent Seven Seas | 2008 | – | – | – | – | – | – | – | – | – | – | – |
| | 2011 | – | – | – | – | 1 | – | – | – | – | – | 1 |
| Royal Caribbean International | 2008 | 96 | 8 | 3 | – | 17 | 19 | – | 7 | 3 | 11 | 164 |
| | 2011[b] | 197 | 2 | 3 | 2 | 27 | 18 | 5 | 38 | 6 | – | 298 |
| Other | 2008 | 1 | – | – | 3 | – | 1 | – | – | – | – | 5 |

(continued)

**Table 1** (continued)

| | Year | Assault | Assault w/SBI | Death | Overboard | Sexual assault and rape | Sexual contact | Sexual-other | Theft | Theft over $10K | Other | Total |
|---|---|---|---|---|---|---|---|---|---|---|---|---|
| Total | 2008 | 115 | 16 | 9 | 7 | 73 | 78 | 7 | 89 | 12 | 18 | 424 |
| | 2011 | 247 | 5 | 11 | 8 | 89 | 57 | 8 | 126 | 16 | – | 567 |

[a]Based on crime reports provided by the FBI in response to a Freedom of Information request by International Cruise Victims Association. The first set of data covered 1 October 2007–30 September 2008. The second set was for 2008. Crime reports to the FBI are voluntary; the industry commitment made in March 2007 is to report to the FBI only crimes against U.S. citizens

[b]Data include five cases disclosed in discovery in a lawsuit that were not included in the FBI data. These include three rapes, one sexual assault, and one case of sexual-other (i.e., indecent exposure)

## 3.4 Other Risks

Cruise ships have other risks, though most pale in comparison to those discussed. Ships have accidents—running aground or colliding with an object or another ship—and some have sunk. While some incidents attract media attention, most remain hidden.

Many accidents such as fires and propulsion problems appear random; others may have greater likelihood on some ships. For example, ships that have sunk in the past decade have been older ships owned by small companies (see www.cruisejunkie.com/Sunk.html). Two cruise ships sank in 2007: Louis Cruises' *Sea Diamond* after running aground off Santorini in April (two passengers perished) and GAP Adventures *Explorer* off Antarctica near the South Shetland Islands after hitting ice and evacuated in the middle of the night.

Both incidents underlined the importance of safety equipment and procedures. Evacuation of *Sea Diamond* was reportedly disorganized and not well facilitated by officers or staff. Abandoning *Explorer* was hampered by lifeboats that didn't easily deploy and engines that wouldn't start, which could have been catastrophic had weather and ice conditions been bad. Relatively new ships also have had their share of problems. Princess Cruises' *Crown Princess* was in service about a month as scores of passengers were injured when the ship listed 24 degrees. The senior watch officer on the bridge had disengaged the automatic steering mode of the vessel's integrated navigation system and took manual control (NTSB 2008). And Hurtigruten's *Fram* was less than a year old when on December 27, 2007 it lost power for 2 hours while on the northern tip of the Antarctic Peninsula and drifted toward a towering wall of ice. The collision bent the railing and a lifeboat was completely crushed.

When restarted, the ship headed for King George Island; the following cruise was cancelled. All ships have accidents and incidents. A comprehensive breakdown presented by Klein (2013) to the U.S. Senate indicated the following between January 2009 and June 2013:

- Cancelations, Itinerary Changes, Missed Port Calls (not weather-related) (N = 271)
- Mechanical Problems, including aground, collisions, fire, power loss (N = 353)
- Deaths on Shore, including dive/scuba, parasailing, snorkeling (N = 37)
- Miscellaneous, including accidents ashore, onboard falls, thefts >$10K, injuries on shore excursions (N = 353)

It is worth keeping in mind CCL's response following the "Poop Cruise" on *Carnival Triumph* in 2013: "[T]he ticket contract makes absolutely no guarantee for safe passage, a seaworthy vessel, adequate and wholesome food, and sanitary and safe living conditions" (Griffin and Bronstein 2013).

# 4 Smoke, Mirrors and Obfuscation

There are other issues worth discussion. These are not felonious, but demonstrate the cruise industry's propensity for misrepresenting its product and its tendency to exploit workers in the interest of maintaining profitability.

## *4.1 Illness Outbreaks*

The complexity and variety of illnesses on cruise ships has shifted over the past three decades. In the 1980s and 1990s outbreaks were commonly caused by food borne bacteria such as Shigella, Salmonella and Escherichia coli. With better food processing and refrigeration, and more careful testing and treatment of drinking water loaded from shore, incidents caused by bacteria have reduced significantly.

The incidence of illness caused by norovirus however has increased significantly. In contrast to four or five norovirus outbreaks between 1999 and 2001, in 2002 the U.S. Centres for Disease Control (CDC) identified 29 illness outbreaks (most caused by norovirus); there were 44 cases of gastrointestinal illness on cruise ships world-wide in 2002. The number of outbreaks since has fluctuated with a high of 54 in 2006 and low of 14 in 2014.[1]

Because outbreaks on cruise ships are highly visible, especially when more than 20% of passengers become ill, norovirus has been nicknamed the "cruise ship virus." The cruise industry claims the label is unfair because the virus is often found in institutional settings. Although this is technically correct, their defence fails to acknowledge that cruise ships are perfect incubators for norovirus and a host of other viruses and bacteria because of the constant socialising within closed spaces.

The cruise industry claims passengers bring norovirus with them. This was first asserted in November 2002 after three successive illness outbreaks sickened more than 400 passengers and 50 crewmembers on HAL's *Amsterdam*. The company's vice president of public relations declared at a press conference, "The ship is not sick. There are sick people getting on the ship" (LaMendola and Steighorst 2002). With large scale illness outbreaks affecting other cruise ships as well, the industry's trade group, International Council of Cruise Lines (ICCL), adopted HAL's defence, and the industry's excuse that "passengers bring it" became common (Klein 2008).

The industry's position implicitly assumes outbreaks are random, but this is not the case. Notably, the frequency of illness outbreaks is related to cruise length; shorter cruises have the lowest rates (Cramer et al. 2006). While it is tempting to conclude that short cruises are safer, this might not be the case. To register as an outbreak, more than 3% of passengers or 2% of crewmembers must report illness; the 3% figure is more easily reached over a longer period of time. Thus, while the

[1] See www.cruisejunkie.com/outbreaks2017.html

rate of outbreak is higher for cruises that are longer, the risk may be greater on a short cruise where the 3% threshold is reached within a very short time.

It may be more enlightening to look for a relationship between illness outbreaks and cruise line or cruise ship. Data reveals Princess Cruises and HAL are disproportionately represented as a percentage of all reported outbreaks, together accounting for 167 cases, or one-third of all illness outbreaks recorded from 2002 through 2014. Both cruise lines have smaller passenger capacity than Carnival Cruise Lines (CCL) and Royal Caribbean International (RCI), but their share of outbreaks is greater (Klein et al. 2017).

Evidence of ship-specific outbreaks further supports the view that illness outbreaks are not entirely random. Within a single cruise line there can be wide difference between ships. For example, HAL has the highest rate of illness outbreaks, but three or four of its ships are disproportionately represented. It is an empirical question as to why these ships have more frequent outbreaks than others (Klein et al. 2017).

Outbreaks reflect how easily norovirus can be transmitted from person to person or via food in a closed environment such as a cruise ship. The continuation of outbreaks on consecutive cruises with new passengers suggest that environmental contamination occurs. Infected crewmembers seem the most likely reservoirs of infection for passengers (MMWR 2002). This view is supported by research finding nearly half of all norovirus outbreaks are linked to ill food-service workers (Widdowson et al. 2005), indicating that even if passengers bring infection on-board, it is the ships that keep it alive, mostly likely through inadequate hand washing and sanitisation processes.

The industry would argue against this conclusion, insisting crewmembers are not a key because of the relatively small number of reported illness among crew compared to passengers. However, those who choose to work at sea may be naturally less susceptible to gastrointestinal upsets, or are simply more stoic. More likely however is that there are strong disincentives against crew members reporting when they are ill (CDC 2002). If they depend on tips, they may work even when they are ill. Some risk losing their job if absent for more than 2 or 3 days and may be pressured to return to work even when unwell. A number of health inspections indicate crew are not removed from work when ill (Cruise Law News 2015). This poses a serious problem for controlling spread of the virus. Not only are ill crewmembers likely to work, but those 'quarantined' in their cabin—a cabin normally shared with other crew members—for 48–72 hours, are likely to return to work when their symptoms ease, but while they are still contagious. The virus can easily be reintroduced and carried over from one cruise to another, especially by kitchen workers, food and beverage servers and those engaged in regular, direct contact with passengers. The problem cannot be addressed until the issue is considered more objectively, without attributing the cause as "passengers bring it with them."

Quarantine practices for passengers are also disincentives to reporting illness, further complicating containment. If passengers report the slightest sense of illness, they risk being quarantined in their room for several days, missing ports. Some keep their illness a secret and continuing with their vacation.

## 4.2 Medical Care and Liability

A cruise ship is surprisingly not required under international maritime law to provide medical services. The only legal requirement is under the Standards of Training, Certification and Watchkeeping for Seafarers (SCTW) Convention, which requires identified crewmembers have various levels of first aid and medical training. Regardless, modern cruise ships maintain an infirmary and almost all have a physician and nurse. These medical professionals work under contract as concessionaires and receive a fee plus commissions on medical services, prescriptions and medical supplies.

There is wide variation in the training and background of medical personnel. Some cruise lines draw their physicians and nurses from the U.K., the U.S., and/or Canada and pay $10,000 or more a month; all are board certified in one of these countries. In contrast, personnel on other cruise lines are drawn from a range of countries, have salaries reportedly as low as $1057 a month, and are not necessarily board certified. A 1999 *New York Times* article reports that only 56% of doctors on CCL's ships had board certification or equivalent certifications, and 85% of the physicians on RCI were board certified (Frantz 1999).

There are cases of malpractice on cruise ships. Passengers may assume they have the same rights and protections as on land, but that is not the case. Even though a physician wears the uniform of a senior-ranked officer, is introduced to passengers on-board as the ship's physician, and like other senior officers may host a dinner table for invited guests, the cruise lines (without exception) say the physician is a private concessionaire and they accept no liability for mistakes made. This was supported by the Florida Supreme Court in February 2007 and the U.S. Supreme Court in October 2007.

Passenger rights when there is medical malpractice was put into flux in November 2014 with a U.S. Court of Appeals for the Eleventh Circuit decision in *Franza vs Royal Caribbean Cruises* (D.C. Docket No. 1:13-cv-20090-JAL; Case 13-13067). In this case a passenger was misdiagnosed and the provision of medical care inordinately delayed, both contributing to the passenger's death. The decision effectively removed a cruise line's ability to claim a physician is an independent concessionaire and that it was therefore not liable for that physician's actions. Instead, the cruise line can now in theory be held liable for medical malpractice (Dickerson and Cohen 2015). The impact of the ruling remains to be seen. Whether a passenger succeeds in suing a cruise line, and under what conditions, remains unclear.

## 4.3 Myth of All-Inclusive

Cruises have historically been marketed as an all-inclusive product. In earlier times this claim wasn't as outrageous as it is today. In the late-1990s, cruise lines introduced "extra tariff" restaurants as an alternative to the traditional dining venues included in the cruise fare. They also created a range of revenue centres (see Klein 2008) and introduced the practice of charging gratuities (more than $70 a week per person) to a passenger's onboard account. The latter replaced the existing system where passengers gave gratuities directly to those who provided service. The result is that the cruise line now determines how much is passed on to the service provider; invariably they receive significantly less than the amount collected by the cruise line.

The key point here is that many cruise ships earn the bulk of their profit from onboard spending—an estimated $60 profit per person per day. Traditionally, the largest sources of profit are bars and restaurants, the casino, and art auctions, however revenue centres proliferated in the 2000s and 2010s. Today revenue is generated from a range of onboard activities such as yoga and fitness classes, self-improvement classes, in-room gambling and pay-per-view TV, premium entertainment (i.e., extra tariff shows), wine-tasting events, and cooking workshops, to name a few (Klein 2008).

Revenue is also generated from onshore. Most cruise ships have shopping programs from which they derive significant income from the onshore stores where their passengers shop. As well, shore excursions sold on board hold back as a commission 50–70% of the amount paid by a passenger. This means a shore excursion provider likely receives less than $25 from the $50 paid by the passenger to the cruise line. The result is a passenger expects a $50 product onshore, but the tour provider can't do that when they receive at best half that amount. The passenger is unlikely to blame the cruise line for the shortfall in product, instead blaming the shore excursion provider and the destination for "ripping them off."

## *4.4 Exploitation of Workers*

Cruise lines take great pride in touting the diversity of their crewmembers. Most passengers assume these crewmembers are treated fairly and are paid a livable wage. A typical onboard labourer works a mandatory 308-hours work month (77 hours a week) and receives as little as US$1.50 an hour; they may work 10 months without a day off. Those in service roles may fare better, depending on the cruise line and the colour of their skin, however because they do not receive gratuities directly the cruise line controls what they are ultimately paid. These crewmembers also have a mandatory 308-hours work month; they may earn as little as US$2 an hour; some may earn as much as US$4.50 an hour.

Aside from the level of income, crewmembers work in a quasi-militaristic structure with a clear hierarchy that places them at the bottom—the darker one's skin colour often means the lower one's status and the absence of opportunity for career development. It is a difficult work environment at best.

An illustration may be helpful. Holland America Line prides itself on Indonesian room stewards and dining room waiters. On a cruise aboard the *Veendam,* I asked a busboy handing out trays at the Lido what it was like working with a surveillance camera on him—there is a camera in the ceiling, like those in casinos, monitoring activity in the Lido. His response was dispassionate and simple: "The Dutchman is always watching." It became clear that the traditional colonial relationship between the Dutch and Indonesians was replicated on these ships. The Indonesian staff was naturally reverent and deferential to the Dutch bosses, not just as their employer but also as the colonial power under which they grew up. This same hierarchy is played out on other ships, often with those in control being White or from countries of the developed world and those under their supervision from countries of the developing world of "global South" (see Klein 2002).

## 5 Summary

As seen, cruise industry practices are at variance with how the industry represents itself and how it wishes to be seen by consumers and others. The issues discussed are not an indictment of the industry, suggesting it should cease to exist. Top the contrary, bringing these into the forefront are hopefully an impetus for the cruise industry to act better; to bring into alliance and coordination with the image it presents its practices and product delivery.

## References

Adams, M. (1990, February 5). Rape case threatens cruise industry image: Girl, 14, says crewman assaulted her. *Miami Herald* (Broward Edition), p. 1.

CDC. (2002, December 12). *Telebriefing transcript: Outbreak of gastrointestinal illness aboard cruise ships*. Atlanta, GA: Centres for Disease Control. Retrieved October 22, 2015, from www.cdc.gov/media/transcripts/t021127.htm

Cramer, E. H., Blanton, C. J., Vaughan, G. H., Bopp, C. A., & Forney, D. L. (2006). Epidemiology of gastroenteritis on cruise ships, 2001–2004. *American Journal of Preventative Medicine, 30* (3), 252–257. https://doi.org/10.1016/j.amepre.2005.10.027

Cruise Junkie. (2017). *Comprehensive list of persons overboard, 1995–2017*. Retrieved September 25, 2017, from www.cruisejunkie.com/Overboard.html

Cruise Law News. (2015). *Jim Walker's Cruise Law News: Breaking news and legal commentary regarding cruise ship passenger and crewmembers around the world*. CDC Press Release for Cruise Industry backfires. Retrieved October 22, 2015, from www.cruiselawnews.com/2014/06/articles/norovirus/cdc-press-release-for-cruise-industry-backfires/

Dickerson, T. A., & Cohen, J. A. (2015, March 3). Medical malpractice on the high seas. *New York Law Journal*. Retrieved March 4, 2015, from www.newyorklawjournal.com/id=1202719354971?keywords=barbetta&publication=New+York+Law+Journal

Dupont, D. K. (2003, July 24). Pollution case haunts Carnival. *Miami Herald*. Retrieved July 24, 2003, from www.miamiherald.com

Elliot, H. (2007, October 18). Cruise ships threaten Seychelles. *The Times*. Retrieved October 19, 2007, from http://travel.timesonline.co.uk/tol/life_and_style/travel/holiday_type/cruises/article2688149.ece

Frantz, D. (1999, October 31). Getting sick on the high seas: a question of accountability. *New York Times*. Retrieved October 22, 2015, from www.nytimes.com/1999/10/31/us/sovereign-islands-special-report-getting-sick-high-seas-question-accountability.html?pagewanted=all

Griffin, D., & Bronstein, S. (2013, December 18). Exclusive: Carnival knew of fire danger before cruise, documents show. *CNN Investigations*. Retrieved September 24, 2017, from www.cnn.com/2013/12/17/travel/carnival-cruise-triumph-problems/index.html

ICCL. (1999, July 27). *Statement of the International Council of Cruise Lines regarding recent environmental settlement*. Retrieved July 31, 1999, from www.iccl.org/press-room/press13.html

Klein, R. A. (2002). *Cruise ship blues: The underside of the cruise industry*. Gabriola Island, BC: New Society.

Klein, R. A. (2005). *Cruise ship squeeze: The new pirates of the seven seas*. Gabriola Island, BC: New Society.

Klein, R. A. (2007, March 27). *Crime against Americans on cruise ships*. Testimony before the Committee on Transportation and Infrastructure, United States House of Representatives, Subcommittee on Coast Guard and Maritime Transportation.

Klein, R. A. (2008). *Paradise lost at sea: Rethinking cruise vacations*. Halifax, NS: Fernwood.

Klein, R. A. (2013, July 24). *Cruise industry oversight: Recent incidents show need for stronger focus on consumer protection*. Testimony before the Senate Committee on Commerce, Science, and Transportation.

Klein, R. A., & Poulson, J. (2011). Sex at sea: Sexual crimes on cruise ships. *Journal of Tourism in Marine Environments, 7*(2), 67–80.

Klein, R. A., Lueck, M., & Poulston, J. (2017). Passengers and risk: Health, wellbeing, and liability. In R. K. Dowling & C. Weeden (Eds.), *Cruise ship tourism* (2nd ed., pp. 106–123). Wallingford: CABI.

LaMendola, B., & Steighorst, T. (2002). Cruise line blames passengers for 3rd viral outbreak on ship. *Sun-Sentinel*. Retrieved November 12, 2002, from http://www.sun-sentinel.com/news/yahoo/sfl-rxship12nov12,0,6638757.story?coll=sfla%2Dnewsaol%2Dheadlines

MMWR. (2002). Outbreaks of gastroenteritis associated with noroviruses on cruise ships – United States 2002. *Morbidity and Mortality Weekly Review, 51*(49), 1112–1115.

NTSB. (2008). *Marine accident report: Heeling accident on M/V Crown Princess, July 18, 2006*. Washington, DC: National Transportation Safety Board (Report #MAR-08-01). Retrieved January 11, 2008, from www.ntsb.gov.Publictn/2008/MAR0801.htm

Perez, E. (2003, August 28). Carnival fires pollution auditors over false compliance reports. *Wall Street Journal*, D1.

Senate Commerce Committee. (2013, July 24). *Cruise ship crime: Consumers have incomplete access to cruise crime data*. Staff report prepared for: Senator John D. Rockefeller IV, Chairman, Senate Committee on Commerce, Science and Technology.

U.S. GAO. (2000). *Marine pollution: Progress made to reduce marine pollution from cruise ships, but important issues remain*. Washington, DC: U.S. General Accounting Office.

Widdowson, M.-A., Sulka, A., Bulens, S. N., Beard, R. S., Chaves, S. S., Hammond, R., & Glass, R. I. (2005). Norovirus and foodborne disease, United States, 1991–2000. *Emerging Infectious Diseases, 11*(1), 95–102.

**Ross A. Klein** is Professor of Social Work and an international authority on the cruise industry and cruise tourism. He has published ten books and monographs, more than four-dozen articles and book chapters, and has testified four times before the US Congress. He is found online at www.cruisejunkie.com.

# 'Missing in (Cruise-) Action': Exploring Missing Passenger Incidents on Board Cruise Ships

**Sandra Wittlinger and Alexis Papathanassis**

## 1 Introduction

"Cruising is an increasingly popular style of vacation enjoyed by millions of people; the cruise industry is currently experiencing worldwide 3.4% annual passenger growth with an estimated 20 million passengers in 2013, with its greatest growth in Australia, New Zealand, and Asia" (Klein 2013). "Never before have I been a part of or seen an industry that is so good at listening and reacting to what its customers want, and this is why we are going to see our industry continue to grow," Cindy D'Aoust CEO of CLIA said in 2016. Moreover, "the cruise industry profited from its image as a safe travel option and generated high revenue and passenger growth last year, according to FVW's annual dossier on the German tour operator market (2017). For the next few years, 85 new cruise ships are commissioned by shipping companies all over the world (Cruise Industry News 2016). With these new generations of 'superliners', it will be possible to accommodate even more passengers, which could cause a number of problems (e.g. MSC Meraviglia which can accommodate 5714 passengers and 2244 crew members). With this exponential growth of the industry, crime rates on cruise ships are already high and are expected to increase, according to the US Department of Transportation. 421 offences were reported to the Federal Bureau of Investigation (FBI) within a single year! This included smaller offences like bodily harm or theft, but half of these offences were classified as constituting serious crimes, like 154 cases of sexual assault (Klein 2012), but also attempted murder, as well as murder on board a cruise vessel. Moreover, this statistic only takes into account ships, which are sailing into US ports, US sea territory or cases involving a US citizen. This is why our paper focuses

S. Wittlinger (✉) · A. Papathanassis
Cruise Tourism Management, Bremerhaven University of Applied Sciences, Bremerhaven, Germany
e-mail: swittlinger@studenten.hs-bremerhaven.de

 
A. Papathanassis et al. (eds.), *Yellow Tourism*, Tourism, Hospitality & Event Management, https://doi.org/10.1007/978-3-319-94664-1_2

on people who were exposed to crime on board, especially overboard cases, as there is a surprisingly high number of missing person cases in this industry. 30% of such overboard cases are mysterious in nature (Klein 2016). However, these mysterious disappearances are just within the known cases. The actual number of overall missing person cases might be much higher. There are no internationally-enforced laws regarding safety and security standards dealing with this matter (W. Gregor, personal communication, June 12, 2017). Still, the Cruise Line International Association (abbr. CLIA) propagates that "there are all these regulations the cruise industry is suffering from, although there aren't any" (R. Klein; W. Gregor, personal communication, 2017).

## 2 Methodology

Before proceeding with outlining the methodology adopted for this piece of research, It needs to be stated that this paper only focuses on persons who went overboard on cruise ships excluding incidents on ferry boats or other occurrences like theft or sexual assault.

### *2.1 Data Collection*

The data/incidents coded and imported in the statistical program PSPP, were mined from various online sources (i.e. http://www.cruisejunkie.com, http://www.cruiselawnews.com, http://www.internationalcruisevictims.com). As the literature on this particular topic is practically non-existent, we opted for a mixed-methods approach. At a first phase, quantitative research on passengers going overboard on cruise vessels was conducted to examine the magnitude and trends of such incidents, followed by qualitative content analysis of expert interviews on the findings.

### *2.2 PSPP Data Sets*

The first data set included 268 incidents, occurring between February 1995 and May 2017, and consisting of:

- 12 accidental falls
- 167 overboards
- 58 missing passengers
- 23 suicides by going overboard
- 5 murders or attempted murders
- 6 cases with no further information published

In addition, other attributes were taken into account, such as: whether it was a crew member or a passenger going overboard, which company and on which ship the incident happened. All available vessel-related data was also added (i.e. gross tonnage, knots, all berth, low berth and number of crew on board) to aid the explorative analysis. Within the second data set, victims' attributes such as: age, gender, location of disappearance, as well as more precise incident codes were collected. Updating the data for completeness, we added five more incidents, occurring in 2015, as well as the incidents reported between May 2017 and mid-July 2017. The latest numbers concluding 274 incidents:

- 12 accidental falls
- 120 overboards
- 49 missing passengers
- 18 suicides by going overboard
- 4 murders or attempted murders
- 5 incidents where there is no information at all (unknown)
- 5 suicides after a casino loss
- 15 intoxication overboards
- 32 cases which were mysterious
- 14 in which the people arguing with their beloved before going overboard.

The third set of data included:

- overall passenger number within a year in the cruise industry
- number of passengers or crew members who went missing each year
- yearly market capacity in total
- number of ships operating each year between 1995 and 2017 if data were available.

Due to an interview with James Walker (personal communication, June 5, 2017), who stated that he sees a correlation between mysterious overboard cases and gender (i.e. victims are mainly young women), we decided to conduct a separate set of data on mysterious disappearance cases between the years 1995 and mid of July 2017. This set of data included 32 cases. The given data was analysed by importing all data-sets in PSPP, and extracting descriptive statistics and conducting bivariate correlation testing and/or one-way ANOVA to discover potential relationships between the different variables.

## 2.3 *Cruise Expert Interviews*

To aid the interpretation of our results, we also conducted semi-structured interviews involving different cruise industry experts that have consistently highlighted and analysed this type of incident. We interviewed:

- Ross A. Klein, Professor at the Memorial University of Newfoundland and expert in crimes on board of cruise ships,
- Jim Walker, a maritime lawyer from Miami, who represents cruise victims in court.
- Wolfgang Gregor, former captain of a cruise ship, manager and author of the book "Der Kreuzfahrtkomplex – Traumschiff oder Alptraum"

Furthermore, and in order to obtain a more balanced view on the matter, we attempted to get in touch with various cruise lines, as well as CLIA; all of which declined the request for an interview or a statement to this topic. The coding process of the semi-structured interviews resulted to 21 axial codes, reflecting four major categories: Life on Board, Jurisdiction, Economics, and Media. All the corresponding open codes, and their allocation are illustrated in the Table 1.

**Table 1** Coding summary

| Axial codes/categories | # of sources | # of codes | Major categories |
|---|---|---|---|
| Overboard | 3 | 41 | Life on board (114) |
| Alcohol misuse | 2 | 15 | |
| Crime | 2 | 14 | |
| Investigation | 3 | 15 | |
| Safety on board | 2 | 15 | |
| Humanity | 1 | 9 | |
| Behaviour on board | 2 | 7 | |
| Safety and security act | 3 | 20 | Jurisdiction (69) |
| Security on board | 3 | 7 | |
| National law | 2 | 15 | |
| International guidelines | 2 | 9 | |
| Flagg countries | 1 | 6 | |
| Law enforcement | 3 | 13 | |
| Profitability | 3 | 16 | Economics (75) |
| Pressure on personell | 2 | 23 | |
| Cronyism | 1 | 7 | |
| Working conditions | 2 | 16 | |
| Growth in cruise market | 2 | 13 | |
| Media involvement | 3 | 6 | Media (29) |
| Disguise | 3 | 16 | |
| Manipulation | 2 | 8 | |

Number of categories comprising each major category in parenthesis

**Table 2** One-way ANOVA missing persons in total, years of cruising

| Years of cruising | Sum of squares | df | Average of quarters | F | sig. |
|---|---|---|---|---|---|
| Between groups | 921.33 | 13 | 70.87 | 7.04 | .003 |
| Within groups | 90.67 | 9 | 10.07 | | |
| Whole | 1012.00 | 22 | | | |

Source: Author's research

# 3 Hypotheses

Fourteen different hypotheses, reflecting the significance of vessel- and victim-related factors were generated and tested. None of the tested factors revealed a statistically significant relationship to missing persons. This leaves us with one remaining explanation for the increasing number of missing cruise passengers:

*During the last years more passengers went missing due to more cruising at the sea.*

Using *One-way ANOVA* analysis with the variables: year and total number of missing persons Table 2 shows a significance level of $p = 0.003$. This association has a high significance level (less than 3%). The *F-test* indicates that the average of the variables is significantly different, as 'F' is with 7.04 higher than 1. As it is shown in the first diagram, there is a constant growth of passenger numbers over the last years.

Barack Obama introduced the Cruise Vessel Safety and Security act in 2010, which became active in January 2014. This act forces cruise lines to report crimes on board of cruise ships involving US Citizens or sailing in US waters. Other crimes concerning non-US-Citizens are actually not reported. This has led us to assume that the actual number of reported incidents is underestimated, as overboard incidents of people from different nations carry a high risk of remaining unreported. Moreover, the media does not presumably publish every single incident, mostly because they may never find out about it. The former CLIA President stated in a confidential meeting between CLIA and the ICV in 2007 "that they will not report any person overboard unless the media already knows about it." (Klein, personal communication 6 June, 2017). Focusing only on overboard cases, there are at least three cases of mysterious disappearances, which cruise lines dismiss as a suicide, without any evidence behind this claims.

It is argued that cruise lines often presume suicide as a reason for disappearance, reaching into their bag of tricks and pulling out a good excuse (Cattarius 2011). In the well-known case of Merrian Carvers, Royal Caribbean stated: "The death of Merrian Carver is a horrible tragedy, but, regrettably, there is very little a cruise line, a resort or a hotel can do to prevent someone from committing suicide" (Anglen 2005).

In the case of George Smith IV, a similar statement was given by Michael Crye, representing the International Council of Cruise Lines (the predecessor to today's Cruise Line International Association, CLIA) "(...) it's difficult if someone chooses to do harm to themselves (. . .)", making this statement "without a shred of evidence justifying such a conclusion" (Walker 2009).

In the case of Amber Malkuch, Holland America Line said, that apparently the woman took her own life (Ducey 2009). Alaska State Troopers spokeswoman Megan Peters informed the press, that the investigations are nowhere near determining the cause of death "and if we haven't been able to make a determination, how can the cruise line who isn't trained?" (Ducey 2009). "Unfortunately, there are no independent police authorities onboard cruise ships to gather the true facts and conduct an objective and timely investigation. Cruise lines investigations are often conducted with the cruise line's reputation and legal interests in mind" (J. Walker, personal communication, June 6, 2017).

For Wolfgang Gregor it is highly questionable that people would attend a cruise vacation only to commit suicide; also due to the fact that death due to drowning is one of the agonizing deaths. Investigations on individual cases uncovered that deaths and missing person cases, especially of young people, are mostly unexplained (2016). "Unfortunately, it also appears that a cruise is a perfect location for a murder, particularly when there are few automatic man-overboard cameras installed on ships, which would document and possibly, deter criminal activity" (J. Walker, personal communication, June 5, 2017). "It's the ideal place to commit a crime, and that is the last message the cruise industry wants to get out." stated Kendall Carver (Yoshino 2007). The disposal of a corpse on a cruise ship is much easier than somewhere else, even more, if one has a cabin with a balcony. Referring to the question if the inhibition-levels regarding capital offences are decreasing, Frank Neubacher, dean of the institute of criminology, university of Cologne, states in the book 'Kreuzfahrtkomplex', that it will help a planning perpetrator, if they become aware of the fact how to get rid of the corpse (Gregor 2016).

A normal city with this level of population would have a police station representing the state's interests. A cruise ship with sometimes more than 6000 passengers and crew members on board has no police station (Cattarius 2011). According to Kendall Carver, entering cruise ships, is most of the time the equivalent of entering a foreign legal framework, as the passengers are exposed to the law enforcement of third world countries. In most cases they do not have any evidence, witnesses, a corpse or traces (Cattarius 2011).

However, these are dreadful examples on how cruise companies may have acted terribly wrong in different situations. Research has shown, that the number of known missing person cases has not increased drastically over the last years, but has steadily increased, in line with total number of persons traveling by cruise ships, as shown in Fig. 1. Nevertheless, it is a safe assumption that there is an even higher number of unknown overboard cases, which is not distinctively different than what is assumed by the cruise experts. Figure 2 shows the exact number of overboard cases from 1995 up to July 2017. As one can see, the swaying numbers are constantly rising, which could be attributed to the rising passenger numbers and the overall cruise capacity growth.

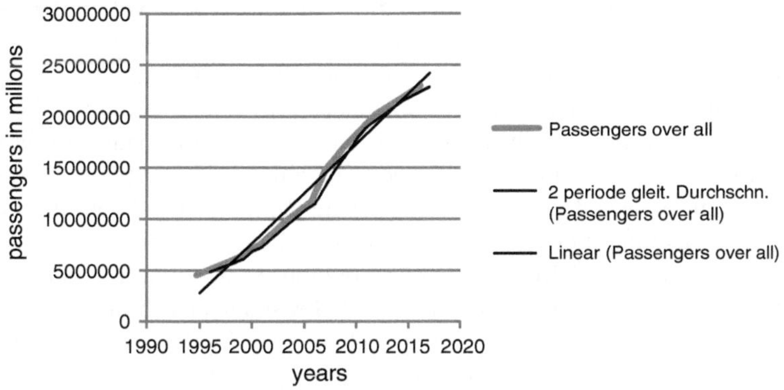


**Fig. 1** Over all passenger numbers. Data source: Cruise Market Watch (http://www.cruisemarketwatch.com/growth)

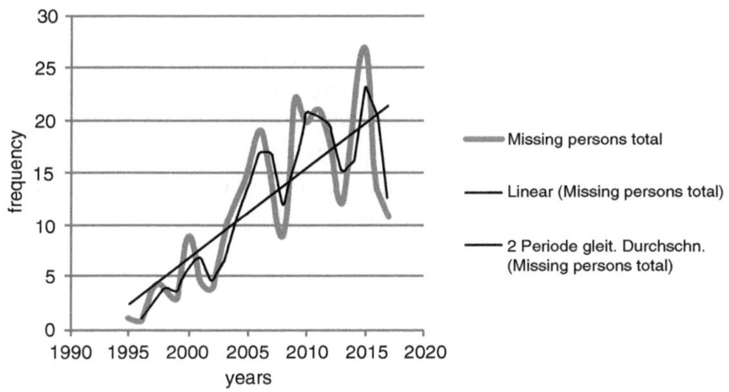


**Fig. 2** Missing persons in total

## 4 Conclusion

During the interviews with the cruise experts, our impression was that there are many more unknown cases of missing persons on board of cruise ships and the reported ones are only a fraction of the total magnitude of this phenomenon. Nevertheless, one also needs to take into account, that all these experts are professional-critics and their activism against cruise industry is associated with financial and/or reputational rewards (A. Papathanassis, personal communication, September 28, 2017). This sheds a critical light to their impartiality and credibility of their statement. However, there are indeed enough known cases, in which the cruise lines acted irresponsibly during or after an overboard case. Unfortunately, no cruise company was willing to give a statement on this sensitive topic. This can also be interpreted as intentional lack-of-transparency from the part of the cruise sector, supporting its critics (A. Papathanassis, personal communication, September 28, 2017).

Our analysis revealed no statistically significant relationship within the 14 different hypotheses, failing to prove that the numbers of persons overboard has disproportionately increased over the last few years, and that other factors like for example ships or the shipping company itself, may indeed play a role. Although the number of missing persons did actually increase, it increased proportionally to the overall number of passengers and the cruise capacity in general. This supports the assumption of a given, expected ratio between cruising capacity and the number missing persons. Of course falling overboard is nothing which occurs on a daily basis, or at least not that we know of. But in case of an overboard situation it is fair to say that one's destiny is sealed. Not only because of the small possibility of detecting a person going overboard (lack of warning technology adoption), but also due to the very long response time of the cruise lines and the procedural formalities they need to follow before attempting a rescue mission.

Cruising will most probably continue to grow within the next few years and the passenger numbers will rise as well. Cruise corporations, especially the larger ones, have the moral obligation to care for their passengers' safety and well-being by implementing improved safety and security measures on board. A pioneer for installing a modern man-overboard-system will be MSC on their new ship MSC Meraviglia. This system will include integrated video surveillance system to optimize security monitoring on board, which will allow for a timely intervention in the unlikely event a person or object falls overboard (Seatrade Cruise News 2017). Regrettably these Systems are not mandatory and not every cruise line is willing to install such a system considering the costs of such systems.

## References


Anglen, R. (2005, November 10). Daughter vanishes while on Alaskan cruise – The strange disappearance of Merrian Carver. *AZ Central*. Retrieved July 9, 2017, from http://archive.azcentral.com/specials/special14/articles/1110vanished.html

Bond, M. (2017, October 9). MSC Cruises deploys man overboard detection technology. *Seatrade Cruise News*. Retrieved from http://www.seatrade-cruise.com/news/news-headlines/msc-cruises-deploys-man-overboard-detection-technology.html

Cattarius, C. (2011, October 16). *Leere Kabinen. Der Tagesspiegel*. Retrieved June 5, 2017, from http://www.tagesspiegel.de/weltspiegel/reise/leere-kabinen/4760856.html

Cruise Industry News. (2016). *Annual Report 2016*. Retrieved April 12, 2017, from https://www.cruiseindustrynews.com/flip/cina16/#p=6

Ducey, L. (2009, August 16). Was cruise ship passenger's death suicide? Investigators don't know. *Seattle Pi*. Retrieved July 9, 2017, from http://www.seattlepi.com/local/article/Was-cruise-ship-passenger-s-death-suicide-1305758.php

FVW Dossier. (2017, January 12). Double-digit growth for German cruise market. *Fvw touristic & business travel*. Retrieved July 11, 2017, from http://www.fvw.com/fvw-dossier-double-digit-growth-for-german-cruise-market/393/167747/11245

Gregor, W. (2016). *Der Kreuzfahrtkomplex – Traumschiff oder Alptraum*. Hamburg: Tredition.

Klein, R. A. (2012, March 1). Oversight of the cruise industry. Testemony before the Committee on Commerce, Science, and Transportation, United States Senat. Retrieved from http://www.cruisejunkie.com/Senate2012.pdf.

Klein, R. A. (2013). Crime at sea: A comparison of crimes on carnival cruises 2007–2011. In A. Papathanassis (Ed.), *Cruise business development: Safety, product design and human capital* (pp. 17–28). New York: Springer.

Klein, R. (2016). Chapter 2, Crime at sea: A comparison of crime on carnival cruise lines, 2007–2011. In *Cruise business development* (p. 22). New York: Springer.

Walker, J. (2009). “Suicide” – One of the Cruise Lines’ Favorite excuse when a passenger disappears at sea. Retrieved July 12, 2017, from https://eproofing.springer.com/books_v2/mainpage.php?token=U5Mqc-U7aOwA4SyTxKPG53Mpy8NI32ATR_uyQTwbeaU

Yoshino, K. (2007, January 20). Cruise industry’s dark waters – What happens at sea stays there as crimes on liners go unresolved. *Los Angeles Times*. Retrieved July 8, 2017, from http://articles.latimes.com/2007/jan/20/business/fi-cruise20

# Crime Control and Tourist Safety: A Case-Study of the Romanian Seashore

**Kamer-Ainur Aivaz, Mariana Juganaru, and Ion Danut Juganaru**

## 1 Introduction

Lately, we have witnessed an increase in the debates and concerns regarding security and safety, in more and more areas (economic, political, social, environmental), at various levels of approach (international, national, regional) and reaction (separately by each state or as the joint effort of several countries). This is, perhaps, a natural reaction, if we consider the changes made in the international conjuncture over the past three to four decades. The media informs us about many different security problems manifested everywhere in the world, which creates the impression that they have become part of our daily lifestyle.

Tourism is one of the economic activities in which the security and safety issues have generated the most diverse consequences. Firstly, the formation of a negative image has led to further mistrust and even the refusal of tourists to visit certain countries/areas/tourist destinations and secondly, the indicators of tourist traffic and the related economic outcomes in some destinations have decreased.

This research refers to an aspect of the many which are included in the concept of "security and safety in tourism", which is *criminality*, and its case study is the tourist destination represented by the towns/resorts on the Romanian Black Sea coast: Constanta, Mamaia, Eforie, Techirghiol, Mangalia, Neptun, Costinesti and Navodari. In the paper, we have included a theoretical part, on interdisciplinary approaches, in order to present the content of the concept of security and safety (for highlighting its role and its importance on tourist activity) and a research model of distribution of the main types of crimes, on years and localities, as working methods using correspondence factor analysis (CFA) and multiple correspondence factor analysis (MCFA).

K.-A. Aivaz (✉) · M. Juganaru · I. D. Juganaru
Faculty of Economic Sciences, University of Ovidius, Constanta, Romania
e-mail: kameraivaz@univ-ovidius.ro

 
A. Papathanassis et al. (eds.), *Yellow Tourism*, Tourism, Hospitality & Event Management, https://doi.org/10.1007/978-3-319-94664-1_3

The database processed in this study ("The situation of criminality in seaside towns") is taken from the data provided by the Constanta County Police Inspectorate and refers to the registration as physical indicators of some crimes within the period 2012–2016. Note that in the Criminal Code of Romania (Law 286/2009) are mentioned and provided penalties for the crime of "theft" (art. 228), "aggravated theft" (Art. 229) and "theft with the intent to use" (Art. 230). In the records of the Constanta County Police Inspectorate, the crimes of "theft" are organised on years, on towns/resorts and on the following ***types***: total vehicle theft; vehicle theft; theft from vehicles; theft from hotel and motel rooms and camping; theft from trading businesses (companies); pickpocketing; other theft crimes. Each of the types of theft mentioned is presented broken down into the following ***categories***: "thefts with unknown author or caught in the act"; "thefts committed during the day or the night"; "thefts committed on the beach/in hotels, motels, camping/in public places/in parks/ in other places". The names of the ***types*** and ***categories*** of thefts belong to the authors of the study and were used to carry out this research, aiming to ensure thecorrelation of the database of the Constanta County Police Inspectorate with the statistical methods used. From the entire database, we have selected three ***types*** of theft: "theft from cars"; "theft from hotel and motel rooms and camping"; "pickpocketing", since we consider them as being more representative considering the topic of this study. We also mention that we selected the towns/resorts where tourist activity takes place. From the administrative point of view, these cities are considered tourist cities: Constanta, Navodari, Eforie, Techirghiol, Costinesti and Mangalia. Mamaia is a resort and it belongs (from the administrative point of view) to Constanta; Eforie Nord and Eforie Sud are resorts of Eforie town, and Neptun is a resort belonging to Mangalia town. We also mention that these records began to be made in this format by the Constanta County Police Inspectorate in 2012.

## 2 Literature Review

In our theoretical literature review, we have noticed that, both in theory and in practice, there is a tendency to use one of the concepts "*security*" or "*safety*" prevailingly, considering that they are synonymous and interchangeable, but in many important documents issued by international bodies/institutions, we find that the expressions are used together—"*security and safety*". For a correct understanding of the analysis performed and presented in our study, we specify that, most of the time, we have used only one of the two concepts, considering that the information is clear and complete. The current concept of "security and safety" is very complex in terms of the forms of manifestation, of the responsibilities, of the ways of preventing and reducing the negative effects.

Safety issues in tourism began to be approached more obviously by different specialists in the 1980s of the past century (Cismaru 2011). Coincidence or not, in the same period became more apparent the tackling of sustainable development issues (tourism being an activity directly concerned by this concept). Thus, it is stated that sustainable development ensures economic and social development and environmental protection at the local, national, regional and global levels, but it also requires changes in mentality, behaviour and structures, which should be able to ensure an effective and viable development (Baddache 2006). At the same time, the power that sustainable development has in terms of the continuous improvement of people's lives and of their relationships, in harmony with the natural environment, is recognised. It is interesting to recall that the World Tourism Organisation (UNWTO) has addressed in the 1980s and 1990s, security issues in tourism as a component of the quality of tourism services (Cismaru 2011). Considering the mentioned points of view, it can be observed that the two concepts, security and sustainable development, have several common features: both include concerns cantered on the "quality" of tourism services and thus of life; they consider changes of mentality, behaviour and structures at local, national, regional and global levels, which act towards increasing security and ensuring sustainable development. The importance of the link between these two concepts has more recently been presented in the paper "Security and Tourism: Concerted Local Policies", developed following the implementation, with the support of the European Commission, of the project EFUS (European Forum for Urban Security). This project was implemented in the period 2013–2015 and combined an exchange of views on security and tourism between seven tourist cities: Alba and Rome (Italy), Barcelona (Spain), Brasov (Romania), Munich (Germany), Saint-Denis (France), ASBL BRAVVO of Brussels (Belgium). The recommendations set forth in this publication (as a result of the activities: local audits, field observations and discussions with experts in tourism and criminology), aim to support the local strategy regarding security in tourism and to contribute to the sustainable development of cities (seen as tourism destinations) and of the quality of life for tourists and locals (www.efus-network.eu).

An increase of the concerns with security in tourism is distinguished with the advent of more specialised papers published in the early 2000s, precisely because of the increasing importance of this issue, given that, in the world, forms of insecurity began being manifested: economic crises, terrorist attacks (the worst being the one of September 11, 2001 in the US), organised crime, pandemics, natural disasters and others. The analysis of security in tourism can be approached on several directions. The first direction refers to the study of security issues that may affect the tourism activity. This includes issues /concerns regarding the classification of security issues, causes/reasons that generate them, their manifestations, the intended targets etc. Another direction is represented by the study of the impact that security issues can have on tourists, the population, businesses and the economic, social, political and natural environment. The last direction refers to the study of the reaction/behaviour of economic agents /operators in tourism (primarily), and of other factors involved in the tourism activity, in terms of the manifestation of security issues on short, medium and long term, in order to devise appropriate security strategies, either to prevent security problems or to reduce the negative image of tourist destinations that have experienced security problems (Cismaru 2011).

Along with the concept of security, in the specialised literature (and in daily talk), the following concepts are also found: insecurity, security issues, threats, risk, crises.

In people's perception, security is generally associated to the measures of ensuring its (which gives them a positive state of mind and helps meet the need for security), while insecurity means the lack of security. Tourism insecurity refers to the threat of production and/or the actual production of events with negative consequences (Cismaru 2011). Any source of insecurity can be addressed as a matter of security.

At EU level, security is treated as an important issue, precisely because it is considered a fundamental right of citizens. At the same time, it is noteworthy that at EU level several initiatives have come forward and various steps have been taken to concretely improve tourism security within the EU (Cismaru 2011). However, if we consider the security issues which have taken place in the European area in the past 2–3 years: the bombings in France (2015 and 2016), Belgium and Germany (2016), the increase in the number of attacks in cities and resorts in Turkey (2015 and 2016) etc., it appears that the efforts which have been made are not enough and it is required to come up with novel approaches. It is advisable, on the one hand, to shape security strategies for the safety and protection of the individual (as a tourist, a member of the local community or an employee in tourism activities) and, on the other hand, to consider security strategies focused on the safety and protection of the tourist destination (through the active involvement of all operators/participants to the tourist activity, in view of increasing the security level of the tourist destination). These steps should be supported by investments in people, security services and security equipment and technologies (Cismaru 2011).

It is obvious that modern man has more free time and, at the same time, that tourism tends to become the main form of leisure activities. Experts believe that currently, in developed countries, tourism occupies about 30% of the spare time (Minciu 2005). Also, it is stated that tourism should be understood and addressed as a "must" for people (Cismaru 2011). These views can be supported if we refer to the benefits of tourism, in terms of meeting the need to spend time pleasantly, while considering the economic, social, political, cultural, technological changes which are specific to the current period. In the context of these approaches and starting from the assertion that marketing is considered the science and art of "meeting the customers' needs" (Kotler and Armstrong 2008, p. 5), we shall discuss some concepts (needs, motivations, tourist behaviour) to understand the current trend of tourism to be manifested as a "necessity".

Thus, it is known that man has many needs, which are constantly changing due to the action of a considerable number of factors, and in approaching the system of needs must be considered the three-dimensional complexity of humans as biological, social and rational beings. A model for the classification and hierarchisation of the system of needs (common in marketing, but also in many other scientific disciplines), is the well-known "pyramid" of A. Maslow. This concept was coined in the study "*A Theory of Human Motivation*" (1943), by the American psychologist Abraham Maslow, who was concerned with deciphering the motivations that are behind human actions. The contribution of Maslow's theory resulted, on the one hand, in the classification of needs into five categories: (1) basic/physiological needs, (2) personal safety/security needs, (3) social/belonging needs, (4) the need for social recognition/esteem/self-esteem/self-confidence and (5) the need for personal growth/self-actualization (Kotler et al. 2010; Datculescu 2006; Dayan and Bouqurel 2008) and, on the other hand, in placing these types of needs in a pyramid on five levels, in the order of the pressure that each category of needs exerts in the direction of meeting the respective need. Despite the proven flaws and the criticisms of specialists, we believe that Maslow's pyramid and currently remains the most widely used model of needs analysis. It is important to also point out that for a correct/full approach of needs it is best to take into account several of their features: the multidimensional nature manifests itself both individually and collectively, their ranking should not be viewed rigidly (in that the order of needs may vary from one person to another and from one stage to another), needs are interdependent, they are interdependent, they do not exclude each other, at any given time they can occur as several needs (sometimes all categories of needs), and any purchase/consumption of a product/service means simultaneously meeting several categories of needs (Datculescu 2006; Juganaru 1998). It can be noticed that on the second level of Maslow's pyramid are located needs related to safety/security. They refer to the physical and mental safety of the individual and can be expressed as the need for order, justice, stability and protection from dangers. If we relate to tourism, we see on the one hand, that all five categories of needs in Maslow's hierarchy are expressed by the individual right from the moment of the search for and selection of a tourist destination and are materialized when he/she becomes a tourist, and on the other hand, that the tourist activities help meet these needs.

Another concept, which is most of the times used for understanding consumer (tourist) behaviour, is *motivation*. It is held that "motivation is the driving force behind any behaviour" (our translation) (Datculescu 2006, p. 53). In the marketing approach, motivation is considered as the totality of reasons, at the basis of which lie the needs of individuals. The reason and motivation form motives that trigger certain reactions and behavioural manifestations in terms of the choice and/or consumption of certain goods and services (Teodorescu 2003). We must also keep in mind that everyone has a multitude of reasons, which they combine differently from one period to another, depending on a range of factors. Identifying and understanding the reasons cannot be considered the only explanation which concern the processes associated to consumer behaviour. Meanwhile, it is estimated that reasons must be regarded as the result of the manifestation of several factors of very diverse nature, which emphasizes the fact that the identification of the reasons is a difficult, but important endeavor in behavioural research (Teodorescu 2003). In tourism, knowing/identifying the reasons for travel allows for the identification of market segments or target groups of tourists grouped by similar characteristics. This can be further useful in the research on supply and demand on the tourist market, in the drafting of strategies aimed at satisfying the demand of the tourist segments with offers of attractive tourist packages.

Current consumer behaviour (particularly that of tourists) is the result of the manifestation of needs and reasons (seen as a system and in motion), but certainly bears the mark of technological progress. We may observe a series of changes that have occurred in consumer behaviour, even if only by reference to what computer technology has meant that after the 2000s, namely: the increase of the degree of equipment with personal computers and mobile phones and of the access to internet connections. This "new wave in technology" gave consumers/tourists new possibilities to get informed, to express themselves and more, to communicate with each other. Networks of social dialogue or social media platforms were formed and expanded rapidly worldwide. Consumers have begun to inform and influence each other more and more, while the influence that companies have (by means of various promotional techniques) over the consumer is decreasing. The development of social media platforms reflects the trend of shifting consumer confidence from the company to other consumers. It can be said that, currently, consumers are also marketers on social media, when they express their opinions and influence/advise other consumers on different offers (Kotler et al. 2010). When referring to the tourism activity, we may observe that the new wave of technology has allowed tourists to connect with each other within communities. For offerors (operators and /or tourist destination), it is important to know how tourists establish links within the community. They can be linked with each other or with a leader or by an idea (Kotler et al. 2010). In these circumstances, social media platforms can be a source of data for qualitative marketing research.

Because of serious events, particularly terrorist attacks, which have intensified in the past years in several countries and which have affected people's safety, including that of tourists, we may observe that many tourists have begun to exhibit a real 'obsession' with security (Popescu 2011). Under these circumstances, some destinations are registering changes (decreases) of the indicators of tourist traffic, precisely because the need for security was, for many tourists, the main motivation or criterion for selecting the destination, and not the aspects related to natural or anthropogenic conditions or attractions, attractive offers, recreational facilities etc. (as was the case a few years ago). In other words, more secure destinations are preferred, to the detriment of the unsafe ones, and the safety/security level provided was capitalized as an element of competitiveness of tourist destinations.

Thus, it is becoming increasingly evident that the safety of tourists is also a component of the demand (based on the need for safety/security), but also an increasingly critical component of tourism offers (manifested at macro- and micro-economic levels). It can be observed that, in the past years, the differentiation of offerors/tourism destinations has been made by tourists (by label/brand and the need for security), but is put into practice by economic operators participating in the tourism activity and by specialised bodies of the state, by providing a secure environment to meet the expectations of tourists. At the same time, in carrying out their activities, companies that work in the tourism/tourism destinations are forced to comply with the imposed regulations (national and international) in terms of providing a level of safety, but more importantly, they need to demonstrate and to communicate that they can ensure the safety and security of tourists. The taking on of security and safety in tourism as a strategy can enhance the quality of services, of the value offered to tourists, which is reflected in the increased competitiveness and business development of the company (Danciu 2013).

## 3 Research Methodology

The Factorial Correspondences Analysis is a descriptive method of multi-diversified data analysis, that characterizes the links between two non-numeric variables (categorical). In our study, these two variables (categories) are: the origin country and the touristic destination.

The method aims to describe the statistical links (the associations) between two non-numeric variables (categorial) and to highlight the similarities and the differences between the statistical units; the method also allows to identify the "responsible" variables for these approaches or oppositions between units, using a factorial axes system which, starting a from a large data table, concentrates the initial information in a graphical form easy to read.

FCA is applied in particular on the data presented in the form of contingency tables, which show the distribution of statistical units, according to the simultaneous variation of two categories of the same variable (in this case the distribution of "the number of non-residents tourists arriving in Romania", by their origin country and touristic destination).

Thus, the factorial correspondences analysis provides a description of the data contained in a contingency table, unravelling the latent structure (hidden) of data, by reducing the dimensionality and the geometric representation (visual) of the categories in a metric space.

The method involves the following steps:

- Calculating the categories profiles of the first variable (meaning the relative frequencies of the "origin country" category), process which shows the distribution of the other variable categories ("touristic destination") among the first variable categories. It has to be calculated, also, the mass of categories of the first variable and their marginal proportions, which indicates their percentage in the total of the observed units. The same process has to be done for the second variable;
- Calculating the distances between points, respectively the distances between the variables categories, represented in the same metric space;
- Looking for a multidimensional space that adjust best the points and the distances between them

Each category of a variable (situated on the row or on the column) can be interpreted as a vector (or a point), in an area with so many dimensions as how many values has its profile (equal to the number of categories of the other variable), of whose coordinates are given by the values of its profile. For example, the "spas" category is represented by a vector with 33 values (corresponding to the 33 countries from which we have non-residents tourists accommodated in the establishments of touristic reception), thus forming theits profile, which is a column profile. The "Germany" category is represented by a vector with 6 values (6 touristic destinations), thus forming its profile, which is a row profile.

The table of row profiles (Table 2), has as components, the partial relative frequencies (fj/i), calculated as the ratio of the partial absolute frequencies (nij) and the marginal frequencies (ni.), for each value of X variable (origin country). A row profile shows, for each xi value (origin country), the percentage of statistical units on the yj values of Y variable (touristic destination). Similarly, the components in the table of column profiles are defined as values (fj/i), calculated as the ratio of the partial absolute frequencies (nij) and the marginal frequencies (ni.), for each yi value of Y variable (touristic destination). A column profile shows, for each yi value, the percentage of statistical units on xi values of X variable (origin country). Each row profile consists of a series of values $f_{j/I}$, where $f_{j/i} = \frac{n_{ij}}{n_{i.}}$ are relative for Y variable, depending on the X = xi level.

A row profile can be represented as a xij point, in the Y variable space. Xij points have a "mass" equal with the marginal frequency fi, showing the proportions of statistical units, which records the xi value of Y variable. The evaluation of the association between two row profiles (of two categories) is carried out by calculating the distance between the points they represent. To calculate the distance between two points, xij and xi,j, the coordinates of xij points have to be transformed, in FCA, after the relation:

$$x'_{ij} = \frac{f_{j/i}}{\sqrt{f_{.j}}}$$

The distance between two categories is usually calculated, as achi-square distance, but, considering the transformation of coordinates, the distance $\chi^2$ becomes an euclidean distance in Rp and is calculated as follows:

$$d^2\left(x'_{ij}, x'_{i'j}\right) = \sum_{j=1}^{p} \frac{1}{f_{.j}} \left(f_{j/i} - f_{j/i'}\right)^2$$

The gravity center of the row profiles cloud (Gi), which defines the average profile, is called centroid and is given by:

$$\text{Gi} = \sum_{i} f_{i.} x'_{ij}$$

One of the objectives of the FCA method is to analyse the links between the two variables, in other words, of the associations between them. Two variables are considered independent if, for each value xi, respectively yj, the distribution of the statistical units by values of Y variable, respectively X variable, is performed in the same proportion.

Testing the hypothesis of independence or dependence between variables involves formulating the following statistical hypotheses: the null hypothesis, H0, which admits that there is an independence between the considered variables (between the statistical variables there are no links) and the alternative hypothesis, H1, which admits dependent variables (there are links between statistical variables). In order to test these hypotheses, $\chi^2$ statistics is used. A calculated value of $\chi^2$ statistics for an assumed risk and v = (m − 1) (p − 1) degrees of freedom, leads to a rejection of H0 hypothesis. It can be considered, in this case, that there are links (associations) between X and Y variables. These associations are described by interpreting FCA results.

The factorial correspondences analysis method involves the representation of a cloud of n Xi points in a vectorial space Rp, the points being the elements of the original data table. Each point has a mass, a ni frequency. In the vectorial space Rp are defined the distance between points, the total inertia (variance) of the cloud of points, the axes of inertia and are identified the responsible points for the formation of factorial axes. The distance between the row profiles, respectively the column profiles represents an approximation of $\chi^2$ distance. Within the correspondences analysis, the concept of variance is defined depending on the distances $\chi^2$ and is called inertia. The variance measures the dispersion of points around the average value. The total inertia measures the dispersion of the categories profile (row or column profiles) around the centroid.

The graph representation of the row and column profiles is realized in an Euclidean space of reduced dimensions, providing a perceptual map, in which categories with similar distributions are placed in close positions, while categories with different distributions are placed in distant positions. This situation shows that the proximity between two row profiles (column profiles) indicates an association between them. The interpretation of this proximity has to be made with caution because a closeness of the points doesn't always show significant linkages. Categories are represented as points in a reduced dimensional space, and the factorial axes are ordered (ranked) in descending order according to their contribution (their importance) in explaining the total variance of the obtained cloud of points.

## 4 Data, Results and Discussion

This study, aimed at analysing the distribution of three crime types (thefts from cars, theft from hotel and motel rooms and camping; pickpocketing) in eight towns/resorts from Constanta county (Constanta, Mamaia, Eforie, Techirghiol, Mangalia, Neptun, Costinesti, Navodari), over a period of five years (2012–2016), is based on the hypothesis that there are differences and similarities in terms of data structure between the year of the crime and the town where it was committed.

The statistical methods used for processing the database, represented by the recordings of "theft" crimes, centralized by Constanta County Police Inspectorate are:

- correspondence factor analysis (CFA), in order to analyse three types of crimes, individually (separately), i.e.: thefts from cars; thefts from hotel and motels rooms and camping; pickpocketing.
- multiple correspondence factor analysis (MCFA)—a multivariate analysis applied to the study of the associations between the three categorical variables (in our study, these are represented by the crime type, year and town/resort where they were committed).

Data processing, testing the indicators' significance and the graphical representations were performed by the SPSS statistical software (Field 2009).

## 4.1 Factorial Analysis of the Crime: "Thefts from Cars"

The data presented in Table 1 represent the absolute values of thefts from cars, recorded in each town/resort, every year and per the entire analysed period. The interpretation of these data enabled us to notice the following aspects:

- over the period under review (i.e. 2012–2016), the crime "theft from cars" decreased (almost by 50%) in 2013, compared to 2012 (from 157 crimes to 88); then, it recorded a significant increase in 2014 (about 3 times, i.e. from 88 crimes to 242), followed by a significant decrease in 2015 (168 thefts) and in 2016 (147 thefts).
- overall (per total towns/resorts), this crime recorded the highest level in 2014. It is noteworthy that the number of crimes decreased from one year to another, between 2014 and 2016, in the context of an increase in the total number of tourists (overall towns/resorts) during the same period, recording 880,381 tourists in 2014, 1,019,233 tourists in 2015 and 1,159,824 tourists in 2016 (according to data provided by NIS-DJS Constanta).
- several towns/resorts (i.e. Eforie, Neptun and Navodari) recorded another development, compared to the general one, the highest percentage in terms of this crime being recorded in 2015 (not 2014, as shown by the overall data).
  - by analysing the total number of the thefts from cars, recorded in each town, between 2012 and 2016, it is revealed that most were committed in Constanta (240) and Mamaia (193) and the fewest—in Techirghiol (4). A high value (130 thefts) was recorded in Eforie (which consists of two resorts, i.e. Eforie North and Eforie South). This value is greater than the sum of the thefts recorded in Mangalia (71) and Neptun (49), given that they have an accommodation capacity greater than Eforie North and Eforie South. The ranking of the towns/resorts analysed by the number of thefts from cars is as follows: Constanta, Mamaia, Eforie, Navodari Mangalia, Neptun, Costinesti and Techirghiol.

The data presented in Table 2 reveal the percentage of thefts from cars, per year, over the entire analysed period, recorded in each town/resort included in our analysis. In other words, Table 2 shows the specificity of each year. By analysing the percentages presented in this table, the following issues are revealed:

- over the period 2012–2016, the highest total percentage is recorded in Constanta (29.9%), Mamaia resort (24.1%) and Eforie (16.2%), representing 70% of all the thefts from cars committed on the Romanian seaside. Given that, administratively,

**Table 1** Correspondence table of thefts from cars, per towns, 2012–2016

Correspondence table

| | Town/resort | | | | | | | | |
|---|---|---|---|---|---|---|---|---|---|
| Year | Constanta | Mamaia | Eforie | Techirghiol | Mangalia | Neptun | Costinesti | Navodari | Active margin |
| 2012 | 45 | 37 | 29 | 0 | 7 | 11 | 7 | 21 | 157 |
| 2013 | 24 | 36 | 13 | 2 | 1 | 6 | 2 | 4 | 88 |
| 2014 | 88 | 61 | 28 | 1 | 25 | 11 | 9 | 19 | 242 |
| 2015 | 36 | 35 | 30 | 1 | 22 | 13 | 6 | 25 | 168 |
| 2016 | 47 | 24 | 30 | 0 | 16 | 8 | 5 | 17 | 147 |
| Active margin | 240 | 193 | 130 | 4 | 71 | 49 | 29 | 86 | 802 |

Source: Authors' own processing by SPSS, data provided by Constanta County Police Inspectorate

**Table 2** Row profiles table for the years when "thefts from cars" were committed, per towns/resorts (Row Profiles output)

| Row profiles | | | | | | | | | |
|---|---|---|---|---|---|---|---|---|---|
| | Town/resort | | | | | | | | |
| Year | Constanta | Mamaia | Eforie | Techirghiol | Mangalia | Neptun | Costinesti | Navodari | Active margin |
| 2012 | 0.287 | 0.236 | 0.185 | 0.000 | 0.045 | 0.070 | 0.045 | 0.134 | 1.000 |
| 2013 | 0.273 | 0.409 | 0.148 | 0.023 | 0.011 | 0.068 | 0.023 | 0.045 | 1.000 |
| 2014 | 0.364 | 0.252 | 0.116 | 0.004 | 0.103 | 0.045 | 0.037 | 0.079 | 1.000 |
| 2015 | 0.214 | 0.208 | 0.179 | 0.006 | 0.131 | 0.077 | 0.036 | 0.149 | 1.000 |
| 2016 | 0.320 | 0.163 | 0.204 | 0.000 | 0.109 | 0.054 | 0.034 | 0.116 | 1.000 |
| Mass | 0.299 | 0.241 | 0.162 | 0.005 | 0.089 | 0.061 | 0.036 | 0.107 | |

Source: Authors' own processing by SPSS

Constanta and Mamaia form one city, one can retain that more than half of these crimes (54%) was committed here;
- in 2013, Mamaia recorded the highest percentage in terms of this crime (40.9%), compared to other towns/resorts, i.e. higher than the one recorded in Constanta (27.3%);
- in 2012, 2014, 2015 and 2016, the highest percentages in terms of thefts from cars were recorded in Constanta;
- in 2016, Eforie recorded (after Constanta) the highest percentage of thefts from cars (20.4%), being situated ahead Mamaia (16.3%);
- no theft from cars was recorded in Techirghiol, in 2012 and 2016.

The data from Table 3 show, for each town/resort, the percentage of thefts from cars, recorded each year, over the analysed period. These data are useful for determining what is specific to each locality. The following aspects are revealed:

- in Constanta, the highest percentage in terms of this crime was recorded in 2014 (36.7%), and the lowest—in 2013 (10%); similar values were recorded in 2012 (18.8%) and 2016 (19.6%).
- in Mamaia, the highest percentage in terms of this crime was recorded in 2014 (31.6%), and the lowest—in 2016 (12.4%); values close to this percentage were recorded in 2012 (19.2%), 2013 (18.7%) and 2015 (18.1%);
- in Eforie, the highest percentage in terms of this crime was recorded in 2015 and 2016 (23.1%); values similar to the maximum ones were recorded in 2012 (22.3%) and 2014 (21.5%); the lowest values were recorded in 2013 (10%);
- in Techirghiol, the highest percentage in terms of this crime was recorded in 2014 and 2013 (50%) and the lowest level—in 2012 and 2016 (0%);
- in Mangalia, the highest percentage in terms of this crime was recorded in 2014 (35.2%); a value close to the maximum one was recorded in 2015 (31%) and the lowest—in 2013 (1.4%);
- in Neptun, the highest percentage in terms of this crime was recorded in 2015 (26.5%); a value close to the maximum one was recorded in 2012 and 2014 (22.4%) and the lowest—in 2013 (12.2%). Typical of this town/resort is that the changes in percentages are not very high, from 1 year to another, as recorded in the other analysed towns/resorts;
- in Costinesti, the highest percentage in terms of this crime was recorded in 2014 (31%), and the lowest—in 2013 (6.9%);
- in Navodari, the highest percentage in terms of this crime was recorded in 2015 (29.1%) and the lowest—in 2013 (4.7%). It is noteworthy that both Costinesti and Navodari present great differences between the percentage recorded in 2013 and the ones recorded in the other years. Also, five towns, i.e. Eforie, Mangalia, Neptun, Costinesti and Navodari, recorded the lowest percentages of thefts from cars in 2013.

In order to apply the correspondence factor analysis, it is necessary to test the hypothesis of the independence between the variables studied, i.e. "town" and

**Table 3** Column profiles table for the towns/resorts where "thefts from cars" were committed, per years (Column Profiles output)

Column profiles

| Year | Town/resort | | | | | | | | |
|---|---|---|---|---|---|---|---|---|---|
| | Constanta | Mamaia | Eforie | Techirghiol | Mangalia | Neptun | Costinesti | Navodari | Mass |
| 2012 | 0.188 | 0.192 | 0.223 | 0.000 | 0.099 | 0.224 | 0.241 | 0.244 | 0.196 |
| 2013 | 0.100 | 0.187 | 0.100 | 0.500 | 0.014 | 0.122 | 0.069 | 0.047 | 0.110 |
| 2014 | 0.367 | 0.316 | 0.215 | 0.250 | 0.352 | 0.224 | 0.310 | 0.221 | 0.302 |
| 2015 | 0.150 | 0.181 | 0.231 | 0.250 | 0.310 | 0.265 | 0.207 | 0.291 | 0.209 |
| 2016 | 0.196 | 0.124 | 0.231 | 0.000 | 0.225 | 0.163 | 0.172 | 0.198 | 0.183 |
| Active margin | 1.000 | 1.000 | 1.000 | 1.000 | 1.000 | 1.000 | 1.000 | 1.000 | |

Source: Authors' own processing by SPSS

"year". This hypothesis is tested based on the calculated statistics $\chi^2$ and it requires the formulation of the following statistical hypotheses:

- The null hypothesis, $H_0$: the hypothesis of independent variables (there is no connection between the town and the year of the crime);
- The alternative hypothesis, $H_1$: the hypothesis of dependent variables (there are connections between the town and the year of the crime).

The value of the test statistics, shown in Table 4, column Chi Square $\chi^2 = 61.376$ is greater than the tabulated value $\chi^2_{0.05;28}$ (for a risk of 0.05 and $v = 28$ freedom degrees), which shows that the hypothesis $H_0$ is rejected. Thus, with a probability of 95%, we can guarantee that, in terms of the crime "theft from cars", there are connections between the variables considered, namely between towns and years. In other words, the towns have retained the same profile (in terms of this crime type), from 1 year to another.

The connections between these variables will be described by the results achieved by the correspondence factor analysis for row-profiles and column-profiles. In factorial analysis, the main objective is to search for the axis that highlights the greatest differences between statistical units, in terms of the recorded variables. For the first factorial axis, we achieved a maximum inertia (spreading) value of the point cloud explained this axis. Basically, the units with the highest spreading are grouped on this axis. Each factorial axis is ranked in the descending order of the dispersions of the individuals' projections on these axes (Pintilescu 2007).

The eigenvalues represent the variance explained by each factorial axis, and the eigenvectors associated to these values define the factorial axes. The highest eigenvalue (column *Inertia*) shows the variance of the first factorial axis, and the sum of the eigenvalues measures the total inertia of the point cloud. The first factorial axis explains 57.7% of the total variance. In the CFA, the number of factorial axes is chosen in accordance with Benzécri's criterion, i.e. we choose those factorial axes that explain together at least 70% of the total variance (Benzecri 1992). In this situation, we need two factorial axes, explaining together 83.6% of total variance. For each category of variables (town/resort and year), we will calculate the coordinates on the factorial axes and the contributions of points to the inertia of an axis.

### 4.1.1 The Coordinates of Points on the two Factorial Axes (Column *Score in Dimension*) Show the Position of Points in the Area Represented by the Axes

By analysing the values of the coordinates of points on the factorial axes, as shown in Table 5, we may highlight the years among which the greatest differences/similarities were recorded in terms of the towns/resorts where the crime "theft from cars" was committed. These points will be located at the ends of the graph when it comes to differences, or they will be located in the same quadrants, within a small distance from each other, as far as similarities are concerned.

**Table 4** Calculated statistics $\chi^2$, eigenvalues and inertia explained by each factorial axis (Summary output)

| Summary | | | | | | | | |
|---|---|---|---|---|---|---|---|---|
| | | | | | Proportion of inertia | | Confidence singular value | |
| | | | | | | | | Correlation |
| Dimension | Singular value | Inertia | Chi square | Sig. | Accounted for | Cumulative | Standard deviation | 2 |
| 1 | 0.210 | 0.044 | | | 0.577 | 0.577 | 0.036 | 0.018 |
| 2 | 0.141 | 0.020 | | | 0.258 | 0.836 | 0.035 | |
| 3 | 0.099 | 0.010 | | | 0.128 | 0.964 | | |
| 4 | 0.052 | 0.003 | | | 0.036 | 1.000 | | |
| Total | | 0.077 | 61.376 | 0.000[a] | 1.000 | 1.000 | | |

Source: Authors' own processing by SPSS
[a]28 degrees of freedom

**Table 5** CFA results for the variable "year" when "thefts from cars" were committed

Overview row points[a]

| | | Score in dimension | | | Contribution | | | | |
|---|---|---|---|---|---|---|---|---|---|
| | | | | | Of point to inertia of dimension | | Of dimension to inertia of point | | |
| Year | Mass | 1 | 2 | Inertia | 1 | 2 | 1 | 2 | Total |
| 2012 | 0.196 | 0.029 | −0.302 | 0.008 | 0.001 | 0.127 | 0.004 | 0.316 | 0.321 |
| 2013 | 0.110 | −1.136 | −0.354 | 0.032 | 0.674 | 0.098 | 0.925 | 0.060 | 0.985 |
| 2014 | 0.302 | −0.129 | 0.514 | 0.013 | 0.024 | 0.566 | 0.083 | 0.883 | 0.966 |
| 2015 | 0.209 | 0.398 | −0.363 | 0.015 | 0.158 | 0.196 | 0.468 | 0.260 | 0.728 |
| 2016 | 0.183 | 0.406 | 0.103 | 0.009 | 0.144 | 0.014 | 0.719 | 0.031 | 0.750 |
| Active total | 1.000 | | | 0.077 | 1.000 | 1.000 | | | |

Source: Authors' own processing by SPSS
[a]Symmetrical normalisation

The contribution of a point to the inertia explained by a factorial axis (Column *Contribution Of Point to Inertia of Dimension*) shows the contribution of the category (year) to the factorial axis dispersion. The points with high contributions on a factorial axis (those with a contribution greater than $1/m = 1/5 = 0.02$) are those points that contribute to the formation of the respective axis (column *Contribution from* Table 5). These are called explanatory points of the formation of the respective axis, as they exercise the greatest influence in shaping the profile (structure) of the year when the crime was committed (Pintilescu 2007).

Thus, the first factorial axis is explained in the ratio of 67.4% by 2013, 15.8% by 2015 and 14.4% by 2016. According to the CFA method, between these years, there are differences regarding the structure of the crimes committed per towns/resorts, the coordinates of these points being located in different quadrants. The second factorial axis is explained in the ratio of 56.6% by 2014 and 19.6% by 2015. The CFA method allowed us to identify the years that distinguish themselves among those included in our analysis, regarding the structure of thefts from cars, per towns/resorts. Moreover, CFA method allowed us to notice that these two years (i.e. 2014 and 2015) differ in terms of the structure per towns.

### 4.1.2 CFA Results of the Variable "Town/Resort" (*Overview Column Points* Output)

By analysing the values of the coordinates of points on the factorial axes, we highlighted the towns/resorts among which there are the greatest differences/similarities in terms of the crime "theft from cars".

Table 6 reveals that the greatest differences occur between Mamaia resort and Mangalia town and between Techirghiol and Mangalia. Moreover, Techirghiol

**Table 6** CFA results for the variable "town/resort" where "thefts from cars" were committed

| Overview column points[a] | | | | | | | | | |
|---|---|---|---|---|---|---|---|---|---|
| | | Score in dimension | | | Contribution | | | | |
| | | | | | Of point to inertia of dimension | | Of dimension to inertia of point | | |
| Town/resort | Mass | 1 | 2 | Inertia | 1 | 2 | 1 | 2 | Total |
| Constanta | 0.299 | −0.077 | 0.442 | 0.010 | 0.008 | 0.415 | 0.038 | 0.834 | 0.871 |
| Mamaia | 0.241 | −0.592 | −0.103 | 0.019 | 0.401 | 0.018 | 0.952 | 0.019 | 0.972 |
| Eforie | 0.162 | 0.241 | −0.369 | 0.007 | 0.045 | 0.157 | 0.279 | 0.438 | 0.717 |
| Techirghiol | 0.005 | −2.381 | −0.992 | 0.009 | 0.135 | 0.035 | 0.668 | 0.078 | 0.746 |
| Mangalia | 0.089 | 0.744 | 0.405 | 0.018 | 0.233 | 0.103 | 0.589 | 0.117 | 0.706 |
| Neptun | 0.061 | 0.049 | −0.534 | 0.003 | 0.001 | 0.124 | 0.012 | 0.944 | 0.956 |
| Costinesti | 0.036 | 0.195 | 0.035 | 0.001 | 0.007 | 0.000 | 0.300 | 0.006 | 0.307 |
| Navodari | 0.107 | 0.579 | −0.438 | 0.011 | 0.171 | 0.147 | 0.687 | 0.263 | 0.950 |
| Active total | 1.000 | | | .077 | 1.000 | 1.000 | | | |

Source: Authors' own processing by SPSS
[a]Symmetrical normalisation

clearly distances itself from the other towns/resorts analysed by recording the lowest criminality rate (see Table 1 and Fig. 1). Also, as shown in Fig. 1, Mangalia also distances itself from the other towns, which means that Mangalia is different from the other towns/resorts.

Also, by analysing the results presented in Table 6, we can appreciate that Constanta, Eforie and Navodari also contribute to the formation of the second factorial axis (of the second group, in terms of spreading) with 41.5%, 15.7% and 14.7% (column Contribution Of Point to Inertia of Dimension 2). By analysing the coordinates of these points (columns Score in Dimension 1 and 2), we noticed that, between Constanta and Eforie and between Constanta and Navodari, there are the most significant differences, by years, in terms of the crime "theft from cars". Meanwhile, we also noticed that, between Eforie and Năvodari, there are similarities regarding the structure of the analysed years, the coordinates of these points being located in the same quadrant.

The graphical representation of row profiles and column profiles in the factorial axes system shows a summary of the initial data table (Table 1). The distance between row profiles (year) and column profiles (town), representing an approximate of the distance $\chi^2$, shows the distance or the proximity between points. Thus, the distribution of points may indicate an association or an obvious distinction between them. However, the interpretation of the association should be made with great caution, because the proximity of these points does not always show that there are significant connections between the row profile and the column profile. The only situation when such an interpretation may be performed without reservations is in the case of two profiles whose categories are located at the ends of the graph (Pintilescu 2007).

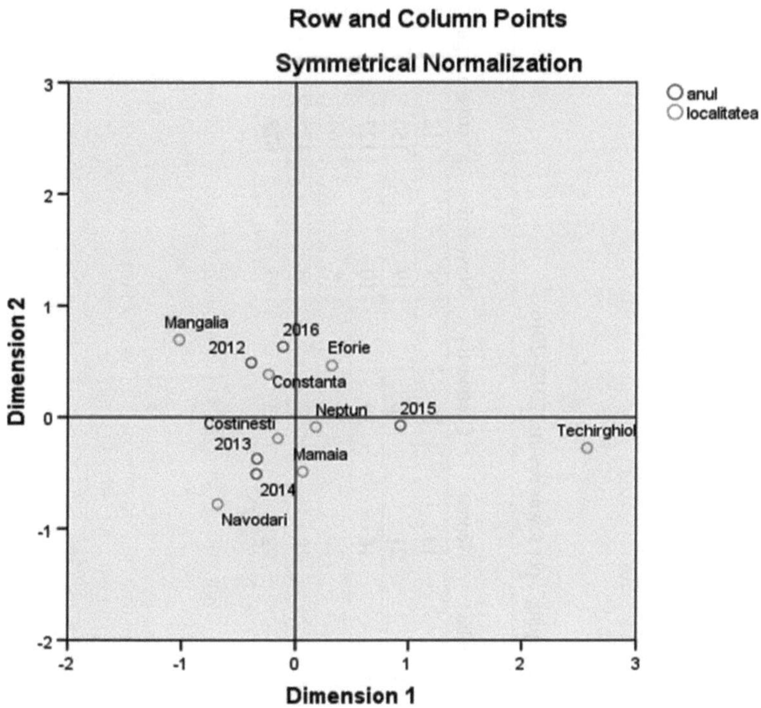


**Fig. 1** Graphical representation of variables in the system of the first factorial axes, for "thefts from cars". Source: Authors' own processing by SPSS

## *4.2 Analysis of the Crime "Theft from Hotel and Motel Rooms and Camping"*

The data presented in Table 7 represent the absolute values of "thefts from hotel and motel rooms and camping", recorded in each town/resort, every year and per the entire analysed period.

The interpretation of these data enables us to distinguish the following aspects:

- for the period under review (2012–2016), the crime "theft from hotel and motel rooms and camping", per total towns/resorts, recorded the highest level in 2015 (164 thefts) and the lowest level—in 2012 (112 thefts). It is noteworthy that similar values were recorded in 2015 (164 thefts) and 2013 (150), and also in 2014 (127 thefts) and 2016 (125).
- every year, per total towns/resorts, a reverse change was recorded, compared to the previous year: in 2013, the number of thefts increased, compared to 2012 (from 150 to 112); in 2014, it decreased, compared to 2013 (from 150 to 127); then, in 2015, an increase was recorded, compared to 2014 (from 127 to 164), and another decrease occurred in 2016, compared to 2015 (from 164 to 125). As already mentioned, during 2014–2016, the total number of tourists, per total

**Table 7** Correspondence table of the crime "theft from hotel and motel rooms and camping", per towns/resorts, 2012–2016

| Year | Town/resort | | | | | | | | |
|---|---|---|---|---|---|---|---|---|---|
| | Constanta | Mamaia | Eforie | Techirghiol | Mangalia | Neptun | Costinesti | Navodari | Active margin |
| 2012 | 6 | 8 | 31 | 1 | 16 | 13 | 29 | 8 | 112 |
| 2013 | 4 | 29 | 32 | 1 | 14 | 21 | 30 | 19 | 150 |
| 2014 | 3 | 28 | 21 | 0 | 10 | 16 | 39 | 10 | 127 |
| 2015 | 4 | 29 | 56 | 11 | 0 | 26 | 33 | 5 | 164 |
| 2016 | 3 | 20 | 45 | 0 | 16 | 16 | 22 | 3 | 125 |
| Active margin | 20 | 114 | 185 | 13 | 56 | 92 | 153 | 45 | 678 |

Source: Authors' own processing by SPSS

towns/resorts, increased from 880,381 tourists in 2014 to 1,019,233 tourists in 2015 and to 1,159,824 tourists in 2016 (according to NIS DJS Constanta).

- a trend similar to the general one was recorded by the following towns/resorts: Mamaia, Eforie and Neptun;
- the highest absolute values in terms of "thefts from hotel and motel rooms and camping", throughout the analysed period, are recorded in Eforie (185 thefts) and Costinesti (153);
- total similar values were recorded in Mamaia (114) and Neptun (92), and also in Mangalia (56 thefts) and Navodari (45);
- the lowest total number of "thefts from hotel and motel rooms and camping" was recorded in Techirghiol (13), as for thefts from cars;
- as a particular aspect, the next town (after Techirghiol), with the lowest total number of thefts from rooms, is represented by Constanta (20 thefts).

The data in Table 8 reveal the percentages of the "thefts from hotel and motel rooms and camping", per year, over the entire analysed period, in each town/resort.

Thus, we can notice what is specific for each year, in terms of "thefts from hotel and motel rooms and camping". By analysing the percentages shown in this table, the following issues are highlighted:

- over the period 2012–2016, the highest percentages, per total, are recorded in Eforie, with its two resorts, i.e. Eforie North and Eforie South (27.3%), and Costinesti (22.6%). It should be noted that these two towns/resorts hold almost half (49.9%) of all the "thefts from hotel and motel rooms and camping", from the Romanian coast. The ranking of towns/resorts, by their share in thefts from rooms is as follows: Eforie, Costinesti, Mamaia, Neptun, Mangalia, Navodari, Constanta and Techirghiol;
- in 2012, the highest percentages in terms of the "thefts from hotel and motel rooms and camping" were recorded by Eforie (27.7%) and Costinesti (25.9%), and, along with two other towns/resorts, i.e. Mangalia and Neptun, they concentrated 79.5% of the thefts committed in all the analysed towns/resorts;
- in 2013, 74.6% of all the thefts from rooms were committed in four towns, i.e. Eforie (21.3%), Costinesti (20%), Mamaia (19.3%) and Neptun (14%);
- in 2014, the same towns (but in a different order) held 81.8% of thefts from rooms, namely: Costinesti (30.7%), Mamaia (22%), Eforie (16.5%) and Neptun (12.6%);
- in 2015, the same towns, as ranked in 2013 (Eforie, Costinesti, Mamaia, Neptun) concentrated 87.8% of all the "thefts from hotel rooms, motels and campings";
- in 2016, five towns (Eforie, Costinesti, Mamaia, Neptun and Mangalia) concentrated 95.2% of the thefts from hotel and motel rooms and camping.
- only in 2014, the percentage in terms of this crime was higher in another town (i.e. Costinesti, 30.7%) than in Eforie (where it recorded 16.5%); however, in all the other years, the largest percentages were recorded in this town;
- in 2014 and 2016, in Techirghiol, and in 2015, in Mangalia, no "theft from hotel and motel rooms and camping" was recorded.

**Table 8** Row profiles table for the structure of "thefts from hotel and motel rooms and camping", per towns/resorts, 2012–2016 (row profiles output)

| Row profiles | | | | | | | | | |
|---|---|---|---|---|---|---|---|---|---|
| | Town/resort | | | | | | | | |
| Year | Constanta | Mamaia | Eforie | Techirghiol | Mangalia | Neptun | Costinesti | Navodari | Active margin |
| 2012 | 0.054 | 0.071 | 0.277 | 0.009 | 0.143 | 0.116 | 0.259 | 0.071 | 1.000 |
| 2013 | 0.027 | 0.193 | 0.213 | 0.007 | 0.093 | 0.140 | 0.200 | 0.127 | 1.000 |
| 2014 | 0.024 | 0.220 | 0.165 | 0.000 | 0.079 | 0.126 | 0.307 | 0.079 | 1.000 |
| 2015 | 0.024 | 0.177 | 0.341 | 0.067 | 0.000 | 0.159 | 0.201 | 0.030 | 1.000 |
| 2016 | 0.024 | 0.160 | 0.360 | 0.000 | 0.128 | 0.128 | 0.176 | 0.024 | 1.000 |
| Mass | 0.029 | 0.168 | 0.273 | 0.019 | 0.083 | 0.136 | 0.226 | 0.066 | |

Source: Authors' own processing by SPSS

The data from Table 9 shows, for each town/resort, the percentage of the "thefts from hotel and motel rooms and camping", recorded each year, in the period under review.

By means of these data, we can reveal the specific elements of each town/resort, in terms of this crime. We noticed the following aspects:

- in Constanta, the highest percentage in terms of this crime was recorded in 2012 (30%) and the lowest—in 2014 and 2016 (15%); similar values were recorded in 2013 and 2015 (20%);
- in Mamaia, the highest percentage in terms of this crime was recorded in 2013 and 2015 (25.4%) and the lowest—in 2012 (7%);
- in Eforie, the highest percentage in terms of this crime was recorded in 2015 (30.3%), and the lowest—in 2014 (11.4%);
- in Techirghiol, the highest percentage in terms of this crime was recorded in 2015 (84.6%) and the lowest—in 2014 and 2016 (0%);
- in Mangalia, the highest percentage in terms of this crime was recorded in 2012 and 2016 (28.6%) and the lowest—in 2015 (0%)
- in Neptun, the highest percentage in terms of this crime was recorded in 2015 (28.3%); equal values were recorded in 2014 and 2016 (17.4%) and the lowest value—in 2012 (14.1%). Typical of this town is that the changes in percentages are not very significant, from one year to another, as recorded in the other analysed towns/resorts;
- in Costinesti, the highest percentage in terms of this crime was recorded in 2014 (25.5%), and the lowest—in 2016 (14.4%);
- in Navodari, the highest percentage in terms of this crime was recorded in 2013 (42.2%) and the lowest—in 2016 (6.7%). A particular aspect: Costinesti and Navodari recorded each, in 2016, the lowest percentages in terms of the crimes "theft from cars" and "theft from hotel and motel rooms and camping" (see Table 3).

The calculated value of the test statistics, shown in Table 10, column Chi Square $\chi^2 = 96.152$, is greater than the tabulated value $\chi^2 0.05;28$ (for a risk of 0.05 and $v = 28$ freedom degrees), which shows that the hypothesis H0 is rejected. Thus, with a probability of 95%, we can guarantee that, in terms of "thefts from hotel and motel rooms and camping", there is a connection between the variables considered, namely between towns/resorts and years.

The first factorial axis explains 56.8% of the total variance. According to Benzécri's criterion, we need two factorial axes that explain together 83.3% of the total variance (Benzecri 1992). For each category of variables (town/resort and year), we will calculate the coordinates on the factorial axes and the contributions of points to the inertia of an axis.

**Table 9** Column profiles table for the years when the crime "theft from hotel and motel rooms and camping" was committed, per towns/resorts (Column Profiles output)

| Column profiles | | | | | | | | | |
|---|---|---|---|---|---|---|---|---|---|
| | Town/resort | | | | | | | | |
| Year | Constanta | Mamaia | Eforie | Techirghiol | Mangalia | Neptun | Costinesti | Navodari | Mass |
| 2012 | 0.300 | 0.070 | 0.168 | 0.077 | 0.286 | 0.141 | 0.190 | 0.178 | 0.165 |
| 2013 | 0.200 | 0.254 | 0.173 | 0.077 | 0.250 | 0.228 | 0.196 | 0.422 | 0.221 |
| 2014 | 0.150 | 0.246 | 0.114 | 0.000 | 0.179 | 0.174 | 0.255 | 0.222 | 0.187 |
| 2015 | 0.200 | 0.254 | 0.303 | 0.846 | 0.000 | 0.283 | 0.216 | 0.111 | 0.242 |
| 2016 | 0.150 | 0.175 | 0.243 | 0.000 | 0.286 | 0.174 | 0.144 | 0.067 | 0.184 |
| Active margin | 1.000 | 1.000 | 1.000 | 1.000 | 1.000 | 1.000 | 1.000 | 1.000 | |

Source: Authors' own processing by SPSS

**Table 10** Calculated value of statistics $\chi^2$, eigenvalues and inertia explained by each factorial axis (Summary output)

| Summary | | | | | | | | |
|---|---|---|---|---|---|---|---|---|
| | | | | | Proportion of inertia | | Confidence singular value | |
| | | | | | | | | Correlation |
| Dimension | Singular value | Inertia | Chi Square | Sig. | Accounted for | Cumulative | Standard deviation | 2 |
| 1 | 0.284 | 0.081 | | | 0.568 | 0.568 | 0.033 | −0.014 |
| 2 | 0.194 | 0.038 | | | 0.265 | 0.833 | 0.038 | |
| 3 | 0.116 | 0.013 | | | 0.095 | 0.927 | | |
| 4 | 0.101 | 0.010 | | | 0.073 | 1.000 | | |
| Total | | 0.142 | 96.152 | 0.000[a] | 1.000 | 1.000 | | |

Source: Authors' own processing by SPSS
[a]28 degrees of freedom

**Table 11** CFA results for the variable "year" when "thefts from hotel and motel rooms and camping" were committed

| Overview row points[a] | | | | | | | | | |
|---|---|---|---|---|---|---|---|---|---|
| | | Score in dimension | | | Contribution | | | | |
| | | | | | Of point to inertia of dimension | | Of dimension to inertia of point | | |
| Year | Mass | 1 | 2 | Inertia | 1 | 2 | 1 | 2 | Total |
| 2012 | 0.165 | −0.390 | 0.487 | 0.022 | 0.089 | 0.202 | 0.325 | 0.346 | 0.672 |
| 2013 | 0.221 | −0.339 | −0.375 | 0.019 | 0.090 | 0.160 | 0.386 | 0.322 | 0.708 |
| 2014 | 0.187 | −0.344 | −0.512 | 0.021 | 0.078 | 0.253 | 0.302 | 0.455 | 0.757 |
| 2015 | 0.242 | 0.929 | −0.074 | 0.060 | 0.735 | 0.007 | 0.992 | 0.004 | 0.996 |
| 2016 | 0.184 | −0.112 | 0.630 | 0.021 | 0.008 | 0.378 | 0.032 | 0.689 | 0.721 |
| Active Total | 1.000 | | | 0.142 | 1.000 | 1.000 | | | |

Source: Authors' own processing by SPSS
[a]Symmetrical normalisation

### 4.2.1 The Coordinates of the Points on the Two Factorial Axes (*Score in Dimension* Column) Show the Position of Points in the Area Represented by the Axes (Table 11)

The first factorial axis is explained in the ratio of 73.5% by 2015. This high value recorded by 1 year indicates that, in terms of variable "years", we can not comment on the existence of similarities or differences as far as the crime "theft from hotel and motel rooms and camping" is concerned, the percentages between towns/resorts being quite similar every year. In other words, the structure of these types of crimes was relatively constant these years. The second factorial axis is explained in the ratio of 37.8% by 2016, 25.3% by 2014, 20.2% by 2012 and 16% by 2013. The CFA method allowed us to identify these years as those that distinguish themselves among the 5 years analysed in terms of structure, per towns/resorts, as far as this type of thefts is concerned. We found that 2 year groups are similar in terms of the structure per towns/resorts, namely 2012 and 2016, 2013 and 2014 (in Fig. 2, these points are located in the same quadrant).

### 4.2.2 CFA Results in Terms of the Variable "Town/Resort" (Overview Column Points Output)

By analysing the values of the coordinates of points on the factorial axes, we highlighted the towns/resorts among which there are the greatest differences/similarities in terms of "thefts from hotel and motel rooms and camping".

Table 12 reveals that the greatest differences, according to the first factorial axis (column Contribution Of Point to Inertia of Dimension 1) is recorded in terms of the

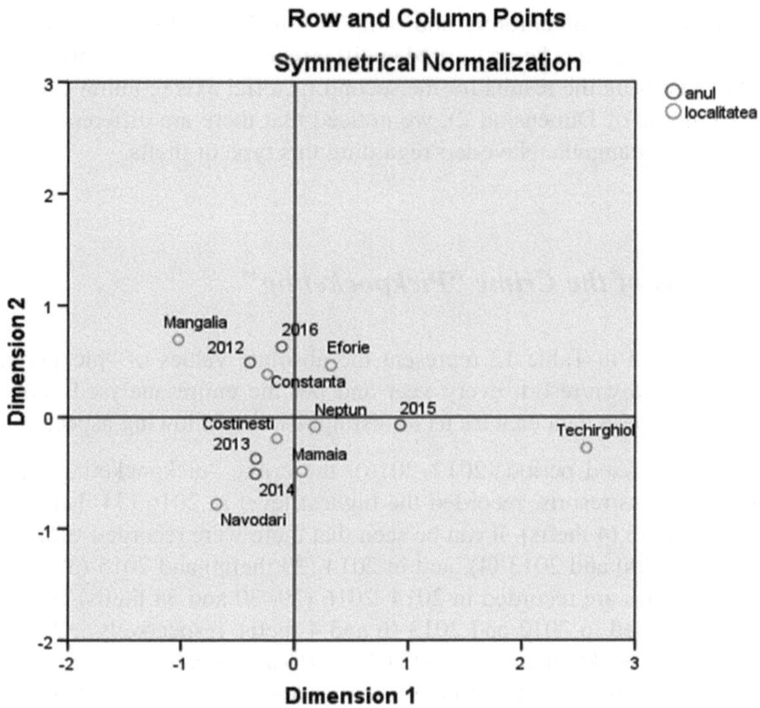


**Fig. 2** Representation of the variables in the system of the first factorial axes for the crime "theft from hotel and motel rooms and camping"

**Table 12** CFA Results in terms of the variable "town/resort" where the crime "theft from hotel and motel rooms and camping" was committed

Overview column points[a]

| | | Score in dimension | | | Contribution | | | | |
|---|---|---|---|---|---|---|---|---|---|
| | | | | | Of point to inertia of dimension | | Of dimension to inertia of point | | |
| Town/resort | Mass | 1 | 2 | Inertia | 1 | 2 | 1 | 2 | Total |
| Constanta | 0.029 | −0.238 | 0.383 | 0.004 | 0.006 | 0.022 | 0.121 | 0.213 | 0.334 |
| Mamaia | 0.168 | 0.065 | −0.491 | 0.013 | 0.002 | 0.209 | 0.015 | 0.592 | 0.607 |
| Eforie | 0.273 | 0.320 | 0.462 | 0.020 | 0.098 | 0.301 | 0.393 | 0.562 | 0.955 |
| Techirghiol | 0.019 | 2.572 | −0.279 | 0.039 | 0.447 | 0.008 | 0.928 | 0.007 | 0.935 |
| Mangalia | 0.083 | −1.021 | 0.692 | 0.032 | 0.304 | 0.204 | 0.759 | 0.239 | 0.998 |
| Neptun | 0.136 | 0.178 | −0.088 | 0.002 | 0.015 | 0.005 | 0.745 | 0.124 | 0.869 |
| Costinesti | 0.226 | −0.155 | −0.190 | 0.010 | 0.019 | 0.042 | 0.160 | 0.165 | 0.325 |
| Navodari | 0.066 | −0.681 | −0.781 | 0.022 | 0.109 | 0.209 | 0.392 | 0.352 | 0.744 |
| Active Total | 1.000 | | | 0.142 | 1.000 | 1.000 | | | |

Source: Authors' own processing by SPSS
[a]Symmetrical normalisation

"thefts from hotel and motel rooms and camping", in Techirghiol and Mangalia, the coordinates of these points being located in different quadrants, far from one another.

Also, by analysing the results for the second factorial axis (column Contribution Of Point to inertia of Dimension 2), we noticed that there are differences between Mamaia, Eforie, Mangalia, Navodari regarding this type of thefts.

## 4.3 *Analysis of the Crime "Pickpocketing"*

The data presented in Table 13 represent the absolute values of "pickpocketing", recorded in each town/resort, every year and per the entire analysed period. The interpretation of these data enables us to distinguish the following aspects:

- during the analysed period (2012–2016), the crime "pickpocketing", per total number of towns/resorts, recorded the highest level in 2016 (34 thefts) and the lowest—in 2013 (4 thefts). It can be seen that there were recorded similar values in 2012 (6 thefts) and 2013 (4), and in 2014 (29 thefts) and 2015 (30 thefts).
- high total values are recorded in 2014–2016 (29, 30 and 34 thefts) compared to the level recorded in 2012 and 2013 (6 and 4 thefts, respectively). On the other hand, it is noteworthy that the period 2014–2016 also recorded an increasing total number of tourists (according to the data provided by INS—CDS Constanta);
- over the entire analysed period, most pickpocketing cases were registered in Mamaia (41) and Constanta (25);
- several towns/resorts recorded a small (and similar) number in such crimes (7 thefts in Mangalia, 6 in Neptun, 5 in Costinesti and 5 thefts in Navodari);
- in Techirghiol, no such theft was recorded between 2012 and 2016. The ranking of towns/resorts by the number of pickpocketing cases is as follows: Mamaia, Constanta, Eforie, Mangalia, Neptun, Costinesti, Navodari, Techirghiol.

The data in Table 14 represent the percentage of "pickpocketing", per year, over the entire analysed period, held by every town/resort.

In other words, Table 14 reveals the specific characteristics of each year. By analysing the percentages shown in this table, the following issues are highlighted:

- in 2012, the same percentage in terms of pickpocketing, i.e. 16.7%, was recorded in four cities: Constanta, Eforie, Neptune and Navodari;
- in 2013, pickpocketing cases occurred only in two towns/resorts, i.e. Mamaia (75%) and Costinesti (25%);
- in 2014, there was recorded the most uniform distribution of the percentage of this crime in the analysed towns/resorts (without taking into account Techirghiol, where no such crime was committed, between 2012 and 2016);
- in 2015 and 2016, the highest percentages were recorded in three towns/resorts: Constanta, Mamaia and Eforie, which, together, totaled 90% in 2015, and 100% in 2016, respectively, in terms of pickpocketing, committed on the seaside;

**Table 13** Correspondence table for pickpocketing, per towns/resorts, 2012–2016

Correspondence table

| Year | Town/resort | | | | | | | | |
|---|---|---|---|---|---|---|---|---|---|
| | Constanta | Mamaia | Eforie | Techirghiol | Mangalia | Neptun | Costinesti | Navodari | Active margin |
| 2012 | 1 | 0 | 1 | 0 | 2 | 1 | 0 | 1 | 6 |
| 2013 | 0 | 3 | 0 | 0 | 0 | 0 | 1 | 0 | 4 |
| 2014 | 4 | 7 | 3 | 0 | 3 | 5 | 4 | 3 | 29 |
| 2015 | 11 | 12 | 4 | 0 | 2 | 0 | 0 | 1 | 30 |
| 2016 | 9 | 19 | 6 | 0 | 0 | 0 | 0 | 0 | 34 |
| Active margin | 25 | 41 | 14 | 0 | 7 | 6 | 5 | 5 | 103 |

Source: Constanta County Police Inspectorate

**Table 14** Row profiles table for the structure of "pickpocketing", per towns/resorts, 2012–2016 (row profiles output)

| Row profiles | | | | | | | | | |
|---|---|---|---|---|---|---|---|---|---|
| | Town/resort | | | | | | | | |
| year | Constanta | Mamaia | Eforie | Techirghiol | Mangalia | Neptun | Costinesti | Navodari | Active margin |
| 2012 | 0.167 | 0.000 | 0.167 | 0.000 | 0.333 | 0.167 | 0.000 | 0.167 | 1.000 |
| 2013 | 0.000 | 0.750 | 0.000 | 0.000 | 0.000 | 0.000 | 0.250 | 0.000 | 1.000 |
| 2014 | 0.138 | 0.241 | 0.103 | 0.000 | 0.103 | 0.172 | 0.138 | 0.103 | 1.000 |
| 2015 | 0.367 | 0.400 | 0.133 | 0.000 | 0.067 | 0.000 | 0.000 | 0.033 | 1.000 |
| 2016 | 0.265 | 0.559 | 0.176 | 0.000 | 0.000 | 0.000 | 0.000 | 0.000 | 1.000 |
| Mass | 0.243 | 0.398 | 0.136 | 0.000 | 0.068 | 0.058 | 0.049 | 0.049 | |

Source: Authors' own processing by SPSS

- throughout the analysed period, it can be seen that the same three locations recorded the largest percentages in terms of this crime: Constanta—24.3%, Mamaia—39.8%, and Eforie—13.6%; together, they represent 77.7% of the pickpocketing cases recorded on the seaside, between 2012 and 2016.

The data in Table 15 show, for each town/resort, the percentages of "pickpocketing" cases, recorded every year, over the period under review. These data are useful for determining what is specific to each town/resort. We noticed the following aspects:

- in Constanta, this crime was not committed in 2013, and in 2015 it recorded the highest percentage in terms of this theft type (44%) throughout the entire period under review;
- in Mamaia, in 2012, no pickpocketing case was recorded, and, in 2013, the percentage of this crime increased significantly from one year to another, i.e. from 7.3% in 2013 to 46.3% in 2016;
- in Eforie, this crime was not committed in 2013; from 2014, a growth was recorded every year, i.e. from 21.4% in 2014 to 42.9% in 2016;
- in Techirghiol, no pickpocketing case was recorded over the period under review;
- in Mangalia, this crime was not committed in two years (2013 and 2016) and it recorded the same percentage (28.6%) in 2012 and 2015; the highest percentage was recorded in 2014, i.e. 42.9%;
- in Neptun, this type of theft was recorded only in two years, i.e. 2012 (16.7%) and 2014 (83.3%);
- in Costinesti, this crime was committed also in only two years: in 2013, it recorded 20%, and in 2014—80%;
- in Navodari, the highest percentage of pickpocketing (60%) was recorded in 2014; in 2012 and 2015, it recorded 20%;
- it is noteworthy that, in all resorts, in terms of this crime, there are great differences between the percentages recorded in 2012 (5.8%) and in 2013 (3.9%), compared to those recorded in the next years, i.e. 2014—with 28.2%, 2015—with 29.1% and 2016—when it reached 33%.

The calculated value of the test statistics, shown in Table 16, column Chi Square $\chi^2 = 51.271$ is greater than the tabulated value $\chi^2_{0.05;28}$ (for a risk of 0.05 and $v = 28$ freedom degrees), which shows that the hypothesis $H_0$ is rejected. Thus, with a probability of 95%, we can guarantee that, in terms of pickpocketing, there are connections between the variables considered, namely between the town/resort where the crime was committed and the year when it was committed. The first factorial axis explains 68% of the total variance. According Benzécri's criterion, we need two factorial axes, explaining together 94.1% of the total variance (Benzecri 1992). For each category of variables (town/resort and year), we will calculate the coordinates on the factorial axes and the contributions of points to the inertia of an axis.

**Table 15** Column profiles table for the years when pickpocketing was committed, per towns/resort (Column profiles output)

| Column profiles | | | | | | | | | |
|---|---|---|---|---|---|---|---|---|---|
| | Town/resort | | | | | | | | |
| year | Constanta | Mamaia | Eforie | Techirghiol | Mangalia | Neptun | Costinesti | Navodari | Mass |
| 2012 | 0.040 | 0.000 | 0.071 | 0.000 | 0.286 | 0.167 | 0.000 | 0.200 | 0.058 |
| 2013 | 0.000 | 0.073 | 0.000 | 0.000 | 0.000 | 0.000 | 0.200 | 0.000 | 0.039 |
| 2014 | 0.160 | 0.171 | 0.214 | 0.000 | 0.429 | 0.833 | 0.800 | 0.600 | 0.282 |
| 2015 | 0.440 | 0.293 | 0.286 | 0.000 | 0.286 | 0.000 | 0.000 | 0.200 | 0.291 |
| 2016 | 0.360 | 0.463 | 0.429 | 0.000 | 0.000 | 0.000 | 0.000 | 0.000 | 0.330 |
| Active margin | 1.000 | 1.000 | 1.000 | .000 | 1.000 | 1.000 | 1.000 | 1.000 | |

Source: Authors' own processing by SPSS

**Table 16** Calculated value of statistics $\chi^2$, eigenvalues and inertia explained by each factorial axis (Summary output)

Summary

| Dimension | Singular value | Inertia | Chi square | Sig. | Proportion of inertia | | Confidence singular value | |
|---|---|---|---|---|---|---|---|---|
| | | | | | Accounted for | Cumulative | Standard deviation | Correlation |
| | | | | | | | | 2 |
| 1 | 0.582 | 0.338 | | | 0.680 | 0.680 | 0.073 | −0.157 |
| 2 | 0.360 | 0.130 | | | 0.261 | 0.941 | 0.086 | |
| 3 | 0.129 | 0.017 | | | 0.034 | 0.975 | | |
| 4 | 0.112 | 0.013 | | | 0.025 | 1.000 | | |
| Total | | 0.498 | 51.271 | .005[a] | 1.000 | 1.000 | | |

Source: Authors' own processing by SPSS

[a]28 degrees of freedom

**Table 17** CFA results in terms of the variable "year" when pickpocketing was committed

| Overview row points[a] | | | | | | | | | |
|---|---|---|---|---|---|---|---|---|---|
| | | Score in dimension | | | Contribution | | | | |
| | | | | | Of point to inertia of dimension | | Of dimension to inertia of point | | |
| Year | Mass | 1 | 2 | Inertia | 1 | 2 | 1 | 2 | Total |
| 2012 | 0.058 | 1.415 | −1.435 | 0.117 | 0.200 | 0.333 | 0.581 | 0.370 | 0.952 |
| 2013 | 0.039 | −0.078 | 2.025 | 0.066 | 0.000 | 0.442 | 0.002 | 0.869 | 0.871 |
| 2014 | 0.282 | 0.954 | 0.348 | 0.164 | 0.441 | 0.095 | 0.908 | 0.075 | 0.983 |
| 2015 | 0.291 | −0.403 | −0.396 | 0.051 | 0.081 | 0.127 | 0.541 | 0.324 | 0.865 |
| 2016 | 0.330 | −0.699 | 0.068 | 0.100 | 0.277 | 0.004 | 0.939 | 0.006 | 0.944 |
| Active Total | 1.000 | | | 0.498 | 1.000 | 1.000 | | | |

Source: Authors' own processing by SPSS
[a]Symmetrical normalization

### 4.3.1 The Coordinates of Points on the Two Factorial Axes (Column *Score in Dimension*) Shows the Position of the Points in the Area Represented by the Axes

The first factorial axis is explained in the ratio of 44.1% by 2014, 27.7% by 2016 and 20% by 2012. The CFA method allowed us to identify these years as those that are distinguished among the 5 years analysed in terms of the structure of pickpocketing, per towns/resorts. Thus, according to the results shown in Table 17 and Fig. 3, there are significant differences between 2016, 2014 and 2012, the coordinates associated with these years being located in different quadrants.

The second factorial axis is explained in the ratio of 33.3% by 2012, 44.2% by 2013, and 12.7% by 2015. We also noticed differences between all these years, in Fig. 3, the coordinates associated with these points being located in different quadrants.

### 4.3.2 The CFA Results in Terms of the Variable "Town/Resort" (Overview Column Points Output)

By analysing the values of the coordinates of points on the factorial axes, there were highlighted the towns/resorts among which there are the greatest differences/similarities in terms of pickpocketing.

According to the first factorial axis, Table 18 reveals the following:

- The greatest similarities occur between Neptun and Costinesti, and between Mangalia and Navodari;
- The greatest differences occur between Costinesti and Mangalia, between Mamaia and Neptun, and between Navodari and Mamaia;

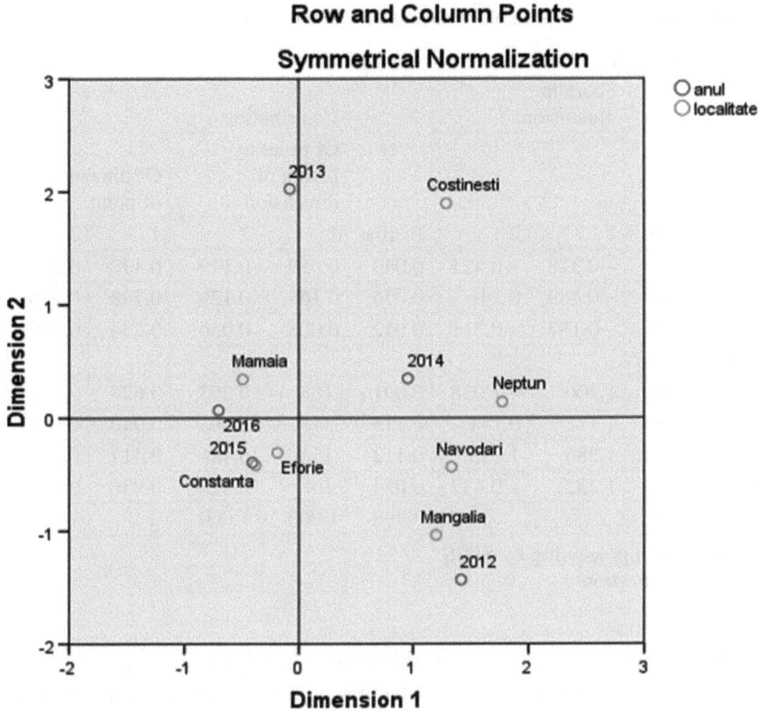


**Fig. 3** Representation of the variables in the system of the first factorial axes, in terms of "pickpocketing". Source: authors' own processing by SPSS

Also, by analysing the results presented in Table 12 (columns Score in Dimension 1 and 2), for the second factorial axis, we also noticed differences between Mangalia and Costineşti.

# 5 Conclusion

Tourism is one of the most important activities of Romanian economy. Internationally, as a tourist destination, Romania is appreciated for its rich and varied natural and anthropic potential. Moreover, it is also seen as a country able to provide safety and security, representing thus an attractive tourist destination. However, this aspect should be carefully managed, exploited and developed by safety and security policies promoted nationally, and with international involvement. This study reveals that the three types of crimes considered in the eight towns/resorts show a downward trend over the period 2014–2016; at the same time, the statistics show a significant increase in the number of (Romanian and foreign) tourists (NIS DJS Constanta).

Unlike the simple correspondence factor analysis, where the association is made for two categorical variables, the multiple correspondence factor analysis (MCFA)

**Table 18** AFC results for the variable "town/resort" in terms of "pickpocketing"

| Overview column points[a] | | | | | | | | | |
|---|---|---|---|---|---|---|---|---|---|
| | | Score in dimension | | | Contribution | | | | |
| | | | | | Of point to inertia of dimension | | Of dimension to inertia of point | | |
| Town/resort | Mass | 1 | 2 | Inertia | 1 | 2 | 1 | 2 | Total |
| Constanta | 0.243 | −0.378 | −0.421 | 0.043 | 0.059 | 0.119 | 0.472 | 0.363 | 0.835 |
| Mamaia | 0.398 | −0.489 | 0.341 | 0.074 | 0.164 | 0.129 | 0.748 | 0.226 | 0.974 |
| Eforie | 0.136 | −0.187 | −0.311 | 0.012 | 0.008 | 0.036 | 0.234 | 0.399 | 0.633 |
| Techirghiol | 0.000 | . | . | . | . | . | . | . | . |
| Mangalia | 0.068 | 1.200 | −1.038 | 0.091 | .168 | 0.203 | 0.628 | 0.291 | 0.919 |
| Neptun | 0.058 | 1.772 | 0.141 | 0.113 | .315 | 0.003 | 0.940 | 0.004 | 0.944 |
| Costinesti | 0.049 | 1.286 | 1.895 | 0.112 | .138 | 0.484 | 0.417 | 0.562 | 0.980 |
| Navodari | 0.049 | 1.332 | −0.437 | 0.054 | .148 | 0.026 | 0.936 | 0.062 | 0.998 |
| Active total | 1.000 | | | 0.498 | 1.000 | 1.000 | | | |

Source: Authors' own processing by SPSS
[a]Symmetrical normalization

can offer an overview of the three variables considered, i.e. the type of crime (thefts from cars, thefts from hotel and motel rooms and camping; pickpocketing), town/resort and year of the crime.

The diagram shown in Fig. 4 shows that the greatest associations occur between the following variables: town/resort and crime type. It can be concluded that certain crimes are committed predominantly in some towns/resorts, or that each town/resort is distinguished by the predominance of certain crime types.

The results obtained by processing the database by CFA and MCFA quantitative methods (according to Fig. 5) allowed us to make a series of qualitative assessments about the criminal profile of each town/resort analysed.

By their location and access routes (Highway Sun-A2), and by the quality of the tourism offer, Constanta and Mamaia are the top tourist destinations on the Black Sea coast. Here lies an important part of the coast accommodation offer, with units that have a high and medium comfort level; the prices are higher (compared to the other towns/resorts); it is dominated by segments of tourists with a high and middle income level, aged between 18 and 60. Tourists are attracted by the entertainment possibilities offered especially in Mamaia, sightseeing and touristic objectives, cultural events, sports and business; tourists prefer short holidays, at weekends, and many of them travel by their own cars (made by famous brands), tempting the criminals. Parking in areas that are not well supervised and the tourists' inattention and lack of information about this crime may be other explanations for the highest levels recorded in terms of the crime "theft from cars". Constanta ranks first, accounting for 29.9%, in terms of the thefts committed; Mamaia ranks second, accounting for 24.1%. In other words, these locations concentrate 54% of all the

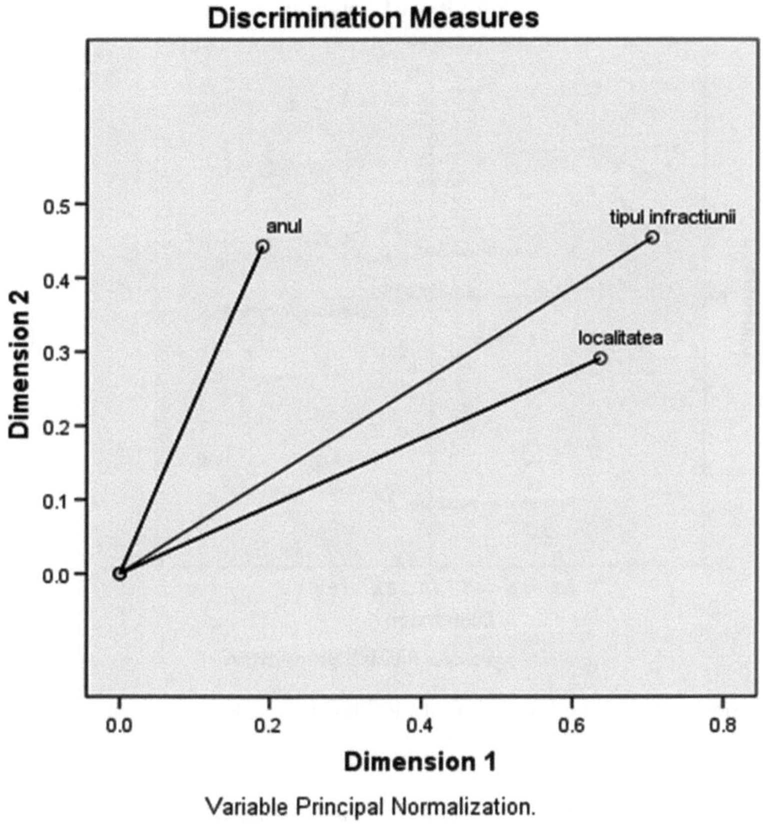


**Fig. 4** Representation of differences in terms of the three analysed statistical variables. Source: authors' own processing by SPSS

thefts from cars, on the entire Romanian coast. The above considerations (as features of the tourist supply and demand) may explain the fact that these two locations also rank as the first two (among the eight towns/resorts) in terms of "pickpocketing". Mamaia holds 39.8% and Constanta—24.3%, which shows a concentration of 64.1% of the crimes committed in the two locations. We may conclude that Mamaia and Constanta are crowded places, with tourists that own money and valuable items, which can be stolen from cars, pockets and bags. It is well-known that, when the tourist is on vacation, s/he changes his/her normal behaviour, meaning that s/he wants to feel less stressed and, therefore, his/her attention can be drawn by the landscape, entertainment, being thus less attentive to what happens around him/her, which makes him/her vulnerable to criminals. Regarding the crime "theft from hotel and motel rooms and camping", Mamaia ranks the third among the towns/resorts analysed (accounting for 16.8%) and Constanta ranks the second to last (accounting for 2.9%). The low levels recorded in terms of this crime in Constanta and Mamaia may be explained by the fact that the accommodation units hire security staff and are

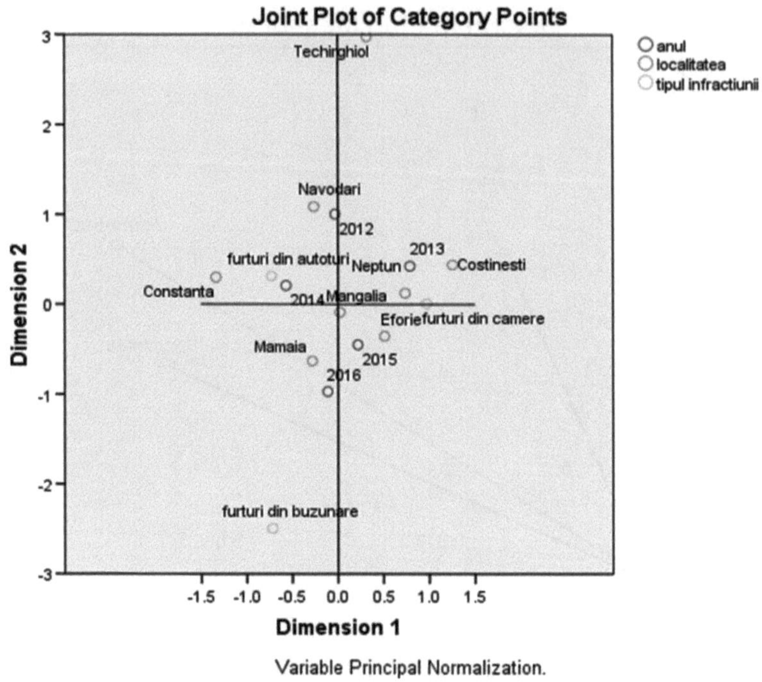


**Fig. 5** Representation of the three statistical variables in the system of the first two factorial axes. Source: authors' own processing by SPSS

equipped with video surveillance systems, appropriate lighting systems at night etc., discouraging thus the possible action of some criminals.

Navodari is no longer the town with school camps, as it was several decades ago. Being situated next to Mamaia resort, at North, over the recent years, new residential complexes and hotel complexes with a high comfort level have been built; these accommodation units are preferred by more exclusive tourists (of all ages), with high and middle income level, who prefer to spend their holiday on wilder, more isolated and quieter beaches. If we consider the characteristics of these tourists and the fact that Navodari can be reached only by car, we can explain why this town ranks fourth in terms of the crime "theft from cars", accounting for 10.7%. Regarding the other two crime types, this town ranks sixth, but it recorded different percentages, i.e. 6.6% in "thefts from hotel and motel rooms and camping" and 4.9% in "pickpocketing". The low percentages recorded in terms of these two crimes can be explained by the fact that, in Navodari, the accommodation assemblies/units are more "closed", they have a more secure operation system, i.e. the control regarding people' entry and exit from the accommodation units is performed more carefully.

Eforie (comprising two resorts, i.e. Eforie North and Eforie South) is located at approximately 15 km South from Constanta. Its tourist offer particularity consists in the access to the Black Sea and to Lake Techirghiol; it has an important accommodation capacity, with different degrees of comfort. It can be reached by car or rail.

The segments of tourists that come here have mostly a middle and a low income level; they belong to all age groups and come here for family holidays, entertainment, rest and treatment. Eforie ranks first in terms of the "thefts from hotel and motel rooms and camping" (27.3%), and third as far as the other two crimes are concerned, accounting for 16.2% in terms of "thefts from cars" and for 13.6% in terms of "pickpocketing". Given these percentages, Eforie is the location with the lowest security level provided to tourists, from all the towns/resorts analysed. We believe that the accommodation units should find solutions in order to reduce the thefts from rooms; tourists must be more alert in regard to the places where they park their cars and how they take care of their personal items; moreover, the local government authorities, together the police, should get involved more, in order to provide tourists an increased safety level (e.g. through proper lighting at night, presence of security staff, installation of video surveillance cameras in the two resorts).

Costinesti is located at 30 km South from Constanta; its accommodation units have an average comfort degree; it is also known as a "youth resort", for its core customer base is represented by the young, who are less demanding, but who are eager to have fun, having a medium income level. In terms of the analysed crime types, Costinesti ranks seventh in "thefts from cars", accounting for only 3.6%. It can be appreciated that the tourists do not come here by expensive cars and, thus, they do not represent an attraction/interest for certain categories of offenders. It ranks second in terms of "thefts from hotel and motel rooms and camping", accounting for 22.6%. This high level of thefts from rooms is explained by the fact that Costinesti is visited mostly by young tourists, who are generally more careless, attracted by entertainment, and also, perhaps, by the lack of security personnel and video surveillance systems in accommodation units. Because in terms of "pickpocketing", it ranks sixth, accounting for 4.9% (the same as that held by Navodari), it can be assumed that, in this resort, tourists do not have money or valuable items in their pockets and handbags, or it may also be assumed that the security services of this resort are well organised.

Located in the South, at a greater distance (about 40 km) from Constanta, Mangalia town and Neptun resort provide accommodation with mostly an average comfort level; some units also provide treatment facilities, which makes them more attractive to segments of tourists (of all ages), with small and medium income level, who want to spend a peaceful (usually with their family) and longer (for treatment and rest) holiday. Also, in these places, there are accommodations with a high comfort level, with outstanding treatment facilities, with a long tradition, with large areas of greenery, as well as with other facilities that attract foreign tourists from different countries. Neptun and Mangalia can be reached by car or train. Using all of these specific supply and demand elements, we can explain the results obtained by our research. Thus, the two towns rank fourth and fifth in terms of "thefts from hotel and motel rooms and camping" (Neptun—13.6% and Mangalia—8.3%) and "pickpocketing" (Mangalia—6.8%, Neptun—5.8%). In terms of the crime "theft from cars", Mangalia accounts for 8.9%, being ranked fifth, and Neptune holds 6.1%, ranking sixth. It can be said that the two towns provide a medium level of tourist safety. In our opinion, first, the accommodation units should be more concerned with taking measures in order to reduce the level of thefts from hotel rooms, and the local administration authorities and the police should get involved more (with personal work methods, equipment), so as to reduce the thefts from cars, pockets, handbags.

Techirghiol is a smaller resort, where tourists (mostly Romanians) come for treatment (especially for rheumatic problems). The accommodation units provide a medium and high comfort level, the target segment of tourists are people older than 40 years, with low, middle, and higher income levels. Techirghiol ranks last in terms of the three types of crimes analysed. There were no pickpocketing cases recorded in this town (in 2012–2016), and in terms of the other crimes, the percentages are very low, i.e. 0.5% for thefts from cars and 1.9% for thefts from hotel and motel rooms and camping. For tourists, Techirghiol is a tourist destination that offers the highest safety level.

The towns/resorts from the Black Sea area, analysed in our study, are some of the most attractive tourist destinations in Romania; these locations represent more than one third of the full capacity of the Romanian tourist accommodation. It is noteworthy that most of the tourist units from these towns/resorts (over 90%) are open only during the summer season. The accentuated intensity of tourist activities over a period of about four months a year is felt by the excessive agglomeration of these towns/resorts, "creating" an attractive environment to potential offenders.

Special efforts are made for proper monitoring and implementation of the measures that provide safety and security to the tourists from this area, during the tourist season. Police and gendarmerie units from each town/resort proceed to increase the number of staff, including by posting additional staff in police and gendarmes, who came from other parts of the country. Local government authorities contribute to the safety and security of tourists by increasing the number of the security and protection staff in public areas and by equipping these towns/resorts with adequate public lighting systems. We believe that, if there were concern to place cameras in different places, in each town/resort (but especially in those places where the analysed crimes reach high levels), the offenders could be identified and they could be easily caught and quickly punished, which would lead to lower crime rates. We also need to develop cooperation between tourist accommodation units, local administration authorities and police and gendarmerie units in order to identify and apply the most appropriate measures whereby to ensure the safety and security of tourists, increasing their satisfaction and promoting the image of the Romanian coastline as a safe tourist destination.

## Bibliography

Baddache, F. (2006). *Le developpement durable au quotidien*. Paris: Editions Eyrolles.

Benzecri, J. P. (1992). *Correspondence analysis handbook*. New York: Dekker.

Cismaru, L. (2011). *Strategii de securitate în marketingul destinaţiei turistice security strategies in tourism destination marketing* (Teza de Doctorat). Universitatea Transilvania din Braşov.

Danciu, V. (2013). Întreprinderea sustenabilă. Noi provocări şi strategii pentru îmbunătăţirea sustenabilităţii corporative. *Revista Economie teoretică şi aplicată* XX, No. 9(586), 4–24.

Datculescu, P. (2006). *Cercetarea de marketing.Cum patrunzi in mintea consumatorului, cum masori si cum analizezi informatia*. Bucuresti: Editura Brandbuilders Grup.

Dayan, A., & Bouqurel, F. (2008). *Studii de piaţă*. Bucureşti: Editura C.H. Beck.

Everitt, B., & Dunn, G. (2001). *Applied multivariate data analysis*. London: Arnold.

Field, A. (2009). *Discovering statistics using SPSS*. London: Sage.

Juganaru, M. (1998). *Teorie şi practica in cercetarea de marketing*. Bucureşti: Editura Expert.

Jugănaru, I. D. (2007). *Politici şi strategii în turismul mondial*. Bucureşti: Editura Expert.

Kotler, P., & Armstrong, G. (2008). *Principiile marketingului*. Bucureşti: Editura Publica.

Kotler, P., Kartajaya, H., & Setiawan, I. (2010). *Marketing 3.0: de la produs la consumator şi la spiritul uman*. Bucureşti: Editura Publica.

Minciu, R. (2005). *Economia turismului*. Bucureşti: Editura URANUS.

Pintilescu, C. (2007). *Analiză statistică multivariate. [Multivariate analysis]*. Iaşi: Editura Universităţii Alexandru Ioan Cuza.

Popescu, L. (2011). Safety and security in tourism. Case study: Romania, forum geografic. *Studii şi cercetări de geografie şi protecţia mediului, 10*(2), 322–328.

Teodorescu, N. (2003). Motiv si motivatie. In: C. Florescu, P. Malcomete, N. Al Pop (coord.) *Marketing Dictionar Explicativ*. Bucuresti: Editura Economica.

# Ethical Tourism: The Theory Vs. The Hedonistic Reality in Popular Greek Tourism Resorts

**Dimitrios Belias, Efstathios Velissariou, Michalis Chondrogiannis, Dimitrios Kyriakou, Labros Sdrolias, George Aspridis, and Athanasios Koustelios**

## 1 Introduction

Tourism is a big business, highly desirable in any country and destination, as it offers: jobs, economic prosperity, incentives to conserve natural resources and to prevent the migration of the local population. Tourism development can help improve the economic and socio-cultural level of residents, by supporting trade, industry and local agriculture, while increasing the demand for local cultural products, the exchange ideas and environmental protection. But there is another side of tourism, less positive, that significantly affects the lives of many people and refers to the loss of traditional habits and cultural features of the destination, increases in crime, prostitution and drug trafficking, misappropriation of land, over-consumption of water and energy, destruction of landscapes for the construction of tourism infrastructure, increases in waste, ecosystem degradation, increase in prices, capital flight and economic inequality (Weeden 2005a, b). Often, the tourist industry has to satisfy extreme desires, many of which are clearly illegal, while others, although not

D. Belias (✉) · E. Velissariou · G. Aspridis
Department of Business Administration, Technological Educational Institute of Thessaly, Larissa, Greece
e-mail: dbelias@teilar.gr

M. Chondrogiannis
Department of Foreign Languages, Translation and Interpreting, Laboratory for Geocultural Analyses, Ionian University, Corfu, Greece

D. Kyriakou · L. Sdrolias
Department of Economic Sciences, Aristotle University of Thessaloniki, Thessaloniki, Greece

A. Koustelios
Department of Physical Education and Sport Science, University of Thessaly, Trikala, Greece

 
A. Papathanassis et al. (eds.), *Yellow Tourism*, Tourism, Hospitality & Event Management, https://doi.org/10.1007/978-3-319-94664-1_4

punishable or subject to prohibitions, they are still morally questionable. Examples include: sex tourism, drug tourism and illegal medical tourism; but also: dark tourism, extreme-risk adventure tourism, gambling tourism and suicide tourism.

One of the key areas of research concerns sex tourism. Despite of the fact that there is a widespread view that sex tourism offends and harms the nature of the tourist industry (Ireland 1993; Rivers-Moore 2011; Abrams et al. 2015), it still seems that many destinations are not doing enough to prevent sex-related crimes. This is something which is quite common in resorts such as Kavos in Corfu and Faliraki in Rhodes, where thousands of drunken young tourists, mostly from Britain, are overindulging in alcohol and hedonistic behaviour. In some cases, those behaviours may result on violent crimes and sex offences. Although this has been a central part of the tourist reality for those resorts there is a lack of research on this. Therefore, the aim of this paper is to fill in this gap by emphasising actions taken so to prevent such incidents. This is a literature review relying on academic journal papers and reports found online at EBSCO and science direct.

## 2 Literature Review

### *2.1 Ethical Tourism*

"As emerging changes in global consciousness demand responses to contemporary challenges such as climate change, consumerism, globalization, sustainability and social alienation, we are increasingly drawn into debates of what it is to be 'good' (ethical)" (Feighery 2011). Ethics in tourism was developed in the 1990s via the AIEST congress in Paris (1992) and the Rio Earth Summit (1992) respectively. Conference delegates agreed to follow the proposed "Agenda 21" which states that Businesses and Industry should adopt to codes of conduct that encourage positive environmental practice (Genot 1995 in Fennell 2006). Although ethical tourism and its importance to the industry have been researched in the context of ecotourism, sustainability, responsibility, pro-poor (Holden 2009), UK ethical consumer trends (Goodwin and Francis 2003) and ethics as competitive advantage (Weeden 2002), a clear definition of ethical travel remains to be made (Lovelock 2008). Hultsman (1995), explains that ethics is a philosophical concept that dwells into the behavioural values and morals of action, linking ethical tourism action as not only knowing what is good (or the right thing to do), but also about behaving and conducting in a good way in tourism (Tribe 2002). Hultsman (1995) presents ethics in tourism as 'a behaviour' making it arguably more challenging to comprehend, measure and analyse. Thus academics are cautious with this topic and this is evident in the lack of research in tourism ethics (Moufakkir 2012).

Some organizations however, such as UK-based Tourism Concern and the charity Tearfund have a clearer understanding of the term "ethical tourism". Weeden (2002) states that "ethical tourism is now an established term, especially for those pressure groups and Christian charities that are concerned with the growth and impact of tourism within developing countries" (p. 143). She continues to explain that the term ethical tourism is derived from sustainable tourism, which became apparent thanks to the global sustainable development initiative of the World Conservation Strategy (WCED) in March 1980 and the creation of the World Commission on Environment and Development (WCED). Ethical tourism is therefore another proposition that has been put in place to address the environmental, social and economic concerns of stakeholders that has derived from mass tourism (Weeden 2005a, b). It is therefore straightforward to understand how ethical tourism is related to sustainable tourism. Nevertheless, ethics require that stakeholders (Maignan et al. 2005) allocate some of the responsibility to the visitors when choosing a tourism product. This is still a grey area in tourism. The industry providers believe that it is the governments who need to be more involved. The tourists and/or visitors believe that it is the responsibility of the industry providers to inform the public of ethical issues. Other stakeholders consider that it is the tourists' who finally need to be responsible in their behaviour as visitors (Tearfund 2002). This, in what may be considered as unethical or irresponsible behaviour does not solve the ethical dilemmas that continue to plague the tourism industry. According to Payne and Dimanche (1996), tour operators who wish to be regarded ethical should: have a relationship with the host community, ensure the fair treatment of employees, embrace clarity in their marketing and actively encourage respect toward the natural environment. Weeden (2002) had similar results where she refers to locally owned organizations, small tour group sizes, fair treatment and wages for staff, along with transparent promotion, as elements that a tour operator should deliver if they wish to be considered ethical. In exploring the attributes associated with a tourist destination as being perceived as ethical, McDonald et al. (2010) found attributes such as: culture-, religion-, environmental-protection, citizens' rights, symbolic monuments and a positive host-attitude toward tourists, in their exploratory work. All the above, constitute examples of what may be considered to be ethical practices for tour operators, along with potential indicators when measuring responsible tourism as well as examples of what denotes an ethical image.

Weeden (2005a, b, p. 235) nevertheless explains that "it is difficult to give a specific example of an ethical holiday." The challenge lies in providing a tangible/measurable aspect in a predominately intangible tourism offering, which reflects varying concepts and philosophies. One of the main difficulties in applying Ethical tourism is addressing three principal impacts: economic, environmental and social as a holistic issue in such a highly-complex legislative environment, spread across an array of sectors, professionals and involving a large number of stakeholders. How can a tour operator control the ethical operations of a supply chain that may commence in France and finish on a remote island in Greece? Is it therefore necessary to address the impacts separately? Or is there an automatic overlap? Another question that may need to be considered is the ethical orientation of tourism businesses. In Fennell and Malloy's (1999) research, not all tour operators were found to be homogeneous in their ethical orientation. Ethical approaches and codes of conducts may correspond to different levels of ethical responsibility, depending on the specifics of tour operator activity and the level of stakeholders' involvement.

This was noted by Fennell and Malloy (1999), where the results showed that ecotourism operators, compared to adventure-, fishing- and cruise-operators, demonstrated a stronger sense of ethical conduct. The authors explained that the findings were partially linked to the application of ethical codes (95% more than the other operators), which the eco-tour operators applied to their everyday business operations. There is a consensus in the literature that adopting ethical codes and conducts, positions tourism companies in a more positive light, adding value, appeal and competitive advantage (Weeden 2005a, b). However, it is not always an easy option for operators in a highly-oligopolistic business environment.

Novelli (2005) relates the application of ethical policies to luxury and a cost that may not see a return on its investment. Being true to one's beliefs is difficult in business, especially when one's livelihood is in question. The operator or manager may have the desire to adopt certain codes and achieve awards and labels that denote a specific quality, standard and expectation. However, the reality of putting these codes into place for a small operator is not always so easy, with many SME's being reluctant to adopt them, due to lack of financial resources, time and/or knowledge. Goodwin and Francis (2003) address the issue of ethically-motivated action. Nevertheless, even in the presence of a strong ethical motivation from the part of the companies, it is difficult to put these codes into place without support. Despite the realistic barriers that come with the application of codes and conducts in ethical tourism, this form of alternative tourism is followed by an array of associations and operators specializing in ethical travel. Jarvis et al. (2010) discuss the benefits of the many tourism certification schemes that have emerged and evolved around the world. These labels and certificates create a form of tangibility and expected quality for the visitor. This is particularly important when visiting new destinations and unknown territories. 'Ethical Traveller' is a non-profit organisation that carries out research on listing the world's ten best ethical destinations. Developing countries are measured on their application of "environmental protection, social welfare and human rights" (Ethical Traveler 2015, p. 2).

The preliminary information is secondary, coming from UNICEF and World Bank reports, which may arguably be biased; notwithstanding, the organisation then carries out primary research interviewing public-sector leaders and travellers. Apart from measuring destinations on the above-mentioned attributes, each destination must also offer "unspoilt beauty, great outdoor activities and the opportunity to interact with local people and cultures in a meaningful, mutually enriching way" (Ethical Traveler 2015, p. 2). These activities denote the interest in this form of alternative tourism and the demand that is generated from the research. To conclude this section, it is important to clarify the main difference between ethical tourism and other alternative tourism forms. With ethical tourism, the stakeholders will be asked to consider the consequences of their actions and examine their own behaviour. They may be asked to reflect on their duties towards other stakeholders, especially those in minority communities. As Lovelock and Lovelock (2013) explain, ethical tourism is more of a humanistic approach, linking oneself with being human and the consequences that come with that. Ethical tourism does nevertheless also consider the environmental and economic impacts that come with the tourism industry. However, this is measured from a behavioural perspective, reflecting on, not only the negative, but also the positive impact that one's behaviour may have on a holiday destination.

Ethical tourism is a way of thinking that may be applied to all forms of tourism. It encourages one to critically reflect on behaviour in order to induce behavioural change. It is more wide-encompassing; it is about morals, rather than being a 'green-being' or a 'justice-being' or an 'eco-being' (Lovelock and Lovelock 2013). This is what differentiates ethical tourism from other alternative forms of tourism. Alternative tourism-forms have been derived from rules and codes stating what can or cannot be done or what is or is not acceptable. Ethical tourism is behaviour; it is part of who we are. There is no one right answer to ethical tourism (Lovelock and Lovelock 2013). However, by applying different or combined theories to an array of situations, stakeholders can take responsibility for their actions, with the support of assisted and guided codes and conducts.

## 2.2 Codes and Conducts of Ethical Tourism

Codes and Ethical Conducts emerged from AT and ST in the late 1970s for both the industry and the tourists. Many of these codes and conducts, which derived from external pressure (Dornier et al. 2010), have evolved over time and generally originate from the industry, governments, NGOs and researchers. The development of codes of ethics came about due to the abuse of power, the exploitation of the environment and the general suspicion of scandalous business conduct (Malloy and Fennell 1998). The objective of these codes is therefore to communicate and regulate industry standards, and to provide guidelines which will aspire and educate all stakeholders (Payne and Dimanche 1998). Having a code of ethics, enables individuals to have an understanding of what is acceptable or unacceptable behaviour. They derive from ethical orientations that denote a sense of intentional or unintentional outcomes (Malloy and Fennell 1998). Not being aware of local values, dress codes and lifestyles, religious beliefs can create offence and frustration between local residences and visiting tourists (Payne and Dimanche 1996).

This emphasizes the importance of tourist education when travelling to a foreign destination. The problem arises when the uneducated tourist believes that they have paid for "their" holiday and all rights are reserved for them. There is at times, a real lack of understanding or arguably a complete ignorance of whose property, home, and land is being visited. It could be argued that it is the responsibility of the tourism companies, who are selling holidays to a particular destination, to inform and guide the tourist of local customs. Or is it the responsibility of governments and foreign investors to include local stakeholders in any planning and development of the destination, which will in turn hopefully lead to better communication between visitors and hosts? The lack of local input and consideration along with uneducated visitors suggests not only a business and marketing disaster, but also a negative social impact on the destination and the negative image and experience that the visitor will take back home (Lovelock and Lovelock 2013). A further ethical problem that may arise, especially when selling an intangible service, such as a holiday, is when the marketing exchange is not transparent. This may appear when the image in the brochure is not the same image in reality and the all-inclusive holiday, is not totally inclusive. These issues formulate an additional side to the ethical problems faced in the tourism industry.

Perhaps some of the questions that need to be asked are (1) what expectations did the visitor have before the holiday experience? (2) was the visitor well informed of local values, cultural norms and the do and don'ts of the destination? and (3) who is responsible for this information; governments, industry and/or individuals? It could be argued that all stakeholders are responsible for their actions. However, when dealing with a consumer group, such as hedonist tourists, behavioural guidelines may be required. The UNWTO published a brochure named: "The Responsible Tourist and Traveller", which was approved by the World Committee on Tourism Ethics (WCTE) in May 2005. This code of conduct works with the Global Code of Ethics, giving tourists and travellers guidelines on how to behave responsibly when traveling. Codes of conducts are also supplied by an array of tour operators who specialize in ethical tourism. However, how is the tourist being informed of these conducts? Should the industry be obliged to provide these guidelines with each holiday booking? After much discussion and input from an array of stakeholders, along with "the perceived need to provide a frame of reference that would govern tourism activity across borders" (Fennell 2006, p. 251), the UNWTO approved the Global Code of Ethics for Tourism (GCET) in 1999. The GCET is a reference of 10 principles covering the economic, social, cultural and environmental impacts of tourism. These code addresses the public sector such as governments; the corporate sector, namely the travel industry and societies in general, conversing with host communities and visiting tourists. The UNWTO (1999) defines the GCET on their website as: "A fundamental frame of reference for responsible and sustainable tourism a comprehensive set of principles designed to guide key-players in tourism development. Addressed to governments, the travel industry, communities and tourists alike, it aims to help maximize the sector's benefits while minimizing its potential negative impact on the environment, cultural heritage and societies across the globe." The GCET is not legally binding; however, it does provide guidelines and reference in achieving responsible and sustainable tourism. Through this achievement, stakeholders can assist in reducing the negative impacts on the industry and create a positive vision for one of the world's largest industries.

Additional support is given via the World Committee on Tourism Ethics (WCTE) which was established in 2004 (UNWTO 2015). The WCTE provides support in the interpretation, application and evaluation of the UNWTO Global Code of Ethics for Tourism. The WCTE also endeavours to encourage the application and commitment of the GCET. This was seen in September, 2011 in Madrid when the UNWTO witnessed the signature of private worldwide companies, pledging the promotion and implementation of the 10 principles listed in the GCET. The Committee vocalised the particular importance of acting responsibly by safe-guarding human rights issues, gender equality, accessibility and protection of defenceless communities. To date (April, 2015) a total number of 399 companies and associations from as many as 55 countries worldwide have signed the Private Sector Commitment to the Code of Ethics (UNWTO 2015). Overall, many different codes and conducts are put in place to encourage and guide public and private sectors to be responsible in their tourism business practices. This responsible attitude provides a sustainable framework to work with. The Brundtl and Report in 1987, delivered by the World Commission for the Environment and Development (WCED), defined the three pillars of sustainability which has encouraged an array of alternative tourism-forms to endeavour in the protection of the environment via ecotourism, generate equality via fair trade tourism and social protection and justice via ethical tourism. As Lovelock and Lovelock (2013) explain, ethics is behaviour and social behaviour in a sense, creates ethical tourism.

With the encouragement of applying the industry's Global Code of Ethics for Tourism, stakeholders may not only see some sustainability of resources, but also support in generating stability for the industry as a whole. However, the reality of adhering to a global code of ethics and rectifying the problem that comes with ongoing impacts is not that straightforward and has received some criticism. As Selmi et al. (2012, p. 135) explain, "The existence of a code is, of course, no guarantee of ethical practices". Lovelock and Lovelock (2013) also highlight that given that the industry has so many different codes and conducts servicing its multitude of sectors, it is surprising that there are still so many ethical problems. A solution could be that stricter rules and penalising legislation is implemented, making the GCET law-binding. Perhaps more realistic guidelines need to be put into place with input from independent, smaller players along with host communities. These are the real contacts that the visitor has with the industry and who are arguably most affected by tourism practices when visiting a destination. Although the content of certain codes and conducts may be put into question and subjected to further discussion, there is evidence that tour operations, associations and travellers are continuing to the sustainability of tourism. This is seen with tour operations who have joined with ATR (Agir Pour un Tourism Responsible; Action for Responsible Tourism) and ATES (Association pour le Tourism Equitable et Solitaire; Association for Equitable and Interdependent Tourism) (Dornier et al. 2010), along with the UK's Tourism Concern and the Association of British Travel Agents (ABTA) who are active in promoting responsible tourism. Websites such as Ethical Traveller encourage, inform and educate visitors along with 'Rough Guide—Better World', one of the travel industry's most used travel guides and social networks enable travellers to discuss, inform and recommend future like-minded travellers. Evidence of having codes and practices in place has also proven to give positive results via a survey carried out by the NGO Tearfund in 2002. The survey's objective was to establish attitudes towards ethical and responsible tourism. Results showed that 45% of respondents would purchase a holiday from a company who applied codes that guaranteed good working conditions for employees, protected the environment and supported local charities. The NGO also indicate that these results would create competitive advantage for a tourism company (Weeden 2005a, b).

## 2.3 Evolution of the Ethical Tourist

The review to date has cited that Fair Trade products, environmentalism, human rights concerns as well and general consumer awareness have made the consumer more ethical in their purchasing of certain goods. Communication through the media tells us that we need to be more responsible as consumers, forcing positive attitudes and images of those companies that are operating responsibly and are involved in ethical actions. This has been applied to the tourism industry where like, the Fair Trade Movement, "enterprises (and associations) can now badge themselves as 'ethical' in terms of environmental standards, work practices and cultural sensitivity" (Gibson 2009, p. 2). The trend for a different type of holiday, for example, one away from the mass of tourists, was described by Krippendorf (1987) as far back as almost 25 years ago, when he applied the need for a different type of tourism experience to Maslow's pyramid of needs. Once the tourists' basic needs such as sleeping, eating and drinking were satisfied, the tourist would require emotional-needs satisfaction. These come in the form of social interaction, self-realisation, knowledge and exploration, creating a tourist typology with independent, respectful and responsible towards the environment and the societal environment being visited. Tourists are becoming much more demanding in general. King (2002) states that 'travel' is much more than visiting a place; it's about restoring oneself, about achievement and experiences. Today 'tourism and travel' are more of a statement, what one would like to see in themselves and their lifestyle (King 2002). The need for a more emotional experience in holidaymaking "is a specific example of the consumer trend towards the purchase of more ethically traded products and increasing pressure across most sectors for evidence of corporate social responsibility" (Goodwin and Francis 2003, p. 272). The growth of tourists visiting developing countries generated a campaign by the association Butcher and Smith (2010) for ethical actions from the tourist as well as the industry. VSO insist that tourists "want to interact with local people and to enjoy a new environment when visiting a developing country" (VSO 1998 in Goodwin and Francis 2003, p. 276).

The association (VSO) believes that tourists require specific information about the local community; how they can get the most out of their holiday and that they receive the guidance and reassurance of visiting particular areas with guaranteed safety. If the tourist does not have the information, then they will stay within the confines of the hotel or complex and not dare or risk the unknown. It could be argued that both the visitor and the host are missing out in emotional and economic opportunities respectively. There is however a paradox in this trend of ethical behaviour; purchasing Fair Trade products has proven to be more egocentric than actually supporting communities in the less developing world. Consumers have a desire to make themselves feel good and 'responsible' (McDonald et al. 2010) be it by purchasing recyclable products, supporting a charity or through their travelling behaviour. "The aspiration to feel good is one of the main drivers of responsible tourism" (Goodwin and Francis 2003, p. 273). Concluding that ethics do not only encourage sustainability, they also assist in the differentiation of goods and services.

'Price' was noted for being be one of the principal factors in influencing and determining holiday destination choice and the purchasing of tourism products (Weeden 2005a, b). However, it has been highlighted through the literature that the 'feel good factor' of being ethical and knowing that your destination choice conforms to ethical actions via its environmental, social and economic equity draws a certain type of tourist to different alternative tourism forms. This was also found in research carried out by Mehmetoglu (2007), who noted that the motivations of nature-focused tourists to Norway, enabled the authors to segment and place the tourists into three classifications; culture- and pleasure- orientated, nature-orientated and low-activity-orientated, determining an offering of different types of nature-based holiday activities.

## 3 Discussion

In Greece and Cyprus there are many area destinations eroded by low-quality tourism and essentially led to decadent tourism. These destinations are Malia in Crete, Faliraki in Rhodes, Laganas in Zakynthos, Kardamena in Kos, the Kavos in Corfu Corfu and Ayia Napa in Cyprus. An important role in Kavos and Faliraki is played by the so-called 'workers', who, for this region, come from England. On most of the cases, those are British workers who often engage in a negotiation with the local bars so to get the best possible price on alcoholic drinks, even if those are not of the approved standards and quality. The result is that many young tourists are getting drunk and out of control, resulting into bar fights, violence and sex crimes. According to Lytras and Papageorgiou (2014), this is a situation where often the tourist groups are getting out of control something which raises ethics issues for the tourist industry.

This brings a major ethical issue since it seems that despite of the disapproval of those practices from the local communities, still it seems that it is a practice widely accepted form the tourist industry. Hence, despite of the ethics which are promoted from the various organizations and from the industry, still it seems that the locals and the intermediaries do not care so much for ethics. Hence, it is reasonable to ask for the use of international tourist standards on ethics so to counter this type of situation in destinations such as: Kavos and Faliraki.

## 4 Conclusions

The World Tourism Organization is recognizing the significant effect of tourism on local communities, the environment and economy in general, introduced in 1999 the Global Code of Ethics for Tourism, comprising 10 articles and designed to minimize potential negative impacts of tourism on destinations and host communities. It is a set of principles, which establish the basis for sustainable development of tourism and addressed to all stakeholders (local and national authorities, local community of professionals, tourism industry, tourists), stressing the rights and obligations of each side. Moreover, a global community of researchers dealing with tourism has identified the great influence of morality in the way that tourists choose the location of their holiday, but also in guiding their behaviour during their travels. Hence, it is important for the authorities on those areas and for the sake of the ethics of the local tourist industry. This is also a topic for a future research, which aims at exploring the views and positions of the people who are engaged on this type of tourism.

## References

Abrams, D., Houston, D. M., Van de Vyer, J., & Vasiljevic, M. (2015). Equality hypocrisy, inconsistency, and prejudice: The unequal application of the universal human right to equality. *Peace and Conflict: Journal of Peace and Psychology, 21*(1), 28–46.

Butcher, J., & Smith, P. (2010). 'Making a difference': Volunteer tourism and development. *Tourism Recreation Research, 35*(1), 27–36.

Dornier, R., Cothias, V., & Loussaïef, L. (2010). The application of collective ethics charters: The case of French adventure tour-operators. *International Business Research, 4*(1), p133.

Ethical Traveler. (2015). *The world's ten best ethical destinations 2015.*

Feighery, W. G. (2011). Consulting ethics. *Annals of Tourism Research, 38*(3), 1031–1050.

Fennell, D. A. (2006). *Tourism ethics* (Vol. 30). Clevedon: Channel View Publications.

Fennell, D. A., & Malloy, D. C. (1999). Measuring the ethical nature of tourism operators. *Annals of Tourism Research, 26*(4), 928–943.

Genot (1995) In Fennell, D. A. (2006). *Tourism ethics* (Vol. 30). Channel View Publications.

Gibson, C. (2009). Geographies of tourism: (Un) ethical encounters. *Progress in Human Geography, 33*, 527–534.

Goodwin, H., & Francis, J. (2003). Ethical and responsible tourism: Consumer trends in the UK. *Journal of Vacation Marketing, 9*(3), 271–284.

Holden, A. (2009). The environment-tourism nexus: Influence of market ethics. *Annals of Tourism Research, 36*(3), 373–389.

Hultsman, J. (1995). Just tourism: An ethical framework. *Annals of Tourism Research, 22*(3), 553–567.

Ireland, K. (1993). Sexual exploitation of children and international travel and tourism. *Child Abuse Review, 2*, 263–270.

Jarvis, N., Weeden, C., & Simcock, N. (2010). The benefits and challenges of sustainable tourism certification: A case study of the green tourism business scheme in the west of England. *Journal of Hospitality and Tourism Management, 17*(01), 83–93.

King, J. (2002). Destination marketing organizations—Connecting the experience rather than promoting the place. *Journal of Vacation Marketing, 8*(2), 105–108.

Krippendorf, J. (1987). Ecological approach to tourism marketing. *Tourism Management, 8*(2), 174–176.

Lovelock, B. (2008). Ethical travel decisions travel agents and human rights. *Annals of Tourism Research, 35*(2), 338–358.

Lovelock, B., & Lovelock, K. (2013). *The ethics of tourism: Critical and applied perspectives.* London: Routledge.

Lytras, P., & Papageorgiou, A. (2014). *Tourism hurting ...The hidden side and defamatory.* Athens: Papazisis.

Maignan, I., Ferrell, O. C., & Ferrell, L. (2005). A stakeholder model for implementing social responsibility in marketing. *European Journal of Marketing, 39*(9/10), 956–977.

Malloy, D. C., & Fennell, D. A. (1998). Codes of ethics and tourism: An exploratory content analysis. *Tourism Management, 19*(5), 453–461.

McDonald, J., Scotto, M. J., & Boyer, A. (2010). *CSR and ethics in tourist destination brand image*. In: actes du Colloque du 7e Congrès de l'ADERSE : RSE & Innovation, Groupe Sup de Co La Rochelle, 24–26 mars 2010.

Mehmetoglu, M. (2007). Typologising nature-based tourists by activity – theoretical and practical implications. *Tourism Management, 28*(3), 651–660.

Moufakkir, O. (2012). Of ethics, leisure and tourism: The 'serious fun of doing tourism'. In *Controversies in Tourism* (pp. 7–22). Cambridge, MA: CAB.

Novelli, M. (Ed.). (2005). *Niche tourism: Contemporary issues, trends and cases*. London: Routledge.

Payne, D., & Dimanche, F. (1996). Towards a code of conduct for the tourism industry: An ethics model. *Journal of Business Ethics, 15*(9), 997–1007.

Payne, D., & Dimanche, F. (1998). Towards a code of conduct for the tourism industry: An ethics model. *Journal of Business Ethics, 15*, 997–1007.

Rivers-Moore, M. (2011). Imagining others: Sex, race, and power in transactional sex tourism. *An International E-Journal for Critical Geographies, 10*(3), 392–341.

Selmi, N., Tur, C., & Dornier, R. (2012). To what extent may sites of death be tourism destinations? The cases of Hiroshima in Japan and Struthof in France. *Asian Business & Management, 11*(3), 311–328.

Tearfund. (2002). "Worlds apart": A call to responsible global tourism. http://www.tearfund.org/webdocs/Website/Campaigning/Policy%2520and%25

Tribe, J. (2002). Education for ethical tourism action. *Journal of Sustainable Tourism, 10*(4), 309–324.

UNWTO. (1999). *Global code of ethics for responsible tourism.* http://www.unwto.org

UNWTO. (2015). *World committee on tourism ethics.* http://ethics.unwto.org/en/content/world-committee-tourism-ethics

Weeden, C. (2002). Ethical tourism: An opportunity for competitive advantage? *Journal of Vacation Marketing, 8*(2), 141–153.

Weeden, C. (2005a). Ethical tourism, is its future in niche tourism? In M. Novelli (Ed.), *Niche tourism, contemporary issues, trends and cases*. Oxford: Butterworth Heinemann.

Weeden, C. (2005b). A qualitative approach to the ethical consumer: The use of focus groups for cognitive consumer research in tourism. *Tourism Research Methods, 179.*

# Security Perceptions of Tourists in the Aftermath of Terrorist Attacks

**Laura Annabel Peters and Alexis Papathanassis**

## 1 Introduction

In a globally driven market with a large number of products, it is essential for suppliers to identify the needs and desires of potential customers. One main element of these needs and wishes is the psychological perspective. The more intangible a good is, the more important is the trust factor. Intangible goods, such as services in general and holidays in particular, cannot be tested in advance, so consumers need to trust the supplier, who is selling only a description of how the vacation might look like (Nepomuceno et al. 2014).

In tourism, one main factors of holiday decision-making is the tourists' safety and security perceptions. Perception can be influenced in many ways (Reisinger and Mavondo 2005). One influencing factor is the occurrence of terrorist attacks; but there can be several other factors that contribute to a feeling of insecurity (Lepp and Gibson 2003). In the following we aim at examining those factors and subsequently formulating tentative hypotheses for further research.

## 2 Research Method

First, a literature review was conducted to synthesise relevant findings derived from former studies, while key themes and research gaps were identified. Due to the fact that the selected topic is rather complex and just experienced travellers, who were

L. A. Peters (✉) · A. Papathanassis
Cruise Tourism Management, Bremerhaven University of Applied Sciences, Bremerhaven, Germany
e-mail: lpeters@studenten.hs-bremerhaven.de



A. Papathanassis et al. (eds.), *Yellow Tourism*, Tourism, Hospitality & Event Management, https://doi.org/10.1007/978-3-319-94664-1_5

already confronted with the issue of security, are able to give a usable and valid feedback, the qualitative research method was adopted.

The data collection method employed consists of conducting and coding data from semi-structured interviews of experienced travellers. The ultimate aim is the creation of a rich picture describing what could be valid for the main part of society. The results of this study, may contribute to measuring the effectiveness of security measures, beyond the deterrence of terrorist attacks, as to include the dimension of instilling a feeling of safety and security for guests.

## 3 Literature Review

### *3.1 Introduction*

Currently, new terrorist attacks around the globe are proliferating the news and media. Often these terrorist attacks take place at holiday destinations. One major reason for this, is the guaranteed international media coverage, given that the victims are mainly tourists from different places of the world (Paraskevas and Arendell 2007). The tourism sector is highly vulnerable to crises such as wars or terrorism. Even if the tourism industry itself (e. g. hotels or tourist beaches) has not actually been a target of an attack, there is still an impact on the industry, especially at the destination that had been attacked (Kılıçlar et al. 2017).

### *3.2 Definition Terrorism*

Terrorism is “the unlawful use of violence and intimidation, especially against civilians, in the pursuit of political aims” (Oxford English Dictionary 2005, p. 785). This definition of terrorism was published in the year 2005. It illustrates the focus and scope shift of terrorism during the last years. In former times, political agendas and conflicts seemed to be the main motive for terror activities. Today, as the terror group the “Islamic State” (IS) is mainly in charge for the biggest parts of ongoing attacks, the definition is not as clear anymore. This group is operating on the fundament of religious conviction and not mainly because of political reasons, even though they abhor the western values including the political direction (Galloway 2016).

Therefore, an adapted definition which is fitting modern terrorism was published at the online dictionary: vocabulary.com. This definition states that a terrorist attack is “the calculated use of violence (or the threat of violence) against civilians in order to attain goals that are political or religious or ideological in nature; this is done through intimidation or coercion or instilling fear” (vocabulary.com, n.d.).

## 3.3 Definition Risk Perception in the Tourism Industry

Risk perception can be defined as the fear of being injured, experience an unwanted dangerous situation or the potential loss of something important (Reisinger and Mavondo 2005). There are several factors that have an impact on tourists' risk perceptions; particularly in terms of safety and security. The main influencing factors investigated by former studies are: terrorism, war, political instability as well as health concerns, criminality (Lepp and Gibson 2003), weather and social hazards. As risk perceptions tend to be subjective, it can vary from tourist to tourist, due to several individual characteristics (Reisinger and Mavondo 2005). Nevertheless, fears of political unrest and/or terrorism seem to be regarded as the greatest risks for tourists (Wolff and Larsen 2013).

## 3.4 Terrorism and the Tourism Industry

Many destinations have suffered in the aftermath of terrorist attacks (Avraham 2016). Experts assume that destinations like Turkey, Tunisia and Egypt are not likely to recover in 2017. German tourists perceive these destinations, as well as the USA and France to be the most dangerous places at the moment (Singer 2017). Thus, the scientific work of Avraham (2016) indicates that the political instability in Egypt, and above all, the terrorist attacks within the destination are the main source of declining tourist numbers.

Most destinations recover rather fast after terrorist attacks. A single attack seems to have no long-term impact on tourist numbers. Nevertheless, the short-term effects are visible (Araña and León 2007; Liu and Pratt 2017). In a survey of 6000 tourists in nine different countries, 97% of the respondents indicated that while choosing a holiday destination, the factor of safety and security is highly- and increasingly-present in their mind (Singer 2017). This suggests that, when attacks occur more frequently, the destination may well suffer from long-term effects (Liu and Pratt 2017). On the other hand, tourists from Russia, the United States of America and China are more likely to tolerate the risk of terror attacks, in case a lower price of the holiday is offered (Singer 2017). But there are also winners of such crises. The tourism market at destinations like Greece, the western Mediterranean or even long-haul destinations like the Caribbean are predicted to have a significant growth in tourist numbers as these destinations are regarded as safer (Singer 2017).

### 3.4.1 How to Recover from Crises

To recover from crises and to increase the safety and security factor has to be the main desire of a destination. Paraskevas and Arendell (2007) indicate that it is the destination management organization's task to create destination wide strategies in order to coordinate stakeholders and to effectively prevent terrorist attacks. These strategies shall be implemented even before incidents emerge. Therefore, destination management organizations should reflect past incidents at other destinations and proactively share crises management knowledge and experience among each other. An issue of crises management is often the absence of communication among the numerous stakeholders and the multiple ways to handle crises. Different hotels, airports, etc. at one destination often do not have a common way to implement security measures and therefore the ability to work together efficiently is not given (Paraskevas and Arendell 2007).

# 4 Research

## *4.1 Interview Participants*

A total of 13 respondents, representing four different nationalities, were interviewed (2 males and 11 females). These interview respondents were of differing ages and professions (eight different professional groups). Furthermore, the interviewees were between the age of 21 and 69 years. The seemingly small number of participants was sufficient to reach data-saturation (i.e. additional interviews do not add novel aspects). At this point it is important to re-state that the purpose of this piece of research is a qualitative exploration of potential factors (tentative hypotheses) affecting security perceptions; and not their quantification and generalisation (Table 1).

**Table 1** Interview respondents: sample characteristics

| Participant | Age | Nationality | Profession | Male/female |
|---|---|---|---|---|
| 1 | 28 | German | Office Clerk | Female |
| 2 | 59 | German | Forwarding Merchant | Female |
| 3 | 69 | German | Pensioner | Male |
| 4 | 28 | German | Student | Female |
| 5 | 41 | German | Travel Agent | Female |
| 6 | 31 | Columbian | Student | Female |
| 7 | 22 | Polish | Student | Female |
| 8 | 25 | German | Student | Female |
| 9 | 26 | German | Student | Female |
| 10 | 24 | German | Student | Male |
| 11 | 21 | German | Student/Receptionist | Female |
| 12 | 30 | German | Administration Secretary | Female |
| 13 | 32 | American | Quality Analyst | Female |

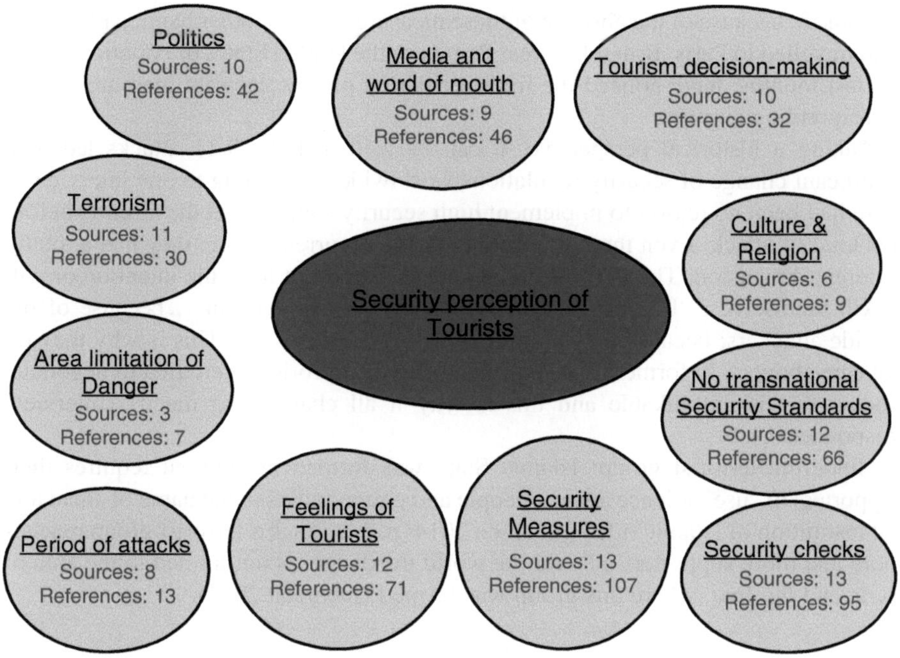


**Fig. 1** Axial codes

## *4.2 Category Formation (Axial Codes)*

To identify the main topics of interest, the transcribed interview texts were coded line-by-line. All the interview transcripts were read line-by-line and analysed sentence-by-sentence in order to discover open codes, which were then organised and grouped into categories. From a total of 526 codes, 11 categories were formed (see Fig. 1). In Fig. 1, the 'sources' refer to the number of interviews where codes fitting the category were present. Furthermore, the 'references' indicate the total number of codes in the category. In the following pages, the key findings regarding the categories are presented and tentative hypotheses are generated on this basis.

### 4.2.1 Terrorism

Terrorism got on a new stage during the last years. Having a look at the attacks, it becomes obvious that their quantity has dramatically increased since the attack in Paris on January the 7th 2015, when two men entered the building of the satirical newspaper "Charlie Hebdo" and killed 12 people (Foster 2017). However, even though a number of terror attacks took place in Turkey, the interviewees reported that they did not notice an implementation new security measures at this certain destination. At the same time, these experienced tourists indicated that they do not feel unsafe because of the absence of these measures. On the other hand, participants who travelled to Paris, Brussels, Great Britain or the United States of America during the last months, have noticed the implementation of new security measures in the corresponding airports.

Taking a historical perspective, it can be said that the 9/11 attacks led to a significant change of security regulations worldwide. According to one interviewee there had been no reason to implement high security standards at the airports before this kind of attack. Even though terrorist attacks occurred before, they had a totally different dimension. The terrorists of former days did not have the intention or will to kill themselves: "It changed to a totally different dimension… because of the suicide attackers; because they are not interested in surviving. This is why they do not care about… In former times in Mogadishu the terrorists even tried to negotiate. Today, this is unthinkable and this is why it all changed so much" (Interview Respondent).

Since the terrorist group: Islamic State was formed in 2006, it requires their supporters to "use violence against people and communities in the name of Jihad and the institution of Islamic rule" (Jabareen 2014, p. 54). As this terrorist group reaches more and more supporters all over the world the danger is not limited to the area of Syria and the Iraq, where this group was formed (Jabareen 2014).

### 4.2.2 Period and Number of Terrorist Attacks

As already mentioned, the aftermath of terrorist attacks is often just visible for a short time. One example for a short-term affected destination is France. This can be seen in a survey of the magazine FVW, which reported that in November 2015, 16% of the survey's participants indicated that they are not willing to travel to France. In February 2017 this number decreased by 6%. On the other hand, destinations like Turkey or Egypt seem to suffer from longer-term effects. The willingness to travel to Turkey is still decreasing (Krane 2017). One reason for this seems to be the large number- as well as the periodical nature of attacks. Nevertheless, one participant acknowledged that in Egypt, tourist numbers seem to recover at the moment. She interpreted this phenomenon as the result of no terrorist attacks over several months in Egypt. Moreover, she believed that if there would be no attack in Turkey for a longer period, people might as well start traveling to this destination again.

### 4.2.3 Area Limitation of Danger

"[…] That was only Istanbul which was a target of many attacks, where a lot of violence took place, but Istanbul is only a very small part of Turkey" (Interview Respondent). During the interviews three participants indicated that the danger of terror attacks or other factors influencing the security of tourists can often be limited to certain areas. According to these interviewees, even if attacks happen or civil unrest takes place at a particular destination, not the whole country is in danger.

Nevertheless, people often misinterpret the situation and perceive the whole country as being unsafe. Another opinion is that only big cities like Paris or Brussels seem to be in danger of attacks. Some respondents reported that the presence of military- and security personnel at bigger cities is much higher than elsewhere. This also leads to the impression that these places are at a higher risk.

### 4.2.4 Politics

"The only reasons for me not to travel to a country are political reasons" (Interview Respondent). This quote illustrates that the political situation often has much more to do with the willingness to travel to destinations than the danger of a terrorist attack. One interviewee who travelled to Moscow described a feeling of being monitored at the destination. Furthermore, some participants indicated that they would not travel to destinations like Turkey, Egypt or the United States of America because they are not willing to support the existing government by traveling there and spending money. However, they underline that their holiday decision does not rely on perceived security risk. Therefore, a change in the political system would often have a higher impact on tourism decision-making than anything else.

On the other hand, the interviewees reported that they believe that an instable political system has also an impact on the probability of a terrorist attack. One respondent reported that many inhabitants are not content with the political system in Turkey and therefore some attacks could be seen as a revolt against the government. One example for this, was the attempt of a coup against the government of Turkey carried out by Turkish military officials on July 16, 2016 (The Washington Post 2016). Additionally, the Turkish government declared to reserve the right to impose a travel ban, which was met by mistrust from the side of potential tourists. Some tourists are scared of travelling to Turkey and then not being able to leave the country again. Furthermore, the Turkish president Recep Tayyip Erdoğan is fighting for the reintroduction of the death penalty, which can be seen as a denial of democracy (Zeit Online 2016). Aside the political instability and institutional lack of reliability, the difference in the political systems plays a role in holiday decision-making as well as in the security- and risk perception of tourists. "[. . .] in Saudi if you would go there. They have different regulations and some things that are illegal in the rest of the world, there, they are legal. So if those kinds of things could affect you directly, then you wouldn't go there. So if the politics have designed a system that works against the tourists, then they would not go" (Interview Respondent). This quote illustrates that even though a political situation can be stable, different laws and regulations can lead to a perceived risk of traveling to those places.

### 4.2.5 Culture and Religion

Culture and religion are important factors for tourists to feel safe at a destination. Due to the fact that destinations like Paris or London seem to have similar cultural values to German cities, tourists from Germany often feel safer at these destinations. Even though, many terrorist attacks took place in Great Britain, most of the interviewees indicated that they would still travel to destinations in Great Britain rather than destinations in Turkey or Egypt. As a reason for this, they mentioned that strict Muslim countries often give the impression of not accepting other religions and that women are regarded as inferior to men. A similar and/or compatible culture and religion at the destination seems to give tourists a feeling of control. It feels like home and they have a familiar daily routine. The study of Jafar Jafari and Noel Scott describes the relationship between religion and the choice of the travel destination. This study points out that there is a significant relationship. Nevertheless, Jafari and Scott also underline that there can be many differences between different Muslim countries, or even in the areas of a certain country and their behaviour towards tourists. This behaviour and the way the community lives their Muslim values and restrictions can be highly influenced by the local government as well as other factors (Jafari and Scott 2014). Moreover, another impression of the interview participants was that countries like France or England give incoming tourists a feeling of being more welcome. Furthermore, a few of the interviewees also explained that destinations like Egypt or Turkey, as they are mainly Muslim countries, could be easily connected to radical terrorist groups like the Islamic State by tourists.

### 4.2.6 Media and Word of Mouth

People often regard news- and others' experiences as the only reliable source of information. As the tourist product is intangible and travellers are not able to test the product in advance, many tourists try to seek for information with their peers and in the media. Many interviewees described that even though they believe that the news often exaggerate the current situation at impacted destinations, they are not willing to find out on their own whether this information is correct or not. One participant described the media like this: "[. . .] So they can always focus on certain events and they tend to focus on things that keep people talking and get people interested and get the noise going about their new story. Nobody talks about the good stuff" (Interview Respondent). This quote suggests that the positive events are often left out by the media because they seem to be not as interesting as the negative events. In contrast to that, most frequent travellers often react differently. Often those frequent travellers reported that they still decided to visit countries like Turkey and were surprised by the misinformation of the press. They described that they never had a feeling of not being safe at the destination. On the other hand, they also indicated that they understand those who are not willing to travel to affected countries, as the media is feeding peoples' anxiety. The study of Tazayian Sayira and Hazel Andrews focuses on the destination of Chilas in Pakistan. This paper illustrates that the image of this destination is mainly impacted by word-of-mouth communication as well as other communication media. Furthermore, the study describes that mainly during and after crises the media plays a very important role. Nevertheless, Sayira and Andrews indicated that the media reports or the information does not always match the reality

(Sayira and Andrews 2016). On the other hand, the interviewees also mentioned the positive effects news reports can have. The media can be used for positive marketing and therefore it can help to repair a destination's image rather fast.

### 4.2.7 Feeling of Tourists

People's feelings such as anxiety, happiness and anticipation, are important factors, which contribute to the degree of holiday enjoyment. Security measures and checks are only some factors that can have both positive and negative impact on these feelings. Many people seem to be rather scared by highly-visible security measures. On the other hand, they strive for a basic safety in the tourism sector. It appears to be very important to implement the right degree of security measure visibility. One participant described that after she went through the normal security checks at the airport, the staff in the plane wanted to check the entire cabin luggage again. "I felt nervous because of that because they wanted to check twice" (Interview Respondent). On the contrary, low degree and visibility of security checks and measures can also generate negative feelings as nothing can be done if a dangerous situation occurs. Terror attacks always generate a feeling of discomfort and the media coverage tends to induce these feelings. But the recovery and the recuperation of feelings of security after such attacks are mediated by totally different factors like the culture and religion of a country. This includes laws and the treatment of women, as well as the overall political situation, as already described in the sections above.

### 4.2.8 Tourism Decision-Making

"I would not stop traveling to places because there was a terrorist attack. [...] This is not really relevant for me [...]" (Interview Respondent). There are several factors influencing holiday decision-making (Reisinger and Mavondo 2005). Nevertheless, holiday decision-making is a very subjective process and varies from person to person. Many people are influenced by the media or by word-of-mouth. Some interviewees explained that they already changed their travel behaviour as a result of ongoing reports about terror attacks, wars or because of political reasons. Moreover, one participant described that she is very upset of not being able to travel to places like Syria, especially Aleppo, as this place is the origin of Christianity. She explained that there is no way that there could be any security measure, which would make her feel safe again within this country. Furthermore, one participant explained that in her opinion it is very easy to find a substitute for destinations like Turkey or Egypt. For her, the usual sun and beach holiday she intends to do when she would travel to Turkey or Egypt, she is able to do anywhere else and this is why she would rather travel to safer places. However, she also pointed out, that this would not be the case at destinations like Paris because in her opinion Paris has way more to offer than other destinations. She reported: "Paris holidays would be mainly a sightseeing holiday [...] and the Eifel tower you are only able to see in Paris" (Interview

Respondent). Furthermore, a very interesting result during the interviews was that almost all of the interviewees indicated that none of the new implemented security measures would have an impact on their own traveling decision or their perception of security.

### 4.2.9 Security Checks

Security checks are the main tool to ensure the safety of tourists. In former times it was common to have security checks only at the airport. Today, not only the existing checks at the airports have been adapted to novel types of risks, but also several new security checks have been implemented in different places such as: subway stations and shopping malls. As one of the interview participants described: "[. . .] everywhere I went like big shopping malls, subway stations etc. they checked almost every purse" (Interview Respondent). Most of the interview participants see the security checks and the majority of corresponding rules and regulations as necessary and important to ensure safety. Other studies describe that there seem to be many people who think differently from our interview participants. Even regular, traditional security measures (i.e. not newly implemented) appear to create tensions between the security staff and the passengers at the airport. Sometimes this even leads to aggressive behaviour between those two parties (Skorupski and Uchroŋski 2016). As soon a security check deviates from the expected routine, it can cause discomfort for the tourists. One respondent described a situation where she was tested on traces of explosive substances. She described the situation as awkward and asked herself why they chose her, as this does not belong to the normal routine of security checks. Another factor which can cause discomfort is that some of the rules and regulations seem to be hard to understand for tourists. One described her incomprehension of the liquids regulation. She does not understand why it is allowed to carry a certain amount of liquids instead of a complete banning of all liquids in the cabin luggage. She added that if there could be dangerous liquids inside a carry-on, they could be dangerous in small potions as well. The system is often not transparent enough and the reasons for changes in regulations are often not well communicated.

### 4.2.10 Security Measures

"I believe that many people demand more safety especially because of the incidents during the last years" (Interview Respondent). Comparable to security checks, security measures appear to be another main part of traveller safety. These security measures can differ a lot from destination to destination. Our interview respondents experienced security measures such as military checkpoints on the streets in Egypt, military staff at the entrance of political buildings as well as security staff at bigger events. Moreover, the German respondents described the German security system as very reliable. Even though, these measures seem to be rather invisible in comparison to other destinations, most of the interview participants reported to feel quite safe in

Germany. Nevertheless, security measures do not always contribute to a feeling of security. Many participants expressed the opinion that none of these measures can eliminate the danger of terror attacks. In addition, they pointed out that newly implemented security measures would not be sufficient a reason for tourists to travel to a destination which they currently choose to avoid; even though, many of the affected destinations introduce new security measures partly in the hope of winning back customers (Goodrich 2002). Several participants indicated that a high degree of security measures, for example at festivals or other party locations, will lead to a loss of the party mood. One of them states: "[. . .] There had been probably undercover security staff but you did not recognise them, which is good. It might sound a bit selfish, but if you want to party then you want to party and not being reminded of the horrible things (meaning the terrorist attacks)" (Interview Respondent).

### 4.2.11 No Transnational Security Standards

"In Brussels when I arrived they opened all the luggage and one lady was checking everything with her hands. And it was very different for me because Hamburg was easier. They are scanning this and that is all. And here she opened everything and she asked about some cosmetics and yes. . . It was stronger, yes" (Interview Respondent). Even though, travellers strive for familiarity regarding security measures and checks, there are many differences around the globe. The Interviewees indicated that in Spanish or German destinations security measures are hardly visible at all. There are just the usual security checks one is subjected going through to the departure area (gates). In destinations such as Egypt a completely different picture can be observed. There are many soldiers on the street equipped with machine guns, as already described in the section above. Another destination with high security standards appears to be Moscow in Russia. One interviewee described that she was forced to hand in her passport at the hotel reception and had to leave it there until she checked out. For her it was a strange situation to walk through an unknown country without having a passport.

Additionally, there was a high presence of security staff at the hotel, who controlled whether they were really guests of the hotel every time they entered. The overall impression formed during our research was that most of the respondents felt rather insecure in the presence of too many visible security measures. High-visibility of security measures can frighten travellers, who may, as a result, interpret the situation to be highly dangerous. This is often the case when travellers are not familiar with it, when comparing them with security measures at their country of origin.

On the other hand, if security checks are not visibly thorough enough at certain airports, this can also contribute to a feeling of discomfort. Participants reported that at some airports in Turkey, for example, they were able to experience inconsequent security checks. Interview participants who already experienced a flight to the USA, mentioned a lengthy procedure consisting of numerous security checks. This procedure already starts with the application for a visa, as tourists have to provide a lot of personal information in order to apply (US Customs and Border Protection n.d.).

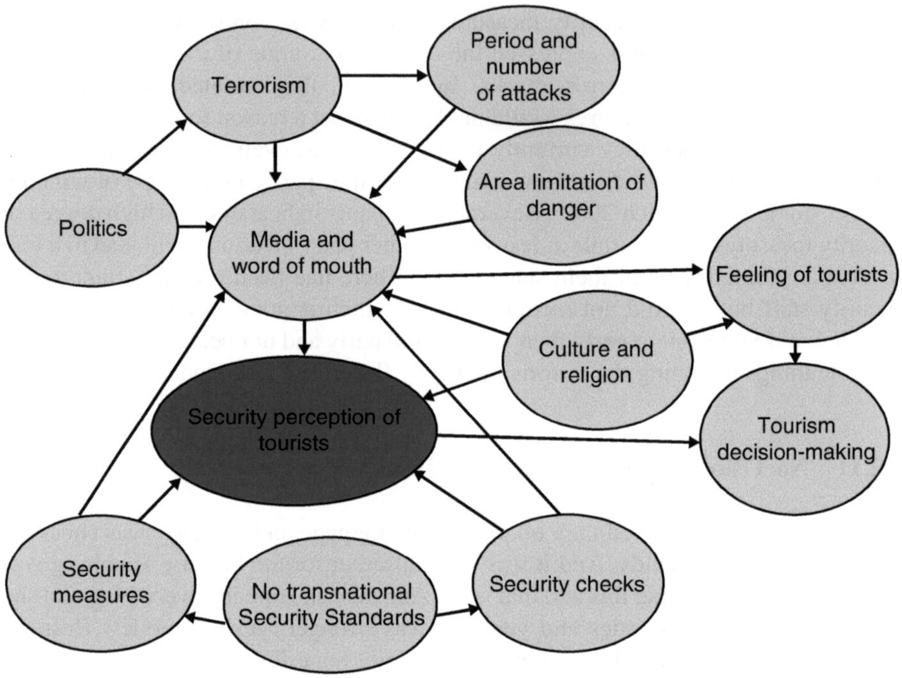


**Fig. 2** Model of relationship between categories

Moreover, the luggage checks are more thorough than anywhere else. Security staff is checking every single piece of luggage before loading it on the plane. The need to have an equal system for every destination is highly recommendable.

## 5 Modelling and Analysis

The model shows the relationships between the different axial codes resulting from our research and represent the tentative hypotheses for further research (Fig. 2).

### *5.1 Tentative Hypotheses*

*Tentative Hypothesis 1: Politics have a major impact on terrorism*

There are several interviewees who gave feedback during the interviews underlining this finding. One of these quotes is the following: "[. . .] Before the change in the political system in Turkey, there had been no risks of terrorist attacks. That means that as long as Erdogan got along with the Kurds and this was the case for a long time and as long as Erdogan wanted to bring the country forward everything was okay and there had been no terrorist attacks" (Interview Respondent).

*Tentative Hypothesis 2: The political situation described by the media has a greater impact on tourists' security perceptions and their holiday selection/decision than terrorism.*

Many of the respondents stated that they would still travel to destinations which had suffered from terrorist attacks. They suggested that other factors, such as the political situation at a destination, play a more important role regarding their security perception and their holiday selection. This can be underlined with the following quote of one participant: "[...] The main point is how the political situation is in the country. This is the sticking point at both destinations (meaning Egypt and Turkey) that there had been a lot of political incorrectness. This is sticking in most of the peoples' heads as well as the current situation regarding Erdogan who is talking about a travel entry ban" (Interview Respondent).

*Tentative Hypothesis 3: Media and word-of-mouth seem to be the main determinants of security perceptions and holiday selection/decision.*

This indicates that tourists are often influenced by the experience reports of other people or by the media coverage. As these two sources are the main sources of information it appears to have a high impact on security perception as well as other feelings of travellers. Many participants claimed that the media is feeding people's anxiety. The following quote reveals the experience of one interview participants with media coverage:

"[...] In my opinion the media is highly involved in people's decision to travel. They prevent people from travelling, because often at the destination the situation is not as bad as described by the media" (Interview Respondent).

*Tentative Hypothesis 4: Culture and religion at the travel destination has a high impact on tourists' security perception.*

This tentative hypothesis refers to a number of our interview participants, who described that the culture at a destination can cause a feeling of discomfort and a reduced feeling of security if it is distant to the culture and religion of one's own home country. Alternatively, cultural distance can also have a positive impact on peoples' feelings. The following quote is underlying that a welcoming and open culture like the culture of France or UK can lead to a positive feeling of travellers, but it also underlines that the absence of it can lead to the contrary. "[...] Great Britain and France are a lot more welcoming to US citizens especially... or citizens of a lot of other places. You don't see the same tensions between their countries or their citizens to other countries the same way you see from Turkey or Egypt" (Interview Respondent).

*Tentative Hypothesis 5: Tourists' security perceptions are key determinants of holiday selection/decision.*

The holiday-travel-decision is mainly based on emotions and feelings. One of the interview participants, who works as a travel agent described the booking situation with her clients: "[. . .] But I can totally understand every client who does not have a good feeling (meaning traveling to destinations like Egypt or Turkey). Going on holidays with an unpleasant feeling is never a good idea because if you are not a 100% sure while booking then you should probably think about traveling to a different destination where you might feel more comfortable" (Interview Respondent).

*Tentative Hypothesis 6: The perceived degree of security-measure standardisation has a significant impact on tourists' security perception.*

The lack standardisation with regard to security checks and measures around the globe, seems to be a source of insecurity for tourists, especially when confronted with unfamiliar situations. Many of our interviewees describe the checks as very scary, because they are not able to see the logic behind it. One respondent said that she was really surprised about the different security checks at numerous airports: "I am consistently astonished by the difference in security checks at the different destinations" (Interview Respondent).

*Tentative Hypothesis 7: Tourists' security perceptions are significantly influenced by others' reported experiences and media reports.*

The media and others' experience reports are the main source of information prior traveling. Especially when tourists have not been to a certain destination before, they are highly influenced by the information they receive. "Do you think the media is influencing a lot the feeling of security of people?" "Yeah." "And why?" "Because media can manipulate other people. When they are saying that there is a lot of security people and that they are saying it is a good place because you can feel comfortable with this and they want to prevent from another situation and people believe that, so they can make you feel sure that it is really safe" (Interview Respondent).

*Tentative Hypothesis 8: The impact of terrorism reports on tourists' security perceptions depend on the frequency and number of attacks, as well as the size of the corresponding geographical impact.*

Our research suggests that tourists seem to have a heightened risk perception only if the impacted destination had suffered from more than one terrorist attack. Moreover, the geographical scope reported in the media appears to also have an impact on security perceptions. One interview participant mentioned that even though terrorist attacks were limited to Istanbul, the media reported that the entire country (i.e. Turkey) is not safe anymore and people are scared to travel to Turkey in general because of this: "[. . .] and so many people are worried because of all the attacks. But these attacks only affect a small part of Turkey, Istanbul. And the rest of Turkey is actually not affected. Turkey does not only consist of Istanbul" (Interview Respondent).

## 6 Limitations

During the initial stages of research, there was the dilemma of whether to limit the respondent sample to frequent travellers, who are presumably more likely to have experiences with security measures and checks. Yet, during the data analysis it became clear that this option might have actually been a research limitation. Inexperienced travellers may have different views on security measures and checks, adding to the diversity of the sample; and hence to the richness of our findings. Another limitation that emerged during the interviews none of the respondents had ever experienced a terror attack themselves or through their friends or family. Nonetheless, the respondents all made clear that a single terror attack at a destination would not have had an impact on their holiday selection/decision. Yet one could be critical of this contention as it rather hypothetical. Another limitation could be the particular time-frame of this piece of research, as in coincided with a number of terrorist attacks, whilst many destinations had to suffer from political conflicts and/or -instability. The corresponding media coverage may have had been very intensive and sensitised the respondents' views and focus on the matter.

## 7 Conclusion

Understanding security perceptions is a highly relevant topic; especially during critical times. There are many factors that contribute to an unsafe or safe feeling that are not readily obvious. The political aspect seems to particularly relevant in the formation of security-related perceptions. It was surprising to discover that a single terror attack does not appear to have a decisive impact on holiday selection or destination decision; as long as the corresponding country itself is perceived as politically-stable. Moreover, experiencing cultural differences seemed very important for the majority of tourists, but can be also associated with safety-related discomfort. Often it might be challenging for destinations to adapt their own laws and regulations to their tourism target markets, but a compromise is worth considering for the sake of tourism prosperity and development. Finally, striving for a standardisation of security systems, especially at airports, is recommendable.

## References

Araŋa, J. E., & León, C. J. (2007). The impact of terrorism on tourism demand. *Annals of Tourism Research, 55*, 229–315.

Avraham, E. (2016). Destination marketing and image repair during tourism crises: The case of Egypt. *Journal of Hospitality and Tourism Management, 28*, 41–48.

Foster, A. (2017, June 23). Terror attacks timeline: From Paris and Brussels terror to most recent attacks in Europe. *Sunday Express*. Retrieved June 2, 2017, from http://www.express.co.uk/news/world/693421/Terror-attacks-timeline-France-Brussels-Europe-ISIS-killings-Germany-dates-terrorism

Galloway, C. (2016). Media jihad: What PR can learn in Islamic State's public relations masterclass. *Public Relations Review, 42*, 582–590.

Goodrich, J. N. (2002). September 11, 2001 attack on America: A record of the immediate impacts and reactions in the USA travel and tourism industry. *Tourism Management, 23*, 573–580.

Jabareen, Y. (2014). The emerging Islamic State: Terror, territoriality, and the agenda of social transformation. *Geoforum, 58*, 51–55.

Jafari, J., & Scott, N. (2014). Muslim world and its tourisms. *Annals of Tourism Research, 44*, 1–19.

Kılıçlar, A., Uşaklı, A., & Tayfun, A. (2017). Terrorism prevention in tourism destinations: Security forces vs. civil authority perspectives. *Journal of Destination Marketing and Management*, 1–15.

Krane, M. (2017, March 3). Gezieltes Misstrauen – Urlaub in Terrorzielen wie Frankreich oder Deutschland lost keine Verunsicherung aus. Bei der Türkei sieht das ganz anders aus. *FVW*. ITB-Ausgabe 2017, pp. 36–40.

Lepp, A., & Gibson, H. (2003). Tourist roles, perceived risk and international tourism. *Annals of Tourism Research, 30*(3), 606–624.

Liu, A., & Pratt, S. (2017). Tourism's vulnerability and resilience to terrorism. *Tourism Management, 60*, 404–417.

Nepomuceno, M. V., Laroche, M., & Richard, M.-O. (2014). How to reduce perceived risk when buying online: The interactions between intangibility, product knowledge, brand familiarity, privacy and security concerns. *Journal of Retailing and Consumer Services, 21*(4), 619–629.

Oxford English Dictionary. (2005). *Terrorism* (6th ed., p. 785). Oxford: Oxford University Press.

Paraskevas, A., & Arendell, B. (2007). A strategic framework for terrorism prevention and mitigation in tourism destinations. *Tourism Management, 28*, 1560–1573.

Reisinger, Y., & Mavondo, F. (2005). Travel anxiety and intentions to travel internationally: Implications of travel risk perception. *Journal of Travel Research, 43*, 212–225.

Sayria, T., & Andrews, H. (2016). Impacts of crises and communication media on place image: A case study of Chilas, Pakistan. *Journal of Destination Marketing & Management, 5*, 351–360.

Singer, R. (President Travelzoo). (2017, March 8). *Safety and security in global travel.* Lecture presented at ITB Berlin, Berlin.

Skorupski, J., & Uchroński, P. (2016). Managing the process of passenger security control at an airport using the fuzzy inference system. *Expert Systems with Applications, 54*, 284–293.

The Washington Post. (2016, July 18). How the Turkish government regained control after a failed military coup. *The Washington Post*. Retrieved July 3, 2017, from https://www.washingtonpost.com/graphics/world/turkey-military-coup/

US Customs and Border Protection. (n.d.). *Official ESTA application*. Retrieved July 6, 2017, from https://esta.cbp.dhs.gov/esta/

Vocabulary.com. (n.d.). *Terrorist act.* Retrieved June 29, 2017, from https://www.vocabulary.com/dictionary/terrorist%20act

Wolff, K., & Larsen, S. (2013). Can terrorism make us feel safer? Risk perceptions and worries before and after the July 22nd attacks. *Annals of Tourism Research, 44*, 200–209.

Zeit Online. (2016, July 22). Türkei verschärft Ausreisekontrollen. *Zeit Online*. Retrieved June 3, 2017, from http://www.zeit.de/politik/ausland/2016-07/putschversuch-tuerkei-ausreisekontrollen-verschaerfung

# Part II
# Tourism Corruption, Holiday Fraud

# The 'Broken Marbles Theory': Exploring Tourists' Perceptions of Corruption and Their Impact on Travel Behaviour

**Alexis Papathanassis and Nicoleta Ramona Dinu**

## 1 Introduction

Tourism represents an attractive option for economic development and prosperity, especially for developing countries. Yet the structural realities of developing economies may coincide with wider corruption, not just in tourism, but in the entirety of their economic activity spectrum. Yet tourism may be particularly susceptible to corruption. Indeed, it has been suggested that corruption is not only endemic to the tourism sector (Din et al. 2016; Harris 2012), but also potentially irrelevant, or even economically beneficial, from a developmental point of view (Uberti 2016; Fisman and Svensson 2007). Nevertheless, for developing economies, corruption represents a significant challenge since it can result to: loss of tax income, destination reputation loss and ultimately guest-dissatisfaction.

Holidays are information-intensive and emotional in terms of their selection and consumption. Reputation and image are both decisive in this respect. In order to understand and effectively tackle corruption in tourism, its behavioural dynamics and outcomes need to be explored. The obvious place to begin, is to study the impact corruption has on tourists themselves. In line, with Papageorgiou's (2008) argument, understanding the 'personal' (individual level), is essential for understanding the industry's dynamics as a whole.

Therefore, the aim of this study is to explore: What do holiday-makers regard as corrupt practices? How do they react to what they perceive as corrupt practice and

A. Papathanassis (✉)
Cruise Tourism Management, Bremerhaven University of Applied Sciences, Bremerhaven, Germany
e-mail: apapathanassis@hs-bremerhaven.de

N. R. Dinu
Faculty of Economic Sciences, University of Ovidius, Constanta, Romania

 
A. Papathanassis et al. (eds.), *Yellow Tourism*, Tourism, Hospitality & Event Management, https://doi.org/10.1007/978-3-319-94664-1_6

why? How do their perception affect, and are affected by, their experiences (or those of others) with corruption? In the following pages the conceptual model of this study is presented, the research methodology is outlined and the results are discussed.

## 2 Conceptual Model

Assuming that a corruption experience reflects a type of, mostly negative, critical incident during one's holiday, exploring its impact on behaviour would lend itself to a 'Critical Incident Technique' (abbr. CIT) as a research methodology. Bitner et al. (1994) defined an 'incident' as an observable fragment of human activity enabling inferences and predictions related to the corresponding actors. 'Critical incidents' are those that make a significant (positive or negative) contribution in the understanding of an activity or phenomenon (Bitner et al. 1994; Grove and Fisk 1997).

In its generic form, this method involves collecting critical incident descriptions and performing content analysis on them, in order to explore the cognitive and behavioural aspects of the phenomenon at hand; in our case 'holiday-corruption'. The conceptual model adopted for structuring this piece of research is simple, but nonetheless useful framework for exploring tourists': experiences (direct or indirect) with corruption, their behaviour towards them and ultimately the impact of (and on) their perceptions. This model is based on Papathanassis (2016a) work, involving the content analysis of 361 TripAdvisor review which identified the following axial codes:

- Perceptions/Attitudes: Stereotyping (i.e. corruption endemic/particular to a culture and/or mentality), Perceived Authority Competence (i.e. accessibility, effectiveness and professionalism of local authorities), Story-telling Exposure (i.e. others reports/recollections)
- Incidents (Types): Victimisation/Exploitation (e.g. Credit card fraud, overcharging in taxis or excursions or restaurants, forced consumption/payment of services, discrimination), Annoyance (e.g. Aggressive selling, illegal vendors, no acceptance of credit cards, bribery-requests), Service Failure (e.g. Unfair cancellation policies, incomplete refunding, non-serious complaint-handling, reservation loss), Mis-information (e.g. Exploitative regulations, incorrect quality ratings/recommendations, unreliable website information), Heritage Mismanagement (e.g. Environmental pollution, loss of authenticity, architectural deterioration, insufficient attraction maintenance)
- Reactions/Behaviour: Publication/Advocacy (i.e. warning others, publicly exposing corruption), Formal Complaint (e.g. police involvement, legal action, formal complaint to management), Empathy (i.e. feeling sorry for the victims and expressing this), Behavioural Adjustment (i.e. adopting corrupt practices and behaviour to gain benefit).

Those axial codes and the resulting conceptual model are depicted in Fig. 1, and constitutes the hypotheses framework for the remaining part of this paper.

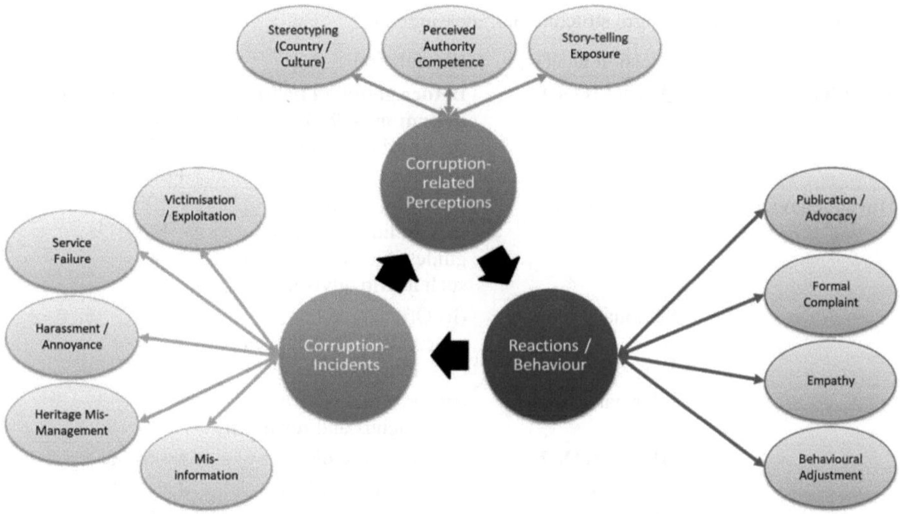


**Fig. 1** The 'holiday corruption triangle'—corruption incidents, tourists' perceptions and reactions

# 3 Methodology

In order to explore and evaluate the conceptual model presented in the previous section, we opted for a quantitative approach based on survey data.

## *3.1 Sampling and Data Collection*

The survey was tested and posted online in 'Google Docs'. The link of the online questionnaire was subsequently posted in various tourism-related Facebook groups, with a request to fill-in and pass it over to others (i.e. 'snowball' sampling method). Between February and March 2017, and after two follow-ups (re-postings online), 268 completed questionnaires were collected and exported in SPSS 2.0 (Statistical Analysis Software) for further analysis. The resulting sample consisted of German- (73%) and English-speaking (27%) respondents. The purpose of distributing the questionnaire in both languages was to enable a more culturally diverse sample.

## *3.2 Questionnaire Design*

The questionnaire consisted of 25 question items, grouped into six questionnaire sections (i.e. 3–4 items per question), each of them corresponding to the elements of the conceptual model. The structure and the measures/questions of the questionnaire are illustrated in detail in Table 1. Regarding the generated data, all survey questions,

**Table 1** Questionnaire design: structure and measurement

| Variable/category | Question label | Formulation | Scale |
|---|---|---|---|
| **REACTIONS** | **QUESTION 1** | **Before going on holiday, I inform myself about the destination/country using:** | 1—Almost Never<br>2—Sometimes<br>3—Moderately<br>4—Extensively<br>5—Very extensively |
| Travel behaviour | Online sources | (i) Online sources (e.g. online destination guides, blogs, review sites such as trip advisor) | |
| | Stationary sources | (ii) Official/off-line sources (e.g. travel agencies, tourist offices) | |
| | Informal sources | (iii) Informal sources (e.g. friends and relatives) | |
| | **QUESTION 2** | **I prefer to book...** | 1—Never<br>2—Rarely<br>3—Occasionally<br>4—Frequently<br>5—Very frequently |
| | Organised- vs. -non-organised travel | (i) Organised holiday packages and tours | |
| | Travel-related cultural distance tolerance | (ii) Holidays in countries which have a familiar and similar culture to mine | |
| | Previous destination experience | (iii) Holidays in countries that I have visited before | |
| **INCIDENTS** | **QUESTION 3** | **During your holidays, have you personally experienced the following:** | 1—Never<br>2—Rarely<br>3—Occasionally<br>4—Frequently<br>5—Very frequently |
| Personal integrity incident | Exploitation/ victimisation | (a) Exploitation and/or victimisation, due to corrupt-practices (e.g. credit card fraud, overcharging in taxis or excursions or restaurants, forced consumption/payment of services, discrimination)? | |
| | Annyoance/ harassment | (b) Annoyance due to corrupt-practices (e.g. aggressive selling/ harassment, illegal vendors, no acceptance of credit cards, bribery-demands)? | |
| Service quality incident | Service failure | (c) Dissatisfaction with services in restaurants, hotels and shops, due to corrupt practices (e.g. cancellation policies, money refunds, | |

(continued)

**Table 1** (continued)

| Variable/category | Question label | Formulation | Scale |
|---|---|---|---|
| | | complaint-handling, reservation loss)? | |
| | Mis-information | (d) Mis-information due to corrupt practices (e.g. exploitative regulations, quality ratings/recommendations, website info)? | |
| Heritage mismanagement incident | Heritage mis-management | (e) Visible deterioration of natural surroundings and cultural heritage due to corrupt practices (e.g. pollution, loss of authenticity, architectural deterioration) | |
| **PERCEPTIONS** | **QUESTION 3** | **During your holidays, have you been told or have heard the following:** | 1—Never<br>2—Rarely<br>3—Occasionally<br>4—Frequently<br>5—Very frequently |
| Storytelling exposure | Exploitation/ victimisation | (a) Exploitation and/or victimisation, due to corrupt-practices (e.g. credit card fraud, overcharging in taxis or excursions or restaurants, forced consumption/payment of services, discrimination)? | |
| | Annoyance/ harassment | (b) Annoyance due to corrupt-practices (e.g. aggressive selling/ harassment, illegal vendors, no acceptance of credit cards, bribery-demands)? | |
| | Service failure | (c) Dissatisfaction with services in restaurants, hotels and shops, due to corrupt practices (e.g. cancellation policies, money refunds, complaint-handling, reservation loss)? | |
| | Misinformation | (d) Misinformation due to corrupt practices (e.g. exploitative regulations, quality ratings/recommendations, website info)? | |
| | Heritage mis-management | (e) Visible deterioration of natural surroundings and cultural heritage due to | |

(continued)

**Table 1** (continued)

| Variable/category | Question label | Formulation | Scale |
|---|---|---|---|
| | | corrupt practices (e.g. pollution, loss of authenticity, architectural deterioration) | |
| **REACTIONS** | **QUESTION 4** | **When faced with corrupt practices during holidays I. . .** | 1—Totally disagree<br>2—Disagree<br>3—Neither agree or disagree<br>4—Agree<br>5—Totally agree |
| Counter/active reaction | Formal complaint | (v) Took concrete action to ensure that those involved in corruption face consequences (e.g. police involvement, legal action, formal complaint to management) | |
| | Publication | (iii) Warned others and publicised/exposed it any way possible (e.g. social media, press) | |
| | Advocacy | (ii) Wondered why the local authorities do not implement sufficient incentives and regulations to prevent corruption | |
| Accept/passive reaction | Behavioural adjustment | (iv) Adjusted to the corrupt practices and try to make the best out of it | |
| | Empathy | (i) Felt sorry for the locals, who live with this kind of thing daily | |
| **PERCEPTIONS** | **QUESTION 5** | **Considering your own holiday experiences, please evaluate the following statements. . ..** | 1—Totally disagree<br>2—Disagree<br>3—Neither agree or disagree<br>4—Agree<br>5—Totally agree |
| Authority competence perception | Experience with authorities | (i) I have had positive experiences and impressions (direct or indirect) with police and security authorities during my holidays and would advise others to involve them when subjected to corrupt practices | |
| | Authority accessibility | (ii) Police and security authorities at holiday destinations are generally accessible, reliable and supportive of tourists | |
| | Authority effectiveness | (iii) Informing managers and other tourism | |

(continued)

**Table 1** (continued)

| Variable/category | Question label | Formulation | Scale |
|---|---|---|---|
| | | stakeholders is an effective way of counter-acting corrupt practices in holiday destinations | |
| **PERCEPTIONS** | **QUESTION 6** | **In your opinion, please evaluate the following statements...** | 1—Totally disagree<br>2—Disagree<br>3—Neither agree or disagree<br>4—Agree<br>5—Totally agree |
| Country-/culture-related inherent corruption | Anti-corruption sentiment | (i) Corrupt countries should be avoided by tourists at all costs; this is the only solution | |
| | Country-/Culture-related stereotyping | (iv) Corruption is not country- or culture-specific; it can occur anywhere and to anyone | |
| Tourism-related inherent corruption | Tourism-related risk acceptance | (ii) Corrupt practices are common to some countries and all tourists should be prepared for it | |
| | Tourist vulnerability | (iii) Tourists are 'easy targets' for corrupted practices and there is always a risk | |

were 5-point Likert Scales, producing ordinal data[1] for the ensuing statistical analysis (i.e. descriptive and inferential statistics).

## 3.3 *Methodological Limitations*

Online data collection and snowball-sampling suffer from limitations such as self-selection bias and decreased representativeness of the results. Nonetheless, the practicality and completeness of online surveys often outweigh their inherent limitations (Sills and Song 2002; Paris 2016). This is essentially a trade-off between practicality and generalisability. Given that the purpose of the survey was mainly exploratory, the trade-off is justified. The aim was to test the interrelationships between perceptions and behaviour, and not to estimate the overall extent of perceived corruption and/or exposure to related incidents in the tourist population.

[1]A variable is regarded to be ordinal when the data it produces (values) represent categories with some intrinsic ranking. Examples of ordinal variables include attitude scores representing degree of satisfaction or confidence and preference rating scores.

Another limitation, particularly relevant for psychometric studies, is the bias and influence of cultural differences. Corruption perceptions and the corresponding behaviours are, most probably, culturally-regulated. Despite the fact that our sample consisted mainly of German-speaking respondents, a third of the sample were international respondents. This measure may not eliminate cultural biases completely, but it dilutes their impact on the results.

# 4 Results and Discussion

## *4.1 Descriptive Statistics and Holiday Corruption*

### 4.1.1 Tourists' Corruption Experiences and Storytelling

The survey data analysis (descriptive statistics) revealed that although not frequent, the majority of respondents had rarely experienced the effects of (what they would regard as) corruption during the holidays (Fig. 2—upper graph). At the same time, they had occasionally heard others report on their experiences with corruption (Fig. 2—lower graph). This disparity between own experience and others' reports of corruption, suggest the multiplication effect of story-telling.

Incidents involving corruption, make good stories to share and are considered interesting for recipients as they serve as a warning and even as a safety advise for others; particularly in social media/review portals. These characteristics render them more likely to be reported and be noticed.

The types of incidents most often experienced by the survey's respondents, involved mainly heritage mismanagement and annoyances in holiday destinations (Fig. 3).

Tolerating distorted, deteriorating and under-maintained attractions (see Fig. 4 for some examples) were presumably perceived by the tourists as incomprehensible/ unacceptable in a tourist destination; and this kind of failure could only be attributed to corruption (and the related ineffectiveness) in public administration.

Similarly, a number of annoyances (e.g. aggressive selling, vendor harassment), can be associated with inability to sufficiently enforce laws and regulations, due to public authority corruption. It appears that a significant amount of corruption incidents involving tourists, could be avoided by improving the effectiveness of local controls and law enforcement. The implicit notion here is that incompetence or inability to 'protect' vital tourism resources (i.e. heritage and the atmosphere/safety of tourism resorts and attractions), can mainly be explained by corruption.

This may, or may not be the case; but ultimately it corresponds to the tourists' perceptions and it is compatible to a systemic definition of corruption (i.e. reflecting a dysfunctionality of the tourism system, originating from mal-practice and

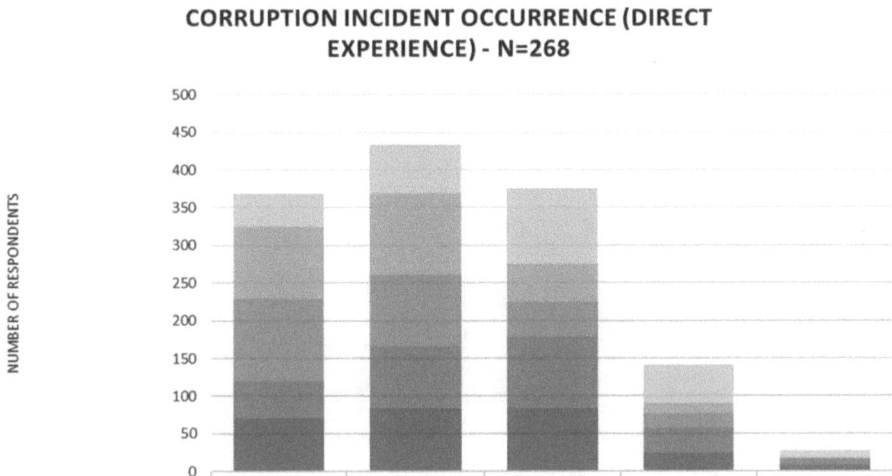


| | Never | Rarely | Occasionally | Frequently | Very Frequently |
|---|---|---|---|---|---|
| Heritage Mis-management | 44 | 65 | 100 | 51 | 9 |
| Mis-information | 96 | 108 | 51 | 13 | 1 |
| Service Failure | 109 | 94 | 46 | 19 | 1 |
| Corruption Annoyance | 50 | 82 | 95 | 34 | 8 |
| Victimisation / Exploitation | 70 | 84 | 83 | 24 | 8 |

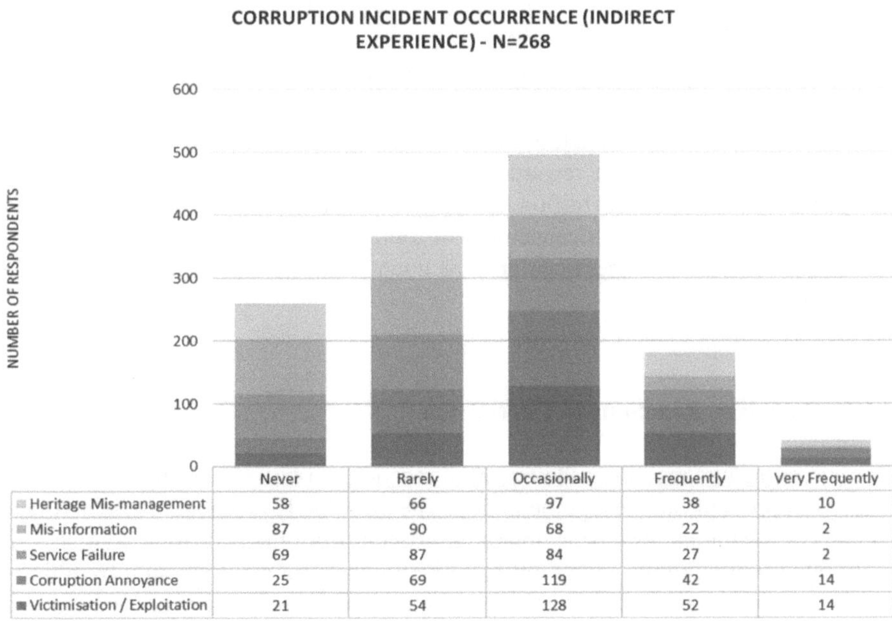


| | Never | Rarely | Occasionally | Frequently | Very Frequently |
|---|---|---|---|---|---|
| Heritage Mis-management | 58 | 66 | 97 | 38 | 10 |
| Mis-information | 87 | 90 | 68 | 22 | 2 |
| Service Failure | 69 | 87 | 84 | 27 | 2 |
| Corruption Annoyance | 25 | 69 | 119 | 42 | 14 |
| Victimisation / Exploitation | 21 | 54 | 128 | 52 | 14 |

**Fig. 2** Holiday corruption incidents—frequencies

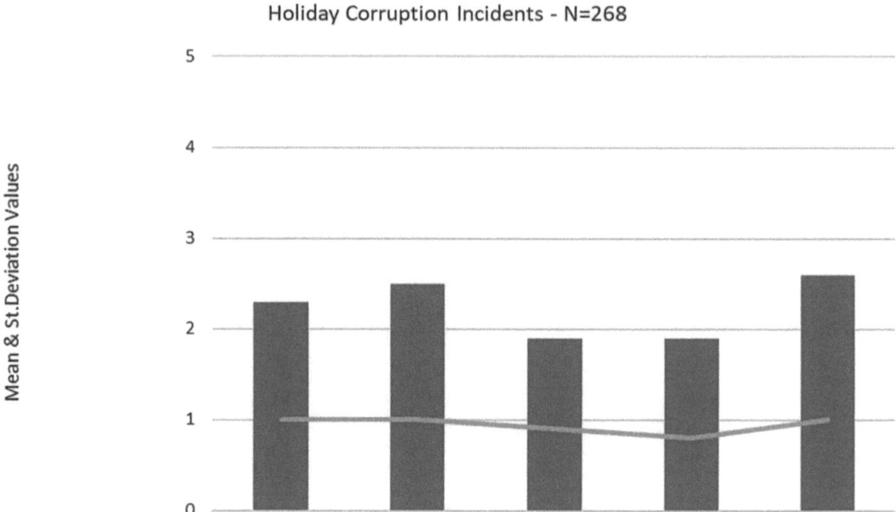


| | Victimisation / Exploitation | Corruption Annoyance | Service Failure | Mis-information | Heritage Mis-management |
|---|---|---|---|---|---|
| Mean | 2.3 | 2.5 | 1.9 | 1.9 | 2.6 |
| Standard Deviation | 1 | 1 | 0.9 | 0.8 | 1 |

**Fig. 3** Holiday corruption incidents—descriptive statistics. Scale: 1—Never/5—Very frequently

ill-intent). In this light, Van Duyne (2001: p. 03) defined corruption as: "an improbity or decay in the decision-making process in which a decision-maker consents or demands to deviate from the criterion, which should rule his decision making, in exchange for a reward, the promise or expectation of it". From the perspective of the tourists (respondents), their assumption is, most probably, that the 'criteria' regarding the management of tourism resources are clear and known; thus failure to adhere to them can only be intentional (i.e. due to corruption) at the governance level.

### 4.1.2 Tourists' Reactions to Corruption

Our survey results regarding the potential reactions to holiday corruption incidents (Fig. 5), support the above argumentation. The most likely reactions would involve a formal complaint and/or a behavioural adjustment from the part of the tourists.

In other words, tourists may opt to actively react against corruption by filling a formal complaint, involving in this way the authorities, or simply passively accept the situation and trying to make the best out of it. A possible interpretation here is that, depending on the trust tourists have towards the local authorities' ability and willingness to react, they will decide to either formally report, or become (active or passive) 'accomplices' to holiday corruption. The third most likely reaction is to

**Fig. 4** Heritage mismanagement examples. (**a**) Heritage deformation example: The architectural character of Rhodes medieval town is deformed due to unregulated/uncontrolled building; even on top of historical ruins). (**b**) Heritage deterioration example: Constanta Casino (Black Sea Coast Landmark) is at risk because of structural corrosion unprotected interior to the weather conditions

| | | Empathy | Advocacy | Publication | Behavioural Adjustment | Formal Complaint |
|---|---|---|---|---|---|---|
| N | Valid | 268 | 268 | 268 | 268 | 268 |
| | Missing | 0 | 0 | 0 | 0 | 0 |
| Mean | | 3.6 | 3.9 | 3.0 | 2.9 | 2.4 |
| Standard error of the mean | | .06 | .06 | .06 | .072 | .07 |
| Standard deviation | | 1.02 | .98 | 1.13 | 1.18 | 1.13 |

Scale: 1 – Totally Agree / 5 – Totally Disagree

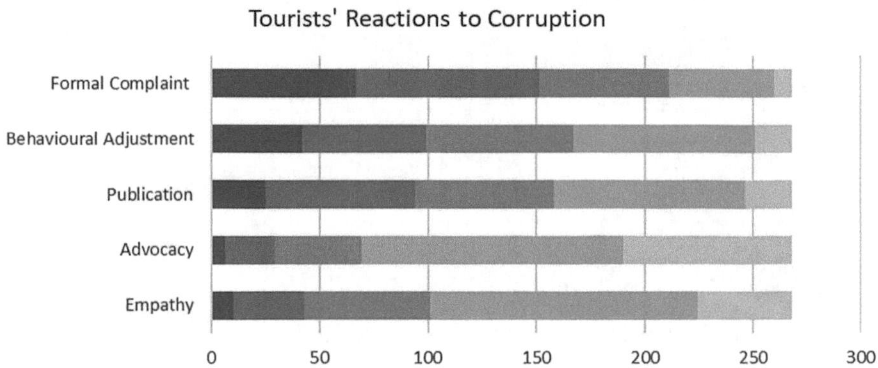


| | Empathy | Advocacy | Publication | Behavioural Adjustment | Formal Complaint |
|---|---|---|---|---|---|
| ■ Totally Agree | 10 | 6 | 25 | 42 | 67 |
| ■ Agree | 33 | 23 | 69 | 57 | 84 |
| ■ Neither Agree or Disagree | 58 | 40 | 64 | 68 | 60 |
| ■ Disagree | 123 | 121 | 88 | 84 | 49 |
| ■ Totally Disagree | 44 | 78 | 22 | 17 | 8 |

**Fig. 5** Tourists' reactions to corruption. Scale: 1—Totally agree/5—Totally disagree

publicise corruption, fuelling holiday-corruption storytelling; which could in turn impact on travel preferences and holiday selection.

## *4.2 Inferential Statistics: Correlation Testing with Travel Behaviour*

The correlation results, referring to the relationship between travel behaviour and holiday-corruption perceptions, experiences and reactions are summarised in Table 2 and discussed in the following pages.

**Table 2** Correlation testing results—travel behaviour and perceptions/reactions

| | N=268 | Residual holiday-related risk corruption acceptance | Cultural/ country-related corruption stereotyping | Storytelling exposure | Authority competence perception (experience, accessibility, professionalism) | Counter/ active reaction (publication, formal complaint) | Accept/ passive reaction (empathy, advocacy, behavioural adjustment) | Personal-integrity incident | Service-quality incident | Heritage-mismanagement incident |
|---|---|---|---|---|---|---|---|---|---|---|
| Pre-travel information intensity | Correlation coefficient | .008 | .011 | .000 | −.034 | .041 | −.109 | −.053 | −.007 | −.028 |
| | Sig. (2-tailed) | .901 | .862 | .996 | .583 | .503 | .075 | .388 | .909 | .646 |
| Organised travel preference | Correlation coefficient | −.136* | .103 | .032 | −.169** | −.081 | .125* | .033 | −.030 | .061 |
| | Sig. (2-tailed) | .026 | .094 | .598 | .006 | .188 | .041 | .593 | .625 | .320 |
| Travel-related cultural distance tolerance | Correlation coefficient | .260** | −.072 | −.058 | .100 | −.022 | −.106 | −.242** | −.079 | −.182** |
| | Sig. (2-tailed) | .000 | .239 | .343 | .102 | .718 | .082 | .000 | .197 | .003 |

*Significance at the 0.05 level; **Significance at the .01 level

### 4.2.1 Pre-travel Information Intensity

Interestingly enough, and unexpectedly, direct experiences with, or exposure to storytelling about, holiday corruption did not reveal any significant correlation to pre-travel information-gathering behaviour. One could expect that the increased perceived risk, due to exposure to corruption incidents, would result to tourists intensifying their information-gathering activities in order to reduce it. Yet, this does not seem to be the case. The obvious explanation for this result could be that instead of aiming at reducing the (perceived) risk of experiencing corruption during their holidays, tourists opt for eliminating it (i.e. risk mitigation, by opting for another, familiar destination), or for 'outsourcing' it (i.e. risk transfer, by opting for organised travel).

### 4.2.2 Travel-Related Cultural Distance Tolerance

The propensity of tourists to refrain from culturally-distant, unfamiliar to them, holiday destinations increases with their exposure to personal-integrity- ($R^2 = -24.2\%$, signifi cant at 1% level) and heritage-mismanagement-incidents ($R^2 = -18.2\%$, significant at 1% level). Simply stated, when exposed to the risk of their own personal integrity/ safety and/or the risk of a deteriorated holiday environment (i.e. attractions and heritage sites), tourists will opt to avoid the risk altogether and simply choose a destination they are familiar and feel more in comfort with. On the opposite side of the coin, this kind of reaction is regulated by an individual tourist's own holiday-risk tolerance level. Tourists with a high acceptance of residual holiday corruption risk (i.e. a certain degree of corruption is acceptable and unavoidable during holidays in general) are more likely to be adventurous with their holiday selection; in spite of exposure to corruption and storytelling about it ($R^2 = 26\%$, significant at 1% level).

### 4.2.3 Organised Travel Preference

Those tourists, with a low tolerance of residual holiday-related corruption exposure risk are also more likely to opt for organised travel ($R^2 = -13.6\%$, significant at 5% level). In relation to 'organised travel preference', there is also a significance inverse correlation with 'authority competence perception' ($R^2 = -16.9\%$, significant at 1% level). This exposes a strategy of 'risk-transfer' from the tourists' part. If local authorities are perceived as competent and willing to deal with and react to holiday corruption incidents, then tourists may choose to travel individually and transfer the residual corruption exposure risk to the local authorities. In the alternative case, where the local authorities are not regarded as competent, the risk is 'transferred' to privately-run packaged-tour operators, who provide structural guarantees and insurances.

### 4.3 *Practical Implications: Holiday Corruption and Destination Development*

The findings here suggest numerous implications for destination development and management. First of all, the re-construction of 'corruption phenomena' at the micro-level, taking into account tourists' perceptions, offers a number of interesting and practically-relevant insights.

Heritage-, environmental- and attraction deterioration are often perceived as the result of systemic corruption, and most importantly are the types of things tourists are more likely to report and tell stories about. Ultimately, this may negatively influence the attractiveness of a destination for new, international, long-haul visitors who may substitute the destination for another, more familiar and culturally-similar one. For emerging destinations, seeking to establish themselves as global holiday resorts, this implies a very concrete recommendation. The maintenance and protection of one's own heritage signifies the importance of tourism for the region and is a symbol of the quality and hospitality experience to be expected by visitors. As such, heritage sites, the natural environment and the public attractions are not merely ticket-revenue-generating resources, but also the very 'brand-promise' of the destination.

We have also seen that, despite an acceptance of a residual risk while on holiday, tourists are rather intolerant of risks related to the safety and personal integrity. Mistreatment, harassment and petty-fraud, may well represent annoyances (compared to more serious crime), but they do nonetheless affect the attractiveness of a destination for potential visitors. This is where effective law enforcement structures at a local level play a role. If tourists are given the possibility to involve local authorities by formally complaining, they are likely to do so; trusting their competence to deal with incidents of this kind. The installation of a tourist police, which is visible, accessible and approachable could have a huge impact in this respect. In the absence, or perceived ineffectiveness, of local authorities, tourists may result to organised travel. In fact, the very perceived local authority's incompetence to counter perceived holiday risks (also corruption related ones) partly constitutes the added-value and attractiveness of packaged holidays, as opposed to individual travel. In turn, a high dependence on packaged tourism leaves a destination in a disadvantageous bargaining position with large tour operators; giving them control of segmentation, distribution and even seasonality of the destination's holiday offering.

It becomes rather obvious, that dealing with holiday-related corruption is a key developmental aspect, not only for the economy as a whole, but also for a particular sector; like tourism. Tourism has proven economically resilient to the ails of developing economies and holds the potential to 'jump-start' a post-industrial-, developing- or post-communist- economy (Papathanassis 2016b). At the end of the day, our research also implies that a lot can be achieved by relatively small-scale measures at the local destination level. Investments in heritage-site management and environmental protection, as well as the installation of specially-trained (tourist) police-officers in tourist hotspots would be obvious short- to medium-term measures in this respect; possibly achieving more than expensive marketing and advertising campaigns.

## 5 Summary and Conclusions

Summarising, this study aimed at exploring tourists' perceptions of corruption during their holidays. Based on the data collected by 268 survey respondents, the main findings are summarised below:

- 73% of the survey respondents have experienced some form of corruption during their holidays; or at least to what they would interpret as corruption
- 81% of the survey respondents have heard other's stories/reports of holiday-related corruption
- Heritage mismanagement (84% of respondents) and annoyances (81% of respondents) are the most frequently reported types of corruption encountered during holidays
- In the absence of (perceived) local authority competence, tourists are less likely to make a formal complaint and more likely to accept, or even participate in, corrupt practices. Alternatively, they might either divert to another destination or opt for organised travel

Simply-stated, the summation of relatively harmless, corruption-enabled incidents, may indeed have significant consequences for a destination's tourism development as a whole. This is analogous to the 'Broken Windows' theory (Kelling and Coles 1998), which postulates that vandalism and petty public offences, have a signalling effect, encouraging more serious crime. It follows that, preventing and monitoring for those smaller forms of public disorder is an effective crime prevention measure, as it creates an atmosphere of lawfulness and order, acting as a deterrent for criminal behaviour. In an analogous manner, desolated attractions and heritage sites, as well as a systematic misbehaviour/malpractice towards tourists (see annoyances) has a signalling effect, pointing towards a more extensive degree of systemic corruption; and a higher expected degree of tourists' exposure its ill-effects; it is not just the 'broken windows' in urban areas, but also the 'broken marbles' in tourist areas!

## References

Bitner, M. J., Booms, B. H., & Mohr, L. A. (1994). Critical service encounters: The employee's view. *Journal of Marketing, 58*, 95–106.

Din, B. H., Habibullah, M. S., Baharom, A. H., & Saari, M. D. (2016). Are shadow economy and tourism related? International evidence. *Procedia Economics and Finance, 35*, 173–178.

Fisman, R., & Svensson, J. (2007). Are corruption and taxation really harmful to growth? Firm level evidence. *Journal of Development Economics, 83*(1), 63–75.

Grove, S. J., & Fisk, R. P. (1997). The impact of other customers on service experiences: A critical incident examination of 'getting along'. *Journal of Retailing, 73*, 63–85.

Harris, L. C. (2012). 'Ripping off' tourists: An empirical evaluation of tourists' perceptions and service worker (mis)behavior. *Annals of Tourism Research, 39*(2), 1070–1093.

Kelling, G., & Coles, C. (1998). *Fixing broken windows: Restoring order and reducing crime in our communities*. London: Simon & Schuster.

Papageorgiou, G. C. (2008). The human dimension of tourism supply-side perspectives. *Annals of Tourism Research, 35*(1), 211–232.

Papathanassis, A. (2016a). Combating tourism-related corruption: Effective countermeasures derived from analysing tourists' perceptions and experiences. *Ovidius University Annals Economic Sciences Series, 16*(2), 248–255.

Papathanassis, A. (2016b). Curing the 'beach disease': Corruption and the potential of tourism-led transformation for developing countries and transitional economies. *Ovidius University Annals Economic Sciences Series, 16*(1), 75–80.

Paris, C. M. (2016). *Surveying backpackers through Facebook: A case for a mixed-mode dual frame procedure. Tourism Travel and Research Association: Advancing Tourism Research Globally*. 63. Retrieved from http://scholarworks.umass.edu/ttra/2011/Visual/63

Sills, S., & Song, S. (2002). Innovations in survey research: An application of web-based surveys. *Social Science Computer Review, 20*(1), 22–30.

Uberti, L. J. (2016). The 'sociological turn' in corruption studies: Why fighting graft in the developing world is often unnecessary, and sometimes counterproductive. *Progress in Development Studies, 16*(3), 261–277.

Van Duyne, P. C. (2001). Will Caligula go transparent? Corruption in acts and attitudes. *Forum on Crime and Society, 1*(2), 73–98.

# 'Blood Antiquities': The Problem of Illicit Trafficking for Tourism

**Ursula Warnke**

## 1 Introduction

Archaeological sites, preserved over thousands years, are now destroyed within few months. Satellite pictures show the pitches of illicit excavations in detail. Objects were removed from their settings in graves, settlements and buildings. The corresponding scientific information without the context is thus lost forever. A single object without the documentation of the archaeological feature is of no value for further research.

The example of underwater cultural heritage, shows the rich cultural treasure lying under water. Worldwide, there are hundreds of sunken cities, due to changing sea levels, shifting landmasses and human activities such as the building of dams. Underwater cities tell a different story from those on land, as they have been protected from many dangers, such as construction projects and expanding cities. Alone in the Mediterranean, we know of 150 sunken cities. This is why for 90% of human history sea levels were much lower, leaving many submerged prehistoric landscapes with traces of human development (i.g. "Doggerland", Black Sea).[1] Three million ancient shipwrecks spanning over thousands of years of history. They tell stories of historic connections between distant civilizations. They preserve distinct artefact collections from those found on land.

All this undiscovered cultural heritage is in great danger. Looting and illicit trafficking damages a large number of archaeological sites. "Illicit traffic results in the irreparable loss of cultural material of great historical and scientific value. Illegal trafficking in cultural property is one of the most important and lucrative

[1] www.splashcos.org (27.12.2017).

U. Warnke (✉)
State Museum Nature and Man, Oldenburg, Germany
e-mail: U.Warnke@Landesmuseen-Ol.de

 
A. Papathanassis et al. (eds.), *Yellow Tourism*, Tourism, Hospitality & Event Management, https://doi.org/10.1007/978-3-319-94664-1_7

transnational criminal activities. It is an international crime that transcends borders, as stolen items are often moved among from one country to another."[2]

Such illegal activities destroy archaeological and historical contexts on a massive scale. Lack of proper (costly) conservation, damages artefacts too. During wars objects are stolen directly from museums and sold for financing the war activities of unlawful groups. In most cases the objects are sold on Ebay and Tourists buy illegal excavated objects during their holidays.

"Looting is most acute in countries which are home to a rich cultural and archaeological heritage, but are missing the appropriate means to protect their cultural resources ("source countries" vs. "market countries"). Illicit trafficking is not limited to the developing world; Countries in Europe or North America are also suffering from an increasing number of thefts and illegal excavations on archaeological sites. On the other hand, the current world economic shift has transformed areas, which used to be considered as source countries, into growing market countries. At the same time, it generates huge profits with minimal risks for the criminals involved, who are often operating in networks with links to other criminal activities."[3] Illicit traffic in cultural goods is a unique phenomenon, with its particularities, own patterns and typology. It is at the third place after smuggling weapons and drugs.[4]

## 2 Who Are the Actors? Who Is Involved?

"The multifaceted aspects of illicit traffic in cultural goods implies that there are diverse profiles, motives and purposes for the people fuelling such illegal activities, regardless of whether they are the thieves, the middlemen or the buyers."[5] Moreover, lenient sanctions applied to illicit trafficking make this activity attractive to a large spectrum of potential 'criminals' that could be categorised by ICOM as following:

### *2.1 Tourists, Random Buyers and Other Ill-Informed Individuals*

Often unsuspecting, tourists and other random buyers can easily be implicated in illicit transactions of cultural goods, a phenomenon aggravated by the rapid growth of mass tourism during the last two decades. These same tourists, given their

[2] www.obs-traffic.museum/what-illicit-traffic (27.12.2017).

[3] www.obs-traffic.museum/what-illicit-traffic (27.12.2017).

[4] https://www.obs-traffic.museum/after-drugs-and-guns-art-theft-biggest-criminal-enterprise-world (28.12.2017).

[5] www.obs-traffic.museum/who-involved (27.12.2017).

inexperience as art and antiquities buyers, are easy targets for dealers offering stolen or illicitly excavated cultural goods. Knowingly or not, such occasional buyers can easily find themselves involved in fraudulent sales, the use of forged documentation and other frauds. Even though they are breaking the law, these buyers are often the good-faith victims of their own limited knowledge of the law and the basic administrative requirements regarding transactions involving art and antiquities.

## 2.2 *Local Communities*

The difficult economic situation prevailing in many developing countries is the primary factor in local communities' involvement in the supply chain. In many regions of the world, members of local communities may turn to looting and selling of archaeological objects for obvious financial reasons.

## 2.3 *Individual Criminals with Financial Motives*

One of the particularities of illicit traffic in cultural goods is its profitability, often described as a trade with maximum profit for minimum risk. Inappropriately indulgent legal sanctions, alongside an abundance of cultural goods that can be stolen or looted and later smuggled, make this illegal activity very attractive for people already involved in other types of crimes.

## 2.4 *Organised Crime*

According to the broad definition provided by the United Nations Convention against Transnational Organized Crime,[6] all international cultural property trafficking is a serious offence that is considered to be organised crime when it involves a group of three or more people.

The role of mafia-type organisations in cultural property crime is a different question. Experts and law enforcement officers have always suspected connections (sometimes occasional) between such criminal groups and illicit trafficking in cultural goods, the logic being that the use of previously existing criminal networks, set up for a diverse range of illicit trades, could also be utilised for the transfer of looted or stolen cultural property. In Italy for instance, despite the long experience in this regard and the expertise of their 'Carabinieri' unit for the Protection of Cultural

[6]http://www.unodc.org/unodc/en/organized-crime/intro/UNTOC.html (27.12.2017).

Heritage,[7] it is impossible to attest to a strong and long-term connection between the traffic of cultural objects and the mafia-like organisations. In South-East Europe for instance, recent cases have shown a clear interaction between the transfer of stolen cultural goods and criminal groups involved in drug or weapon trafficking.

## 2.5 Compulsive Thieves

Cultural objects, particularly those with a high artistic, historical or symbolic value can also favour criminal impulses in people, who would otherwise have no further motive to operate than the compulsive need to obtain a particular art or archaeological piece. The fact that compulsive thieves can be curators, guides or even random visitors acting opportunistically also make them very difficult to anticipate.

## 2.6 Private Collectors

Private collectors are a key element in the wide spectrum of people associated with the illegal trade of cultural goods. The situation has changed in these past years, due to the increasing control on sales and increased awareness of the need to proceed with detailed scrutiny and precautionary measures when acquiring a cultural object.

## 2.7 Art Market

For many years, the art market has been declared as one of the driving forces of illicit traffic in cultural goods, particularly in Western countries. Though financial interests, self-regulation and professional secrecy still prevail in the market, sometimes at the expense of ethics and control of legal provenience, the situation has dramatically changed in the past decade, at least amongst the market leaders. Public awareness, along with the accumulation of cases tarnishing the market's reputation, has had very positive consequences on the profession.

Unfortunately, in addition to a number of small auction houses with less consideration for the ethics of acquisition, the development of information technology has been the source of a new rising trend in the art market: on-line sales. Internet has become an uncontrolled market place for stolen or looted cultural goods.

[7]https://www.obs-traffic.museum/carabinieri-protection-cultural-heritage (27.12.2017).

## 2.8 Scientists and Academics

The role scientists and academics play in the development of the traffic is often underestimated or even completely disregarded. Scientists and academics may be involved in the traffic in many different ways: unregulated and unscientific excavations, sale of objects coming from legal excavations, transaction of looted artefacts, fake expertise or production of forged certificates.

## 2.9 Places of Conservation

Though museums still are the first target of claims for return and restitution of cultural objects legally or illegally removed from their country of origin, their involvement in illicit traffic has dramatically changed in the past decades. The development of ethical standards and strict rules of procedure in the museum world, along with the involvement of top-ranked museums in court cases, has deeply modified the institutional policy of acquisition. Museums can no longer be considered as a common destination for looted or stolen cultural goods, notwithstanding the fact that some members of the museum community may still not abide by the internationally recognised ethical standards such as the ICOM Code of Ethics for Museums.[8]

## 2.10 Public Officials, Diplomats

Just as in the case of academics, the involvement of national and international diplomats remains a taboo and undocumented subject, and a sensitive aspect of the trend. Several cases have already shown the use of diplomatic immunity and diplomatic channels for the easy import, export and transaction of cultural objects of doubtful provenience.

## 2.11 Soldiers, Military

History is full of examples proving the high vulnerability of conflict areas to thefts and looting, given the lack of protection granted to cultural heritage in these particular contexts. Cultural objects are first and foremost sold as a source of revenue to soldiers, whether they are stolen randomly or upon specific order. But they can

---

[8]Download: https://www.obs-traffic.museum/sites/default/files/ressources/files/ICOM_Code_Ethics.pdf (27.12.2017).

also be kept as a "souvenir". The plundering of a country or region's cultural property can also be part of a military strategy, consisting of the destruction of the symbolic value of the enemy's cultural heritage. In this area too, times have changed and progress has been made thanks to the promotion of standards and training manuals for the protection of cultural heritage during conflict.[9]

### 2.12 *Private Companies*

"In the particular case of the looting of underwater archaeological sites, several cases have proven the involvement of private companies initially involved in drilling operations or other kinds of legal underwater activities. Some have been commissioned by the State to specifically search for underwater heritage, with the aim of sharing the findings and saving the wrecks. In this case, companies have been known to sometimes keep hidden part of the findings to illegally sell them in other countries and/or via internet."[10]

## 3 Places of Crime

Thefts of objects take place in a wide variety of places and countries, and these same objects can be sold on diverse platforms and in different parts of the world, depending on current market trends. From sites to museums to churches, from Western to Middle Eastern to Eastern countries, market and source countries vary and shift through time and events. The question of where illicit traffic occurs can be divided into two parts: "Where are the objects taken from?" and "What countries or regions are most involved and affected?"[11]

Theft of objects can happen in different locations: archaeological sites—including underwater ones—, public or private places of conservation (museums, churches, castles, houses, etc.). The smuggling of objects out of archaeological sites is mostly due to a lack of appropriate protection, which can be explained by a lack of funding, size and nature of the area to protect, and absence of inventory and safe storage of excavated objects.

The traffic of underwater heritage represents a particular and growing issue of concern. Shipwrecks and underwater archaeological sites are a very attractive target for looters, particularly for the quality of the objects excavated and the difficulty for national authorities to control their maritime areas.

---

[9]Latest UN resolution (2017) Download: https://www.unesco.de/fileadmin/medien/Dokumente/Kultur/UNSEC_Res2347.pdf (28.12.2017).

[10]www.obs-traffic.museum/who-involved (27.12.2017).

[11]www.obs-traffic.museum/where-does-it-occur (27.12.2017).

Sometimes isolated, with limited security systems, and the necessity to remain relatively open to the public, churches and other places of worship are very vulnerable. In some European countries, churches are the first victims of thefts.

Thefts from museums have significantly decreased over recent years. Nevertheless, the creation of hundreds of new museums in developing countries may pose new challenges in terms of collections' security in the years to come.

## 4 Market Countries vs. Source Countries

Illicit traffic in cultural goods is often organised through a common scheme: the removal from the place of origin, the transit and the acquisition. Within this scheme, one must also consider the specific distinction between three types of countries that can be qualified as:

- Source countries, from which the objects are removed
- Transit countries, through which the objects are transported and transited
- Market countries, in which the objects are bought, traded, or sold[12]

1. *The characteristics of a source country:*
    - Difficulties (technical, human, financial) to ensure the protection of its cultural heritage, (particularly archaeological sites)
    - Weak economy, which can encourage individuals or communities to participate in a lucrative traffic
    - Richness of archaeological heritage and history
    - Abundance of movable cultural property (including religious)
    - Occurrence of a civil unrest, armed conflict or any other man-made or natural disaster.

    The Egyptian revolution (2011) or the Syrian armed conflict are perfect examples of how conflict areas can be suddenly exposed to greater risks and see occurrence of illicit traffic in cultural goods increase significantly. Given those criteria, developing countries are, in general, at greater risk of thefts and looting.
2. *The existence of a transit country* can be based on different factors, such as the geographical position between source and market countries, the presence of existing networks for various forms of traffic and/or criminal organisations, and lesser control in merchandise shipping and receiving.
3. *A market country* is not necessarily the country in which the object is sold, but the country of origin of the person buying the object. Market countries are naturally characterised by the existence of a strong demand for archaeological objects and,

[12]www.obs-traffic.museum/where-does-it-occur (27.12.2017).

in many cases, a structured legal art market. Some objects can actually be sold several times on the black market, sometimes over the course of several decades, before emerging in a legal auction with what seems like valid property titles.

Finally, a weak national legal framework or an absence of measures implemented in line with the existing international legislation (related to the trade of cultural objects) are also a prime element in explaining the development of illicit traffic in cultural goods; in both transit and market countries. One of the reasons that North America and some Western European countries have seen a decline in their illegal trade is due to their reinforcement of national legislation, contributing the a better implementation of international legislation such as the 1970 UNESCO Convention on the Means of Prohibiting and Preventing the Illicit Import, Export and Transfer of Ownership of Cultural Property.[13]

### *4.1 The Case of Conflict Areas*

"Thefts of cultural objects take place all over the world, not only in conflict areas or economically challenged countries. Countries in conflict areas are particularly vulnerable. General chaos or the specificity of the conditions within countries affected by a conflict makes it so that fewer resources, such as guards, can be provided to sites and museums, thus facilitating the work of looters and thieves, whether they are criminals, members of the local population or soldiers from all sides."[14]

## 5 The Characteristics of Illicit Traffic in Cultural Goods

"Unlike the traffic of drugs, weapons or chemicals, the illegal transnational trade of cultural goods concerns a product that is usually considered licit. Moreover, this kind of traffic is often regarded to be a harmless crime and is hardly remarked upon by law enforcement agencies, governmental authorities or the public, despite its size and its obvious monetary value.

As for the trafficked objects, they are hard to identify. Cultural objects were produced in the distant past, sometimes in series, but sometimes with unique and identifiable characteristics. Moreover, many of them, and obviously all the unexcavated archaeological objects, are not inventoried. Furthermore, the value of the goods increases with uniqueness and the passage of time, with some items missing for decades before emerging on the legal market.

[13]Download https://www.obs-traffic.museum/sites/default/files/ressources/files/UNESCO_convention_1970.pdf (27.12.2017).

[14]www.obs-traffic.museum/where-does-it-occur (27.12.2017).

Finally, the fight against illicit traffic is often constrained by a series of legal weaknesses, which diminishes the ability of law enforcement agencies and prosecutors to fight looters and traffickers of cultural objects:

- The main international legal instruments are rarely fully implemented.
- In many countries, theft, concealment and illegal excavations are not considered as serious crimes.
- Penal sanctions are unfortunately very light in a large number of countries.
- Short time limitations make the legal recovery of a stolen object that much more difficult.
- Few countries have specific import procedures for cultural objects.
- Short deadlines for seizing, complicate the work of customs officers in identifying tainted objects."[15]

"A large number of looted or stolen objects often leave the black market to be offered for sale as 'legal' property. The legality of the ownership over a cultural object is usually determined by the supporting documentation (title of ownership, certificate of authenticity, history of the object, export certificate). Therefore, the faking or forging of documents is the most common method used to clean the past of an object, or even create a full fictional history for the item."[16]

## 6 The Fight Against Illicit Traffic

Fighting against illicit traffic has become a real challenge, requiring the use and development of a wide mosaic of tools and practices created and implemented over the last few decades. It is a long-lasting involvement, consisting of complementary cooperative actions, along with the creation of effective instruments, beyond the mere improvement of the tools existing designed to better control the art market and borders.

### *6.1 Raising Public Awareness*

No society has been able to criminalise an activity and fight against it without the agreement and the support of the general population. In order to efficiently fight the illegal trade of cultural property, it must be regarded to be a serious crime by the general public. So public communication is the key element of awareness-raising. The use of new technologies and web instruments, allows national and international actors to easily and quickly contact thousands of people around the globe. Among

[15]www.obs-traffic.museum/how-it-done (27.12.2017).

[16]www.obs-traffic.museum/how-it-done (27.12.2017).

other objectives, public communication is actually a key purpose of the International Observatory on Illicit Traffic in Cultural Goods.

The media remains one of the strongest tools for the mobilisation of both the public and the stakeholders towards the protection of cultural heritage against illicit traffic. Despite their expertise and their understanding of the issue, the sensitisation of experienced professionals is also as important.

## *6.2 Ratification of International Conventions*

The development of a strong international legal basis is at the core of an efficient transnational cooperation for an effective fight against the traffic. The ratification of the two main international instruments, namely the UNESCO 1970 Convention[17] and the UNIDROIT 1995 Convention,[18] is a basic requirement, and countries can't possibly fight the traffic and hope for the restitution of stolen objects without signing off these international instruments.

Though ratification is hardly efficient without a proper implementation, only few of the 125 State Parties of the 1970 Convention have actually implemented the instrument thoroughly. The Convention requires a series of essential measures to be adopted by countries. These vary from the creation of national cultural property inventory, to the creation of specialised services to fight the traffic.

As for the 1995 UNIDROIT Convention, which has so far been ratified by only 35 countries, the possibilities it offers to national authorities and individuals are often misunderstood or underestimated. Nevertheless, the 'spirit' of the convention and its main principles—such as the obligation of due diligence—are gaining ground among the international community and art and heritage professionals. They actually have a growing influence on the evolution of national and regional practices and legal frameworks.

## *6.3 The Role of International Organisations and Cooperation*

For the raising of awareness, the promotion of legal instruments, the development of practical tools, the training of professionals and the enhancement of international cooperation, international organisations play a crucial part. The United Nations Economic and Social Council (ECOSOC)[19] officially recognises an international

[17]Download: https://www.obs-traffic.museum/sites/default/files/ressources/files/UNESCO_convention_1970.pdf (27.12.2017).

[18]Download: https://www.obs-traffic.museum/sites/default/files/ressources/files/UNIDROIT_convention_1995.pdf (27.12.2017).

[19]https://www.obs-traffic.museum/united-nations (27.12.2017).

group of experts made up of six organisations who are working in close collaboration combining their expertise in the area: the International Council of Museums (ICOM),[20] the International Criminal Police Organization (INTERPOL),[21] the International Institute for the Unification of Private Law (UNIDROIT),[22] the United Nations Educational, Scientific and Cultural Organizations (UNESCO),[23] the United Nations Office on Drugs and Crime (UNODC)[24] and the World Customs Organization (WCO).[25]

This international group of leading experts, along with other NGOs and intergovernmental organisations, participate in the international efforts to stop illicit traffic in cultural goods. When dealing with transnational criminals who perfectly know how to take advantage of the legal and operational gaps, international cooperation is an essential element in the following areas: standardisation of the practices and of the legal frameworks, exchange of information, control of the transportation of cultural goods, joint investigations, prosecutions, dialogue for the return or restitution of stolen or looted cultural property, etc.

The International Council of Museums ICOM established the program "fighting illicit traffic". ICOM and its partners work to raise awareness of, and combat illicit traffic in cultural goods in order to ensure the protection of world cultural heritage. For that purpose ICOM implemented its "Red Lists Database",[26] and has an observatory of illicit traffic.[27]

In view of the difficulty to reach a strong international legal consensus in the matter, the number of bilateral and multilateral agreements has been growing over the past few years. The necessity to have a common framework for the control and the status of foreign cultural objects within the common market, has forced EU institutions to tackle the problem, and eventually recast the Council Directive 93/7/EEC on the Return of Cultural Objects unlawfully removed from the territory of a Member State.[28]

---

[20]http://icom.museum (27.12.2017).

[21]https://www.interpol.int (27.12.2017).

[22]http://www.unidroit.org (27.12.2017).

[23]http://www.unesco.org (27.12.2017).

[24]http://www.unodc.org. Download: https://www.obs-traffic.museum/sites/default/files/ressources/files/UNODC_convention_2000.pdf (26.12.2017).

[25]http://www.wcoomd.org (27.12.2017).

[26]www.icom.museum (27.12.2017).

[27]https://www.obs-traffic.museum (27.12.2017). Most parts of this article are taken from this source.

[28]Download: https://www.obs-traffic.museum/sites/default/files/ressources/files/EU_Council_directive_93_7_EEC_1993.pdf (27.12.2017).

## 6.4 *The Role of Governmental Administration*

At the national level, many requirements actually depend on the goodwill of the governments. The ratification and implementation of international legal instruments is the first of them, and implies the enhancement of national legislations, particularly in the following areas:

### 6.4.1 Definition of National Cultural Property

- Legal requirements for the import, export and transfer of ownership of cultural property (export certificates, registers for art and antique dealers, etc.)
- Definition and implementation of strict due diligence procedures for the acquisition of cultural objects
- Setting-up of sanctions in case of a breach of national legislation
- Transposition of professional ethical rules into the national laws

On a more practical level, state administrations are strongly encouraged to take the following measures:

- Setting-up of one or more national services for the protection of cultural heritage
- Establishment and update of national inventories
- Development of conservation institutions
- Supervision of archaeological excavations and promotion of related scientific research—Establishment of ethical rules for art and heritage professionals, including the art market
- Public awareness-raising
- Development and use of practical tools

To support the work of international organisations, law enforcement agencies, state administrations and art and heritage professionals therewith, a wide range of practical instruments have been developed over the past decades, particularly for police and custom agencies.

Inventory being the best way to protect a cultural object, there are dozens of inventory tools already in existence and readily available to help individuals and institutions register and manage their collections. Meanwhile, major law enforcement agencies, UNESCO, museums, cultural heritage organisations, art trade and art appraisal organisations and insurance companies recommend the use of a specific international standard determining the minimum amount of information to document collections of archaeological, cultural and artistic objects: the Object ID Standard or Object ID norm.[29] Developed by the J. Paul Getty Trust, the Object ID Standard

[29] https://www.obs-traffic.museum/object-id (29.12.2017).

simplifies the retrieval of an object in case of theft and is compatible with INTERPOL'S database of stolen works of art.[30]

Along institutional and national inventories, the use of a database of stolen cultural property is another essential requirement to track down stolen objects and prevent their transaction. Notwithstanding the importance of national databases, the use of the Interpol's Stolen Works of Art Database remains the best way for everyone to access to information on stolen objects from all over the world. It is freely accessible online to the public since August 2009 through INTERPOL's secure website.[31] In the list of practical instruments intended for law enforcement agencies, ICOM'S Red Lists[32] help them quickly identify, for a given country or region, the categories of objects particularly exposed to the traffic. In order to improve the control of the export of cultural goods customs can also use the UNESCO-WCO Model Export Certificate for Cultural Objects.[33]

## *6.5 Building Professional Ethics Within the Art and Heritage Community*

"A wide range of codes of ethics and guidelines have been drafted and revised in a number of professional sectors[34]: archaeologists, art historians, museum professionals (ICOM Code of Ethics for Museums),[35] librarians, archivists, art dealers, etc. They are all intended for different contexts, and they address different matters. Though, despite the high number of principles listed in these instruments, there is a clear lack of sectorial and geographical harmonisation related to the prevention of illicit cultural goods traffic, and efforts need to be done in this regard.

Ethical principles come prior to legislation, they are non-legally binding, and the relevant authorities are often unable to monitor, investigate and sanction their respect. Therefore, their effectiveness mostly relies on self-regulation."[36]

[30]https://www.interpol.int/Crime-areas/Works-of-art/Works-of-art (27.12.2017).

[31]https://www.interpol.int/Crime-areas/Works-of-art/Works-of-art (27.12.2017).

[32]https://www.obs-traffic.museum/international-council-museums (27.12.2017).

[33]Download: https://www.obs-traffic.museum/sites/default/files/ressources/files/UNESCO_WCO_Modele_Certificat_Exportation.pdf (27.12.2017).

[34]For example the publication: Countering illicit traffic in cultural goods—the global challenge of protecting the world's heritage. Free Download: www.icom.museum/programmes/fighting-illicit-traffic/icoms-international-observatory-on-illicit-traffic-in-cultural-goods/ (27.12.2017).

[35]www.icom-deutschland.de/schwerpunkte-ethische-richtlinien-fuer-museen.php (27.12.2017) free download: http://www.icom-deutschland.de/client/media/362/code_ethics2013_eng.pdf

[36]www.obs-traffic.museum/how-fight-it (27.12.2017).

## 7 Tourism and Urban Development

"Cultural and heritage tourism is defined as travel directed toward experiencing the arts, heritage and activities that truly represent the stories and people of the past and present."[37]

Tourism and culture are closely connected; the latter provides an incentive for the former. Studies show that 37% of global tourism is related to culture and heritage. 9.5% of global Gross Domestic Product (GDP) comes from tourism. In developing States, tourism can account for up to 25% of GDP. One study has shown that for every $1 that a visitor spends at a heritage site, they may spend up to $12 at surrounding businesses, such as hotels, restaurants, etc. Fisheries often employ less people in coastal areas than tourism (hotel, food, sales, transport, guides). Especially diving tourists spend more money and stay longer.[38]

ICOM worked on a charter with the goal to implement standards to protect heritage while making sure that the communities involved can benefit from a long-term advantage. In this charter, museums have an active part in heritage management.[39] Sustainable tourism development must include the protection and promotion of cultural heritage.

Underwater cultural heritage represents a unique form of cultural heritage that distinguishes those areas that promote it from other destinations. Underwater cultural heritage is especially important for coastal and island States, many of which have established maritime and coastal tourism industries. Maritime heritage demonstrates connections with other regions of the world and promotes unity through shared heritage among nations. Many countries still lack underwater archaeologists and experts. Commercial salvagers and treasure-hunters are often used in place of archaeologists, which leads to the damage and destruction of important sites. The rules in the Annex to the 2001 Convention (UCH)[40] provide important guidelines for heritage management, but they are often not followed.

---

[37] Kamani Perera, The Role of Museums in Cultural and Heritage Tourism for sustainable Economy in Developing Countries; http://www.ne-mo.org/fileadmin/Dateien/public/statements_and_news/Reading_Corner/Cultural_and_Heritage_Tourism.pdf (27.12.2017).

[38] http://www.unesco.org/new/en/culture/themes/underwater-cultural-heritage/publications-resources/ (27.12.2017).

[39] http://icom.museum/programmes/cultural-tourism/ (28.12.2017). Hans-Martin Hinz, Museen und Touristen: Enjoying without destroying, in: ICOM Deutschland. Beiträge zur Museologie. Band 2, Museen und Denkmäler – Historisches Erbe und Kulturtourismus, Berlin 2010, 11 ff., 12.

[40] http://www.unesco.org/new/en/culture/themes/underwater-cultural-heritage/2001-convention/official-text/ (17.12.2017).

## 8 Museums and Tourism

Museums play an important role in helping demonstrate a region's cultural value. For example, the VASA Museum in Stockholm brings an estimated $300 Million each year to the city. Museums featuring underwater cultural heritage present a unique and original experience for tourists. Cultural heritage tourism is one of the vital components of the tourism industry, and is a powerful economic development tool. It has been revealed that museums are now playing a major role not only in the wider sphere of arts, but also within tourism and leisure.[41]

The World Tourism Organization (UNWTO) decided in 1999 the Global Code of Ethics for Tourism[42] what gives a good framework. Museums have a special role to fulfil. They have direct contact to the people. "Museums are recognized as integral partners in sustainable development, advocating a greater respect and understanding of the importance of heritage to the source communities".[43]

[41]Kamani Perera, The Role of Museums in Cultural and Heritage Tourism for sustainable Economy in Developing Countries; http://www.ne-mo.org/fileadmin/Dateien/public/statements_and_news/Reading_Corner/Cultural_and_Heritage_Tourism.pdf (17.12.2017)

[42]http://ethics.unwto.org/en/content/global-code-ethics-tourism Download full text: http://cf.cdn.unwto.org/sites/all/files/docpdf/gcetbrochureglobalcodeen.pdf (28.12.2017).

[43]Hans-Martin Hinz, Museen und Touristen: Enjoying without destroying, in: ICOM Deutschland. Beiträge zur Museologie. Band 2, Museen und Denkmäler – Historisches Erbe und Kulturtourismus, Berlin 2010, 11 ff., 21.

# Tourism and Trafficking of Cultural Goods: An Overview of Regulatory Initiatives

Kalliopi Chainoglou

## 1 Introduction

Culture and cultural heritage are important assets for tourism as they attract millions of tourists every year to visit culture-related destinations. During the past few decades, cultural heritage has been receiving growing attention within the tourism industry and it has been incorporated into tourist-related economic development policies and planning. Cultural tourism, including cultural heritage tourism, has been defined as "visits by persons from outside the host community motivated wholly or in part by interest in historical, artistic, scientific or lifestyle/heritage offerings of a community, region, group or institution" (Silberberg 1995, p. 361).

Cultural tourism not only presents one of the major development opportunities at regional, national and local level, but is destined to benefit local communities and to motivate them to maintain, preserve and manage their cultural heritage (Ezeuduji and Rid 2011, p. 189; Samukelisiwe Nkwanyana et al. 2016). From this perspective, cultural tourism can be a considerable force for the promotion and safeguarding of tangible and intangible heritage, while encouraging the development of arts and other culture-related activities as well as the continuance of cultural practices and traditions, benefiting thus the local/host communities.

Culture and cultural heritage are of immeasurable value to host communities as they form part of their cultural identity and collective memory (Chainoglou et al. 2017); at the same time, they form part of the human history and civilization and should therefore be protected from unlawful appropriation and pillage. Cultural tourism does not always bring benefits; if poorly managed or regulated, cultural tourism can turn into a form of 'yellow tourism' causing short-term and long-term negative impacts on culture and heritage. One of the major threats posed by cultural

K. Chainoglou (✉)
University of Macedonia, Thessaloniki, Greece
e-mail: chainoglou@uom.gr



A. Papathanassis et al. (eds.), *Yellow Tourism*, Tourism, Hospitality & Event Management, https://doi.org/10.1007/978-3-319-94664-1_8

tourism is the trafficking (illicit trade) of antiquities and cultural goods from source to market. According to UNESCO, trafficking in cultural property is estimated at $2 to $6 billion per year (Borgstede 2014). The paper presents policies and laws introduced by international organisations in tackling the problem of illicit trade of cultural goods which can be a by-product of cultural tourism and discusses relevant initiatives at regional (European) level.

## 2 Tourism-Related Threats to Cultural Heritage and Cultural Property

Cultural heritage and cultural goods can be in danger not only of natural disasters, such as earthquakes, but can also be endangered by some major human-induced threats. The latter can relate to the lack of understanding of the subject heritage area, i.e. the conservation heritage issues, the lack of sustainable tourism strategies or the lack of understanding how yellow cultural tourism can feed transnational organised crime and result in the systematic looting trafficking of cultural objects. Regional organisations have acknowledged the possibility of tourism having a negative effect on cultural heritage and have stressed the need for advancing a framework of cultural heritage cooperation at international level. For example, in 2016 the ASEAN Vientiane Declaration on Reinforcing Cultural Heritage Cooperation acknowledged the increasing threats, "as a result of illicit trafficking in cultural property, natural disasters, climate change, unsustainable tourism, rapid urbanisation, to tangible cultural heritage" and expressed the commitment to develop a cooperation framework to "mitigate the impacts of tourism to protect heritage sites from damaging commercialisation" and to promote "law enforcement in eliminating cross-border trade of cultural objects". Along the same lines, the Inter-Parliamentary Union in 2016 affirmed in a Resolution that mass tourism may have adverse impact on heritage itself and that "tourists have a duty to maintain and preserve our common heritage, which should help to create visiting conditions that allow each and every one to respect that heritage and at the same time avoid using it inappropriately or untowardly". In other words, the dynamics behind the relationship between tourism and cultural heritage have to rely on a fine balance between sustainable tourism and the protection, conservation, interpretation and presentation of the heritage (see also the ICOMOS Charter 1999).

When tourism crosses the path of cultural heritage and cultural goods, there are some threats that will bear devastating impact on the cultural heritage concerned. And tourists themselves will have only acted as accelerators to the damage caused to the cultural property in question. One of the persistent criticisms of cultural tourism is the commodification along with the process of re-contextualisation of culture in a given setting. For example, "tour-operators, tour guides, and tourism planners translate, commodify or package particular types of artefacts, spaces, stories and social practices into discourses, products and events that are accessible to tourists.

Tourists, by definition, spend only a short period of time in any particular place and thus they can only experience selective aspects of the host culture" (Picard and Robinson 2006, p.22; Picard 1992); the result is that certain aspects of the cultural resources of a particular country are accorded a narrative different to the one that the host community attaches to them. As touristic aesthetics are overtly imposed on national/local cultural goods and resources, "tourism not only challenges recognised formulations, categories and boundaries of collective identity, but also relocates the very processes of formulating and constructing identity into the new social spaces created by tourism" (Picard and Robinson 2006, p. 22; Picard 1992). Furthermore, the lack of regulation of heritage sites or the ignorance on the part of tourists can endanger the integrity of the cultural heritage sites. For example, when cultural heritage sites are not listed as protected sites they can often be subjected to abusive or non-respectful behaviour by ignorant tourists. Every now and then there are reported cases of tourists climbing on or defacing heritage sites; it is often the case that tourists may illegally remove cultural and archaeological items from heritage sites in order to keep mementos of their cultural visit or to sell them in the black market. In this context, tourists may find themselves being willingly or unwillingly part of transnational criminal rings operating in the black market of selling/receiving cultural goods. As Irina Bokova commented back in 2014 "tourists are easy targets for dealers selling cultural artefacts of doubtful provenance. They are usually unaware that these 'souvenirs' may be stolen heritage—ripped away from their original settings, illegally excavated from archaeological sites, or traded by unscrupulous individuals offering meagre payment." (UNESCO, Antitrafficking Campaign 2014; Husken 2017). Indeed, countries like Cyprus, Greece, Egypt, Italy, Israel, India and Bulgaria that have been receiving millions of cultural tourists over the past decades have experienced the negative aspects of cultural tourism: numerous archaeological sites have been raided, illegal excavations have been carried out either by locals or by cultural tourists and numerous cultural artefacts have been illegally exported and entered the black market (Bowman 2008). And once cultural goods enter the black market, they are indisputably lost forever. The implication is that the physical and immaterial integrity of the cultural heritage in question will be severely affected by the acts of the tourists. Furthermore, if they result in the illegal removal of cultural goods from their place or country of origin, then it will inflict great damage on the rightful owners of this heritage as the latter forms an intrinsic part to their cultural identity and values. Such acts do not violate the cultural heritage and identity of the directly affected communities, but can be detrimental to the whole of mankind as heritage belongs to all humanity and if lost to the black market, then pieces of our shared, common human story are lost too.

The illicit trade of cultural property is a problem that concerns every region of the world and is of growing concern for the international community. At the international level, international organisations have spearheaded efforts to promote cultural heritage protection and the restitution of illegally exported cultural goods. These efforts have been orchestrated by adopting a number of legal and policy instruments that purport to create a framework for the elimination of the illicit trade in cultural objects and the restitution of illegally exported cultural goods. At the same time, it has been acknowledged that the illegal removal of cultural goods has been associated with two facts: (a) at national level, there are still states that have left unregulated the cultural objects markets, (b) at regional level, there is still limited co-operation between states as to law-enforcement operations on cultural-goods smuggling. With these in mind, in 2014, UNESCO, the UN Office on Drugs and Crime, and the World Tourism Organisation (UNWTO), launched a global campaign against illicit trafficking of cultural goods entitled "Travel, Do not Traffic". The purpose of this campaign was to raise awareness regarding illegal export of cultural objects, using the following message (UNESCO, Antitrafficking Campaign 2014):

> Dear tourist, make sure that the souvenir you take hasn't been looted from a museum or illegally excavated from an archeological site. Please check its provenance and verify that it can be exported out of the country! Keep in mind that a cultural object is not simple merchandise: it embodies history and has a symbolic value for the local people. Help stop illicit trafficking!

UNESCO has partnered with Lonely Planet France, in order to achieve wider publicity for this campaign. This awareness-raising initiative aims at making every tourist an active actor in cultural heritage preservation. As the former General Director of UNESCO has said "this campaign will help make any tourist a more respectful of other cultures and ambassador of a more sustainable world. This campaign is not just a campaign on tourism, but on citizenship" (UNESCO, Antitrafficking Campaign 2014). In 2017, the UNWTO ran a similar campaign raising awareness of the contribution that sustainable tourism can make to development in line with the UN Sustainable Development Goals and promoted a mini-code of tourist/traveller ethics on how to be a responsible, respectful and informed traveller; some of the tips given therein included: "Research your destination to learn about local customs, traditions and social conditions; Do not buy counterfeit products or items that are prohibited by national/international regulations; Take photos instead of protected cultural artefacts as mementos of your trip; Respect wildlife and their natural habitats..." (UNWTO, Be a Responsible Traveller 2017).

UNWTO and UNESCO have been working together to run educational and public information campaigns to promote a sense of appreciation of cultural property among the general public and to raise awareness about the strong interlinks between tourism and culture and the need for the development of sustainable cultural tourism strategies. Yet it is observed that at international organisations' level the link between cultural tourism, looting and illicit trade of cultural property, and transnational organised crime is still overlooked despite the evidence of a substantial number of reported cases. And despite the efforts for sustainable cultural tourism strategies and regional co-operation partnerships, actions to curb the trafficking in cultural property have not yet matched the gravity or the extent of the crime or have not been directly associated with tourism-related strategies and policies as such. This is also confirmed by the fact that there are few reliable statistics and exchange of information at regional level which could provide answers to even the most basic questions about the link between cultural tourism, trafficking in cultural property and transnational organised crime.

## 3 Institutional and Legal Responses Concerning the Trafficking of Cultural Goods

At universal level, the trafficking of cultural goods is regulated by various legal instruments. The 1970 Convention on the Means of Prohibiting and Preventing the Illicit Import, Export and Transfer of Ownership of Cultural Property, is one of the first legal instruments that attempted to constrain and prohibit the looting and smuggling of cultural artefacts by introducing a triptych of state obligations: preventive measures, return and restitution, and international cooperation. The 1970 Convention succinctly states that "every state [must] protect the cultural property existing within its territory against the dangers of theft, clandestine excavation, and illicit export" while also avowing that "the protection of cultural heritage can be effective only if organised both nationally and internationally among states working in close cooperation" (UNESCO 1970). The 1995 UNIDROIT Convention on Stolen or Illegally Exported Cultural Objects complements the 1970 Convention by covering aspects of international private law not previously regulated by the 1970 Convention; the purpose of the 1995 UNIDROIT Convention is to harmonise the legal framework on the restitution of cultural objects and to introduce the duty of due diligence on the part of buyers when purchasing cultural objects. Despite these legal developments, the international community has asserted that the looting and trafficking in cultural property falls also within the wider context of transnational organised crime.

Hence, in 2000, when the UN General Assembly adopted the UN Convention against Transnational Organised Crime (2000), it was envisaged that the Convention would "...constitute an effective tool for international cooperation in combating, inter alia, money-laundering, corruption, trafficking in endangered species of flora and fauna, offences against cultural property, and growing links between transnational organised crime and terrorist crimes" (UNTOC, Preamble). Indeed, UNTOC Conference of Parties has described the problem as such: "[Trafficking in cultural property] has links to organised crime, as it relies on modus operandi used by organised criminal groups; the strong demand for illicit objects is highly lucrative for those participating in the trade; its complex nature often requires the involvement of many actors, legal entities and third parties, who tend to operate in a structured and organised way; and the use of modern and sophisticated technologies. There is also evidence that transnational trafficking in antiquities is linked to other illicit activities in which organised criminal groups are involved, including drugs and arms smuggling, violence, corruption and money-laundering" (UN Report 2010).

Furthermore, the UNTOC Conference of Parties has repeatedly asserted that in order to effectively tackle the trafficking in cultural property and its links to organised crime, states must exchange information on all aspects of criminal offences against cultural property, in accordance with their national laws, and to coordinate administrative and other measures taken, as appropriate, for the prevention, early detection and punishment of such offences (UNTOC Conference of Parties 2010, 2012). This Convention offers added value to the prevention, investigation and prosecution of trafficking of cultural property as well as the return and restitution of stolen/trafficked cultural objects through a number of measures such as criminalisation, prosecution, international investigation, extradition, recovery of illicit cultural goods and prevention (Campbell 2013). It goes without saying that the fight against illicit trade in cultural property could not be facilitated without the inter-agency and inter-organisational cooperation developed through the UN Office on Drugs and Crime, Interpol (INTERPOL 2017), the International Institute for the Unification of Private Law (UNIDROIT), the Organisation for Security and Cooperation in Europe (OSCE), and the International Council of Museums (ICOM). The mandate of these agencies and organisations working in the field of trafficking in cultural property is based on the 2015 International Guidelines for Crime Prevention and Criminal Justice Responses with Respect to Trafficking in Cultural Property and Other Related Offences and the decisions of other UN bodies (UN ECOSOC 2004, 2008, 2010; UN General Assembly Resolution 66/180 2012, UN General Assembly Resolution 68/186 2014, UN General Assembly Resolution 70/178 2015a, UN General Assembly (2015b), UN General Assembly Resolution 70/76 2015c, UNESCO (2015a), UNESCO (2015b), UNESCO (2015c), UN Commission on Crime Prevention 2015).

The trafficking of cultural property is not only related to transnational organised crime groups and the financing of mafia syndicates or even insurgent groups but it has been lately linked to terrorist financing too (Chainoglou 2019). Following the unprecedented number of looted artefacts being illegally exported from Iraq and Syria, the UN Security Council has adopted Resolution 2199 (2015a) and Resolution 2253 (2015c) which prohibit trade in cultural property from Iraq and Syria. With Resolution 2199 (2015a), the Security Council condemns the destruction of cultural heritage, whether incidental or deliberate, and including religious sites and objects, in Iraq and Syria, and notes that "ISIL, ANF and other individuals, groups, undertakings and entities associated with Al-Qaida, are generating income from engaging directly or indirectly in the looting and smuggling of cultural heritage items from archaeological sites, museums, libraries, archives, and other sites in Iraq and Syria, which is being used to support their recruitment efforts and strengthen their operational capability to organise and carry out terrorist attacks" and decides "that all Member States shall take appropriate steps to prevent the trade in . . . Syrian cultural property and other items of archaeological, historical, cultural, rare scientific, and religious importance illegally removed . . . from Syria since 15 March 2011, including by prohibiting cross-border trade in such items" (paras. 16–17). With Resolution 2249 (2015b) the Security Council notes that the "eradication of cultural heritage and trafficking of cultural property. . .constitutes a global and unprecedented threat to international peace and security". The UN Security Council Resolution 2322 (2016) calls States to develop broad law enforcement and judicial cooperation in preventing and combating trafficking in cultural property. By Resolution 2347 (2017), the Security Council has attempted to create a comprehensive framework solely focused on the protection of cultural heritage. Resolution 2347 condemns the unlawful destruction of cultural heritage, including the destruction of religious sites and artefacts, and the looting and smuggling of cultural property from archaeological sites, museums, libraries, archives, and other sites, in armed conflicts, notably by terrorist groups. The Resolution affirms that states have the primary responsibility for protecting their cultural heritage within their borders and to advance the protection of cultural heritage, if requested, with the assistance of relevant UN agencies. This is a timely response to the challenges posed in certain regions, like Middle East, North Africa and South Asia, where the looting of archaeological sites has reached an industrial scale. The forecasting for the success of Resolution 2347 (2017) is more than promising. The UN Secretary General in his first report on the implementation of Security Council Resolution 2347 (2017) noted that institutional changes have been taking place in the form of creation of specialized units in central and local administrations, designing tools and training for customs and law enforcement dedicated personnel and public prosecutors, and the creation or improvement of procedures or databases to collect information on criminal activity related to cultural property and its illicit trade. At national level, states have individually taken additional measures ranging from creating national databases to combat illicit trafficking of cultural property and using the INTERPOL Database on Stolen Works of Art, or raising public awareness of illicit trafficking of cultural objects and how to prevent it, mainly within the UNESCO campaign #Unite4Heritage, to disseminating information regarding import and export restrictions governing trade in cultural objects, and financially contributing to the Heritage Emergency Fund, Second Protocol Fund and the International Alliance for the Protection of Heritage in Conflict Areas to support preventive and emergency operations. In this context and as the momentum builds around protection for cultural heritage and the need to halt illicit trade of cultural property, the international organisations at European level have responded more than efficiently.

The most comprehensive initiatives on trafficking cultural goods have been taking place at European level [even prior to UN Security Council Resolution 2347 (2017)]. Two European organisations, the EU and the Council of Europe have adopted legal instruments that are tackling the issue from various perspectives.

At EU level, it has been acknowledged that one of the main problems with illicit trade in cultural property related to the fact there were no common rules with regard to the import of cultural goods from third countries and as a consequence trafficking routes have been developed through the most vulnerable parts of the unevenly regulated EU territories (EU Commission, Mapping of Cultural Heritage Actions 2017a; EU, Illicit Trade in Cultural Goods 2017). While EU customs may intercept incoming illicit cultural goods, they still lack the appropriate legal and operational means as well as the expertise to detect that the cultural goods in question have been stolen, illicitly excavated or that they are accompanied by falsified documentation. One has to remember that once such goods enter through the EU territory, then they may be laundered and resold to private individuals or art dealers and galleries not only across EU but to third countries too. In 2009, the Council adopted Council Regulation (EC) No 116/2009 on the export of cultural goods which sets up uniform controls at the EU's external borders by subjecting the export to the presentation of an export licence which is obtained with the competent authorities in the Member States and valid throughout the EU. Recently, the Council adopted Directive 2014/60 of the European Parliament and of the Council on the return of cultural objects unlawfully removed from the territory of a member state. This Directive is recasting the earlier 1993 Council Directive 93/7/EEC. The aim of this new Directive is to provide for intra-EU national authorities' cooperation mechanisms in consultation with the Internal Market Information System and return proceedings against the possessor to secure the return of a cultural object unlawfully removed from the territory of one EU country to the territory of another EU country on, or after, 1 January 1993. This Directive provides EU member states with more time to conduct search on missing cultural objects that are located in another EU state and sets a 3-year time limit for the central authority of the requesting EU member state to take action on the return of the unlawfully removed property. Furthermore, the EU is taking more robust policy-measures to tackle the interlinked issues of trafficking in cultural goods, combating terrorism financing and protecting cultural heritage, in particular in source countries affected by armed conflict [such as the European Agenda on Security (2015), the Council Conclusions of 12 February 2016 on the fight against the financing of terrorism, the Communication from the Commission to the European Parliament and the Council on an Action Plan for strengthening the fight against terrorist financing and the Directive on combating terrorism (EU Directive 2017)]. The EU policies combine regulatory and non-regulatory policy options, including inter alia operational cooperation between customs and law enforcement authorities i.e. EU Policy Cycle on serious and organised crime 2018–2021, and capacity building and training of the relevant law enforcement authorities on the trafficking of cultural goods (see for example the Technical Assistance and Information Exchange instrument (TAIEX) of the EU, the Post Disaster Needs Assessments and Recovery and Peace-Building Assessments missions of the EU, etc). The latest EU initiative concerns a proposed Regulation on the import of cultural goods which apply to cultural goods meeting a 250 year minimum age threshold (EU Commission Proposal for Regulation 2017b). The proposed instrument introduces a special framework of protection and level of scrutiny before entry in the Union's customs territory for particular cultural goods that are under the threat of trafficking: "the person who seeks to introduce them into the Union's customs territory must provide the following documents in order to prove licit provenance, i.e. legality of export from the source country:—for archaeological objects, parts of monuments that have been dismembered and for rare manuscripts and incunabula, the person must apply to the competent authority designated for this purpose by the Member State of entry for an import licence, by providing proof of licit export of the goods from the source country;—for all other cultural goods, the person must submit to customs a signed statement (affidavit) certifying that the goods were legally exported from the source country, accompanied by a standard Object ID document, describing the object in detail. Customs register and keep a copy of these documents" (EU Commission Proposal for Regulation 2017b, p. 7). Overall, it proposes to ensure that importers, including tourists and travellers, exercise due diligence when buying cultural goods from third countries and to standardise information that certifies the legality of the cultural goods.

At the Council of Europe level, the new Council of Europe Convention on Offences Relating to Cultural Property is a criminal law convention that aims to build on the existing instruments such as the 1970 Convention and the 1995 Convention. The new Council of Europe Convention which was adopted on 19th May 2017 in Nicosia has already been signed by 10 states. Even though this is a regional instrument it is globally-oriented legal instrument that is open to signature and ratification by non-member states of the Council of Europe. The purpose of this Convention is to enhance the law enforcement capacity and to ensure the harmonization of the criminalization of different aspects of trafficking of cultural property given the differences between the states' legal orders across the international community (Caponigri and Pirri 2017). For example, under the Convention, a number of acts have been criminalized such as theft and other forms of unlawful appropriation, illegal importation, illegal exportation, acquisition, placing on the market, falsification of documents, destruction and damage of cultural property, and aiding or abetting and attempt the commission of one of the aforementioned criminal offences. Furthermore, the Convention calls for the investigation and prosecution of these criminal offences ex officio and for international co-operation in these criminal matters to the "largest possible extent". More interestingly, the Convention calls for the monitoring and reporting of suspicious dealings or sales on the internet. Should this Convention be ratified by all 28 EU member states that are at the same time member states of the Council of Europe, and in conjunction with the EU proposed Regulation on the import of cultural goods, then the European framework will be globally the first of its kind in tackling through such comprehensive, transnational and inter-agency means the trafficking of cultural property. Of course, it remains to be seen whether these regulatory instruments of the EU and the Council of Europe will be eventually incorporated by their member states into their tourism strategies and actions plans and how they will be advanced through information-awareness campaigns by the relevant stakeholders, including the tourist operators.

## 4 Summary and Conclusion

The analysis above indicates that it is evident that the trafficking of cultural property is a multi-dimensional phenomenon and it can materialise through various actors. The international organisations have adopted legal and policy instruments that are regulating the import/export as well as the return and restitution of cultural goods. And in order to do so, they have painstakingly promoted the transnational co-operation among the national competent authorities. However, they significantly lack any initiatives in acknowledging the dynamics behind the relationship between yellow tourism and the illicit trade in cultural property. International co-operation should depend also on new stakeholders, such as tourism authorities, tourist operators and tourist operators; moreover, information awareness campaigns should reach out to every tourist/traveller. The existing legal frameworks (whether universal or regional) concerning the fight against the trafficking of cultural goods cannot fulfil their potential without seeking to actively engage all tourism industry actors in the preservation and protection of cultural assets and goods. In parallel, states and international organisations have to develop tools, synergies and policies that promote sustainable tourism while protecting culture and cultural heritage and contributing to the fight against the illicit trade in cultural goods. The implication of this would be to bring the existing legal framework on cultural goods' trafficking in alignment with the UN Sustainable Development Goals. But to do so, this requires further research to be conducted and more data to be collected on the relationship between yellow cultural tourism and the trafficking of cultural goods.

## References

ASEAN. (2016). *Vientiane declaration on reinforcing cultural heritage cooperation in ASEAN*. Available at http://asean.org/storage/2016/09/Vientiane-Declaration-endorsed-by-7th-AMCA-24Aug2016.pdf

Borgstede, G. (2014). Cultural property, the palermo convention, and transnational organised crime. *International Journal of Cultural Property, 21*(3), 281–290.

Bowman, B. (2008). Transnational crimes against culture: Looting at archaeological sites and the "grey" market in antiquities. *Journal of Contemporary Criminal Justice, 24*, 225–242.

Campbell, P. B. (2013). The illicit antiquities trade as a transnational criminal network: Characterizing and anticipating trafficking of cultural heritage. *International Journal of Cultural Property, 20*, 113–153. Available at https://www.cambridge.org/core/services/aop-cambridge-core/content/view/47EFDD1CF26E676A77BFD5D89A493DB7/S0940739113000015a.pdf/illicit_antiquities_trade_as_a_transnational_criminal_network_characterizing_and_anticipating_trafficking_of_cultural_heritage.pdf

Caponigri, F., & Pirri, A. (2017). Summary report of conference on "A new perspective on the protection of cultural property through criminal law". *Rivista di Arti e Diritto Online, 2*, 1127–1345.

Chainoglou, K. (2019). Destruction and reconstruction of cultural heritage in eastern mediterranean: from cultural genocide to war crimes and crimes against humanity. In S. N. Litsas & A. Tziampiris (Eds.), *The new eastern mediterranean*. Cham: Springer.

Chainoglou, K., Wiesand, A., Donders, Y., & Sledzinska, A. (2017). *Culture and human rights: The Wroclaw commentaries*. Berlin: De Gruyter.

Council of Europe. (2017). *Convention on offences relating to cultural property*. Council of Europe Treaty Series no. 221. Available at https://rm.coe.int/CoERMPublicCommonSearchServices/DisplayDCTMContent?documentId=0900001680710435

EU. (2017). *Illicit trade in cultural goods* (Regulation EU 116/2009 and Directive 2014/60/EU). Available at http://www.europarl.europa.eu/RegData/etudes/BRIE/2017/603259/EPRS_BRI(2017)603259_EN.pdf

EU Commission. (2015). *European agenda on security*. COM (2015) 185 final. Available at https://ec.europa.eu/anti-trafficking/sites/antitrafficking/files/eu_agenda_on_security_en.pdf

EU Commission. (2017a). *Mapping of cultural heritage actions in European union policies, programmes and activities*. Available at http://www.dedale.info/_objets/medias/autres/mapping-cultural-heritage-1110.pdf

EU Commission. (2017b). *Proposal for regulation on the import of cultural goods*. COM(2017) 375 final. Available at https://ec.europa.eu/taxation_customs/sites/taxation/files/cultural_goods_proposal_en.pdf

EU Council Regulation (EC) No 116/2009 on the export of cultural goods. *Official Journal of the European Union*. 10.2.2009. L 39/1-39/7.

EU Directive. (2017). Directive (EU) 2017/541 of the European Parliament and of the Council of 15 March 2017 on combating terrorism and replacing Council Framework Decision 2002/475/ JHA and amending Council Decision 2005/671/JHA; *OJ L 88*, 31.3.2017, pp. 6–21.

Ezeuduji, I. O., & Rid, W. (2011). Rural tourism offer and local community participation in The Gambia. *TOURISMOS: An International Multidisciplinary Journal of Tourism, 6*(2), 187–211.

Husken, T. (2017). *The practice and culture of smuggling in the borderland of Egypt and Libya.* https://www.chathamhouse.org/sites/files/chathamhouse/publications/ia/INTA93_4_08_Husken.pdf

ICOMOS. (1999). *International cultural tourism charter-managing tourism at places of heritage significance.* Available at https://www.icomos.org/images/DOCUMENTS/Charters/INTERNATIONAL_CULTURAL_TOURISM_CHARTER.pdf

Inter-Parliamentary Union. (2016). *Resolution on ensuring lasting protection against destruction and deterioration for the tangible and intangible cultural heritage of humanity.* Available at http://archive.ipu.org/conf-e/134/Res-2.pdf

INTERPOL. (2017). *Creating a national cultural heritage unit.* Available at https://www.interpol.int/News-and-media/Publications2/Leaflets-and-brochures/Creating-a-National-Cultural-Heritage-Unit

Picard, M. (1992). *Bali. Tourisme culturel et culture touristique.* Paris: L'Harmattan.

Picard, M., & Robinson, M. (2006). *Tourism, culture and sustainable development.* Paris: UNESCO. Available at http://unesdoc.unesco.org/images/0014/001475/147578e.pdf

Samukelisiwe Nkwanyana, M., Ezeuduji, I. O., & Nzama, A. T. (2016). Cultural heritage tourism in South Africa: Perceived a panacea for rural development? *Acta Universitatis Danubius, 12*(6). http://journals.univ-danubius.ro/index.php/oeconomica/article/view/3550/3742.

Silberberg, T. (1995). Cultural tourism and business opportunities for museums and heritage places. *Tourism Management, 16*(5), 361–365.

UN Commission on Crime Prevention and Criminal Justice. (2015). *Resolution 24/2 Strengthening crime prevention and criminal justice responses with respect to trafficking in cultural property and other related offences, E/CN.15/2015/19.* Available at https://www.unodc.org/documents/organised-crime/mandates_on_trafficking_in_cultural_property/Resolution_24_2_E.pdf

UN Conference of Parties to the Organised Crime Convention. (2010). *Resolution 5/7 Combating transnational organised crime against cultural property.* Available at https://www.unodc.org/documents/organised-crime/COP_5_Resolutions/Resolution_5_7.pdf

UN Conference of Parties to the Organised Crime Convention. (2012). *Resolution 6/1 Ensuring effective implementation of the United Nations Convention against Transnational Organised Crime and the Protocols thereto.* Available at https://www.unodc.org/documents/treaties/organised_crime/COP6/CTOC_COP_2012_15/CTOC_COP_2012_15_E.pdf

UN ECOSOC. (2004). *Resolution 2004/34. Protection against trafficking in cultural property.* Available at https://www.unodc.org/documents/treaties/organised_crime/ECOSOC_res_2004-34.pdf

UN ECOSOC. (2008). *Resolution 2008/23. Protection against trafficking in cultural property.* Available at https://www.unodc.org/documents/treaties/organised_crime/ECOSOC_res._2008-23.pd.pdf

UN ECOSOC. (2010). *Resolution 2010/19 Crime prevention and criminal justice responses to protect cultural property, especially with regard to its trafficking.* Available at https://www.unodc.org/documents/organised-crime/UNODC_CCPCJ_EG.1_2012/ECOSOC_Res_2010_19_E.pdf

UN General Assembly. (2012). *Resolution 66/180 strengthening crime prevention and criminal justice responses to protect cultural property, especially with regard to its trafficking.* Available at https://www.unodc.org/documents/organised-crime/UNODC_CCPCJ_EG.1_2012/A_RES_66_180_E.pdf

UN General Assembly. (2014). *Resolution 68/186. Strengthening crime prevention and criminal justice responses to protect cultural property, especially with regard to its trafficking. A/RES/68/186.* Available at http://www.un.org/en/ga/search/view_doc.asp?symbol=A/RES/68/186

UN General Assembly. (2015a). *Resolution 70/178 Strengthening the United Nations crime prevention and criminal justice programme, in particular its technical cooperation capacity.* Available at http://digitallibrary.un.org/record/821515/files/A_RES_70_178-EN.pdf

UN General Assembly. (2015b). *Resolution 69/196. International guidelines for crime prevention and criminal justice responses with respect to trafficking in cultural property and other related offences, A/RES/69/196*. Available at https://www.unodc.org/documents/organised-crime/trafficking_in_cultural/RES-681-86/A_RES_69_196_E.pdf
UN General Assembly. (2015c). *Resolution 70/76 Return or restitution of cultural property to the countries of origin*. Available at http://www.un.org/en/ga/search/view_doc.asp?symbol=A/RES/70/76
UN Report. (2010). *Use of the United Nations convention against transnational organised crime for protection against trafficking in cultural property: Note by the secretariat*. Available at CTOC/COP/2010/12. https://www.unodc.org/documents/treaties/organised_crime/COP5/CTOC_COP_2010_12x/CTOC_ COP_2010_12x_E.pdf (13 August 2010)
UN Secretary General Report. (2017). *S/2017/969, 17 November 2017, Report of the secretary-general on the implementation of security council resolution 2347 (2017)*. Available at http://www.un.org/ga/search/view_doc.asp?symbol=S/2017/969
UN Security Council. (2015a). *S/RES/2199 (2015)*.
UN Security Council. (2015b). *S/RES/2249 (2015)*.
UN Security Council. (2015c). *S/RES/2253 (2015)*.
UN Security Council. (2016). *S/RES/2322 (2016)*.
UN Security Council. (2017). *S/RES/2347 (2017)*.
UNESCO. (1970). *Convention on the means of prohibiting and preventing the illicit import, export and transfer of ownership of cultural property*.
UNESCO. (2014). *Anti-trafficking campaign: Your actions count – Help fight trafficking!* Available at http://www.unesco.org/new/en/culture/themes/illicit-trafficking-of-cultural-property/meetings/forums-seminars-and-information-meetings/unwto-campaign/
UNESCO. (2015a). *Statement of the 3rd meeting of states parties to the UNESCO 1970 convention, "stop illicit trafficking of cultural property"*.
UNESCO. (2015b). *Bonn declaration on world heritage, 39th UNESCO world heritage committee*.
UNESCO. (2015c). *Declaration on culture as an instrument of dialogue among peoples*, EXPO, Milano, International Conference of the Ministers of Culture.
UNIDROIT. (1995). *Convention on stolen or illegally exported cultural objects*. Available at https://www.degruyter.com/downloadpdf/j/bog.2016.34.issue-34/bog-2016-0039/bog-2016-0039.pdf
UNWTO. (2017). *Be a responsible traveller*. Available at http://www.travelenjoyrespect.org

# Exploring Insurance Fraud and Tourists' Misbehaviour

**Dimitrios Belias, Efstathios Velissariou, Michalis Chondrogiannis, Dimitrios Kyriakou, Konstantinos Varsanis, Labros Vasiliadis, and Athanasios Koustelios**

## 1 Introduction

The insurance market is a privileged context for incomplete information between the agent (the insured) and the principal (the insurer). The insurer does not know everything of the insured person, and in particular the financial risks, which he/she may incur. There are opportunities for strategic behaviour resulting from of an asymmetric risk assessment. The economic literature classifies two types of information asymmetry: moral hazard and selection. The moral hazard concerns the influence of insurance cover on the behaviour of the insured person. The level of self-protection of insured persons may decrease after the signing the insurance

D. Belias (✉) · E. Velissariou
Department of Business Administration, Technological Educational Institute of Thessaly, Larissa, Greece
e-mail: dbelias@teilar.gr

M. Chondrogiannis
Laboratory for Geocultural Analyses, Department of Foreign Languages, Translation and Interpreting, Ionian University, Corfu, Greece

D. Kyriakou
Department of Economic Sciences, Aristotle University of Thessaloniki, Thessaloniki, Greece

K. Varsanis
Department of Business Administration, Technological Educational Institute of Western Macedonia, Kozani, Greece

L. Vasiliadis
Department of Accounting and Finance, Technological Educational Institute of Central Greece, Dirfies Messapies, Greece

A. Koustelios
Department of Physical Education and Sport Science, University of Thessaly, Trikala, Greece



A. Papathanassis et al. (eds.), *Yellow Tourism*, Tourism, Hospitality & Event Management, https://doi.org/10.1007/978-3-319-94664-1_9

contract. Agents may be tempted to engage in riskier behaviour when they have good insurance coverage. In that case, the insurance contract has the effect of increasing exposure to risk. Regarding the phenomenon of adverse selection or anti-selection, the agent who chooses the most attractive insurance contract, has an advantage on information in relation to the insurer (Boyer et al. 1989). Confronted with individuals coming from a heterogeneous background, the insurer is unable to distinguish between them and this creates a high degree of risk. The insurer therefore does not have sufficient information to enable it to achieve a match between the terms of the contract and the individual risks. This situation results in the same contract insurance can be offered to agents with different risks (Abbring et al. 2008).

One of the key issues that the insurance firms have to deal with is the case of fraud. This can be found in many transactions related to tourism. Fraud can appear on the case of a tourist who is taking advantage of moral hazards. One case is of tourists who appear to claim that they have been the victims of rape. This is very frequent with tourists who go to Kavos and other popular Greek resorts. However, there are claims that many of these cases are frauds. This type of fraud case has not been widely examined. Thus, this paper will examine the case of tourism-related frauds, whilst focusing on sex crimes reported on mass tourism resorts such as Kavos in Corfu. Since there is a gap in the literature, the paper aims at setting the necessary background for future research. The methodology adopted for this piece of research, consists of systematically reviewing and analysing secondary data (content analysis). It is important to note that the existing literature on this issue is rather limited. For the case study, the authors have asked the contribution of the local authorities, who have provided data and some views regarding the case of frauds. Moreover, the authors have also requested the views of insurance market experts.

## 2 Literature Review

### *2.1 Theoretical Studies of Information Asymmetry*

The foundation work of Rothschild and Stiglitz (1976) analyses and describes the functioning of a competitive insurance market in the presence of adverse selection. In the model of Rothschild and Stiglitz (RS), the agents are differentiated by their probability of accidents and adverse selection. The two authors consider this variable to be an exogenous, characteristic that agents cannot change and that the insurer cannot observe. The probability of an accident can be either low or high. As a result, two types of agents exist on the market: low- and high-risk agents, who the insurer is not able to distinguish. The authors assume that risk-averse agents are seeking insurance. Each insurer offers a single insurance contract. If balance exists, the RS equilibrium is defined as a menu of contracts; such that each contract is non-deficient and that there is no contract offered outside this menu, which would be profitable. The RS equilibrium, in the presence of adverse selection, is not been mixed; It is a separator. High-risk agents self-select and get their high-cost insurance policy, offering them coverage. Low-risk agents, on the other hand, choose the partial coverage at lower prices. The properties of competitive equilibrium in an insurance market in pre-moral hazard are described mainly in a series of works by Arnott and Stiglitz (1988) and Arnott (1992). Agents assumed to be identical can change their probability of accidents by choosing a level of effort after choosing their insurance policy. This prevention action or level of effort is an unobservable variable for the insurer. In a situation of moral hazard, where the agent is covered, possibly by several insurers, the less the effort. Consequently, the insurer compels each agent by an exclusivity clause, which states that they are the sole insurer for the risk under consideration. The contract offers an insurance contract, whose coverage depends on the level of the prevention cost: If the cost of prevention is low, the agent can be incentivised to make the effort by offering them a contract with partial coverage. Otherwise, it becomes very costly to induce the effort and in this case, the equilibrium contract proposed is a fully hedged contract.

The theoretical work that we have just described assumes a single information-related problem on the insurance market: either adverse selection or moral hazard. In fact, the two phenomena of asymmetry of information can exist simultaneously. Several theoretical works have been developed to study the insurance market, where adverse selection and moral hazard coexist. We quote mainly the works of Chassagnon and Chiappori (2005) and Chassagnon (2005), which develop the competitive aspect. They define the balance of a competitive market, where there are sources of asymmetry of information. They define two types of agents characterised by their probability of ex ante accident, before the choice of the contract. The probability of an accident is not exogenous. It depends on the level of effort chosen by each agent, for a given contract. The level of prevention effort is not observed by the insurer. For a given level of effort, the riskier agent ex ante has an accident probability greater than the least risky agent ex ante. They claim that the cost of prevention depends on both the level of effort and the type of agent.

## 2.2 Delinquency in Tourism

The booming tourism industry is accompanied by a sharp increase of not only the income and living standards of the inhabitants of each tourist area, but also of major problems. This paper focuses solely on issues concerning various types of infringements including insults, violent actions, indignity, and obscene behaviours. The tourist delinquency, used to describe a phenomenon, relates only to tourists who, during single their holidays make deliberate, unprovoked, systematic, repeated delinquent behaviour. The purpose is intentional or inadvertent, unintentional and perhaps sometimes also based on naivety and climatic relaxation that defines the mood of a holiday. To term 'tourist delinquency' is not sufficient to adequately describe the magnitude of the infringements it entails. "The tourist movement often aims to satisfaction extreme desires, many of which are clearly delinquent while other without being punishable or subject to prohibitions, is specific and debatable.

In delinquent behaviours include: sex tourism, drug tourism, and in particular large number disparate pursuits as dark tourism, extreme tourism risk and specific cases such as gambling tourism, tourism of pride parades etc." (Alleyne and Boxill 2003).

Tourist infringements are focused either on actual crimes or conventional crimes. While the first, mainly attack the values of society (life, liberty, property), the second attack both the basic values of society and the safety of others (e.g. violation of traffic regulations, smoking in places prohibited etc.). Generally, delinquent behaviours have to do with: increased incidences of bad behaviour, insult public decency, increased criminality, misbehaviour attributed to alcohol, prostitution, gambling and drugs. It is common knowledge, however, and it seems strange and that many local communities and their authorities ignore, by turning a blind eye to, the delinquent behaviour occurring in their area, especially when they come from tourists (Biagi and Detotto 2012). The reason why such behaviour is tolerated is presumably the expected profit gains for the destination. All is overlooked for the sake of money, but also for a misguided interpretation of 'tourist development'. The majority of tourists feel that the money they spend for the holidays gives them the right to do anything they want. Tourism has brought changes in value systems and behaviour, thereby threatening the indigenous identity of each destination (Biagi et al. 2012).

## *2.3 Types of Tourist Delinquency*

Delinquent tourist behaviour can take place in any tourist destination and in any form. Any kind of infringement may be regarded as either an 'unlucky moment' or as a deliberate act. No tourist deliberately wishes to challenge local police authorities or magistrates, let alone the legal status of a foreign country. The line between legality and illegality can be very thin, and during holidays many let their guard down in order to escape and relax. This can be observed with the plethora of incidents involving tourists: bad behaviour, thefts, drunkenness, vandalism, damage of property, trafficking or drug use, prostitution, insult public decency, fights, traffic accidents, road traffic offenses, physical violence, verbal abuse, insults, threats, sexual harassment, intimidation, threatening behaviour, hate crimes, noise disturbance from vehicles, loitering, abuse of public space with prostitution and sexual acts, illegal and uninsured employment, unintentional injuries (Biagi et al. 2012; Moira et al. 2013).

Young tourists may to fail to make the distinction between acceptable and unacceptable/illegal behaviour. The 'gravity theory' postulates that there are some laws 'eternal' and 'unwritten' laws, which have long existed, regardless whether they are addressed by legislators such as: public indecency and insults. These 'unwritten' laws have been universal to societies throughout the history of mankind. But at the end of the day infringements which carry significance are those which are legally defined such as the following:

- misdemeanours, which include violations of traffic, disruption of the siesta, illegal profession etc. and which punishable by detention or a fine
- misdemeanours, which include offenses such as physical injury, abuse, theft, fraud, manslaughter, etc. and which is punishable by imprisonment or a fine, felonies in which the catalysis of the Republic include financial crimes against the State, manslaughter with intent, drug dealing by profession and habit, rapes, robberies,
- major fraud and forgery, drug trafficking, etc. which are punished by imprisonment (Moira et al. 2013).

## *2.4 The Sociological Dimension of Delinquency*

Humans, as social beings, cannot exist without being integrated in a community. Ontologically, human existence cannot be understood separately from its social environment. Coexistence means individuals interacting within a social space, which can often create many problems. The peaceful coexistence of individuals in a society becomes possible only if each person behaves according to some written regulatory or unwritten rules of conduct that society has set (Cohen 1996). Tourism is defined as social phenomenon, the result of human activities, which need examination and analysis. Tourism and travel generally comprise of a (very old) process based on human curiosity, an interest for the unknown and the discovery new places. Therefore, one should exclude the view that the Tourism is an 'accidental' social phenomenon and instead should be seen as 'contextual' social phenomenon (Walker 2008).

The sociology of tourism, a branch of the social sciences, has been developed recently aiming to shed light into the human dimension of tourism. It focuses on incentives, roles and the behaviour of tourists during their holidays and recreational activities. Every person, a member of society, is an absolute entity, an individual personality, which has their own ideas, principles, reactions, attitudes, impulses. Many times, the observed person may act in a way that affects other people, disturbing the peaceful coexistence of people in society. For sociologists, a behaviour is considered unlawful when it is contrary to the prevailing morality and entails penalties; or when the behaviour of the part of a system has negative effect on one or more parts of a system or the entire system and its maintenance (Ryan 1993). In sociology the word delinquency is synonymous with crime and deviant behaviour and refers to events or actions that cause harm or they affect the quality of life of people in the community. The general conclusion her is that the functioning and the structures of society in which we live influence our behaviour and we certainly all play a role in delinquent behaviour (Moira et al. 2013).

The sociological study of offending behaviour has been regarded as one of the most interesting but also the most difficult to study. The social theory of delinquency, deals with violence and offenses, as a social phenomenon, its extent depending on the degree of a person's acceptance of rules, laws and morals of society. Many sociologists, including Emile Durkheim, tried to analyse the emergence of deviant behaviour in modern industrial societies. When the collective consciousness is not prevalent, there is lawlessness and possibly crime, which is a pathological condition which raises reactions from the community. Therefore, according to Durkheim, there the phenomenon of lawlessness, is socially defined and as such it needs to be studied. Moreover, the rapid changes occurring in modern world often lead to anomia (Moira et al. 2012).

Observed disturbance is a key issue, since it concerns the cohesion of the members of a society or an individual, there are no common accepted rules of social behaviour, as to identify the needs and means of fulfilling individual desires. Many may not abide to those rules, while others can discipline their passions. There is a similar approach from another American the sociologist Merton, who formulated his own theory for deviation, based on the classic concept of lawlessness that Durkheim introduced, in which significance is placed in the terms 'objective' and 'means' for achieving the targets, to explain the tension caused in a person's behaviour conflicting with the rules of society (lawlessness). According to Merton, anomie exists in each period of imbalanced development in the function and structure of a society, where the split of goals and accepted rules of conduct, causes feelings of failure and frustration (Moira et al. 2013).

## 2.5 Psychological and Biological Approach to Delinquency

Delinquent or deviant behaviour is a very interesting case study for sciences such as psychology, which with the aid of theoretical approaches give various interpretations on the causalities of these type of phenomena. Psychology, attempting to explain delinquency, uses various terms such as: delinquency, aggression, deviant behaviour. The main points on which psychology relies on in trying to decode the phenomenon of delinquency and its forms, concern the relationship between environmental conditions and learning by copying other behaviours (Ryan 1993; Moufakkiv 2005). The science of psychology stresses the importance of psychological factors in the genesis of crime and offense; whilst being especially interested mental health, as well as the reactions to the various challenges of the social environment (conflict between individual desires and societal requirements can not the person to balance and so driven crime-offense). Unpleasant memories or impressions from childhood, guilt, beliefs, etc. cause severe internal conflicts in person, who is very likely to break or seek redemption through criminal or delinquent behaviour. There is even the concept of certain individuals being attracted towards crime because of emotional disability or due to various childhood traumas (Gould et al. 2002).

Specifically, psychology approaches crime in two main ways: psychoanalytic psychology and the behaviour psychology. The main difference between the two ways is the importance given to each of the innate factors in their role in shaping personality. "The psychoanalytic psychology argues that the behaviour of person emanates from the space of the unconscious, whose impulses just controlled by the conscious or subconscious part of the personality, according with the requirements of the moral principles of good and evil. The psychology of behavioural supports, that the soul of man at birth is an unwritten plate, upon which, with the mechanism procedure stimulus reaction, scored and formed as learning the different products ideas, intentions and experiences that ultimately compose the behaviour of a person (Moira et al. 2012).

## 3 Discussion: The Case of Kavos

The area of Kavos is very famous as a tourist destination in abroad—principally and perhaps particularly in the UK. It has the reputation of an area where the visitor can have fun because there are plenty of clubs, bars, etc. Over the last decade, this destination is going through downturn because it has been 'stigmatised' as a region predominantly for only young British tourists who create problems. Local government insists on ineffective measures and action proposals, with the consequence that there is no substantial recovery in the region. If there is a potential for a touristic recovery, first all facilities and infrastructure in the area need to be upgraded. The large, UK-based tour operators are selling Kavos as a holiday package. Kavos carries the classic image of many Mediterranean resorts which offer the 3S (i.e. sun, sea and sand), but with an important difference: it addresses only young Brits who are keen on nightlife, without time constraints, loud music and large quantities of alcohol. All these are advertised by the tour-operators and are offered in extremely affordable packages. It is also important to underline that the only image of the area projected abroad is the one provided by the large tour-operators. The suggested target group is the between the ages 18 and 30. The main attractions of the destination are cheap drinks and all-night entertainment (this can be ascertained by a quick review of the brochures of major tour-operators).

This negative image formation is also the result of a chronically deficient local tourism development policy and lack of organised action, which are a common issue for many resorts. The tourism development of the resort was anarchic and unplanned; with dominant tour-operators determining demand. The area of Kavos began to grow rapidly with mass tourism in the early 80s, when tourist arrivals in Corfu were constantly growing and the traditional resorts of British youth tour-operators in other regions of the island (e.g. Benitses) were at their height. As they showed signs of saturation, low-cost accommodation capacities started to be developed in Kavos, betting on the potential of its long, sandy beach. Due to a favourable political and economic environment at the time, many farmers and land-owners in Kavos, built rooms with holiday homes without permission, and leased them (fixed amount per bed covers the entire season) to British tour-operators in exchange for prepayments, which in turn financed the construction of new rooms. Throughout the course of the 80s, and until 1992, the growth rate of arrivals, and bed-nights offered in the region was impressive. 1993 was the first year of decline. The British market monopolised the Cape and even created a kind of 'ghetto' with practically full sovereignty and lively young British tourists (so-called 'lager louts', meaning 'beer mob'). This prevented the coexistence of other tourist nationalities. Tourism seasonality in Corfu inevitably is determined by the operation of charter flights from Britain to Corfu, since the predominant form of tourism on the island is packaged tourism.

It has become commonly acceptable to the society of Kavos that it is about mass tourism and that the rampage and binge drinking night life for young adults, is part of that. The large British travel agencies, have their own excursion offices, staff hotels with own representatives and promote their own restaurants and entertainment venues. The particular target market is not particularly interested in visiting museums, churches, and/or natural attractions. In order to generate excursion income, the so-called 'pub crawl' was invented. It is worth mentioning that the main concern of several bar owners is to secure customers consuming in their businesses, and are therefore forced bribe representatives and agents to ensure the customer flow. Also great are the concerns of the accommodation-owners regarding the destruction and damages caused the drunken tourists. With the existing seasonal competition, combined with difficult years in the tour-operator market, selling at low prices (almost below cost, to at least cover charter seat costs) have become commonplace. The aim is not to attract normal prices, but to gain additional revenue through alcohol sales. The tour-operators, who claim that they themselves do not want problems, pilot, promote holiday packages at a destination, only as long benefit from it. When there is no benefit, they leave behind their 'scorched earth' and pressure the local prices and tax income even lower. Such tactics and such conditions, come at the expense of control and policing, which unfortunately does not exist to the extent that it should. Kavos is, for the last three decades, a tourist destination for young British tourists, who want to enjoy the sun and the sea, combined with low priced drinks, 24-hour fun, countless clubs and bars. This attracts 'passive tourists', who come exclusively and only for resting, without any interest for the cultural or historical aspects of the location, or even an exploration of the wider area. It is no accident fact that the Cape is dominated by British cultural elements (food, shop names, drinks, employees).

One of the key issues of this resort are the numerous rapes and assaults reported to local authorities and the subsequent claims made to insurance firms. Just to give an idea, the local authorities in 2013 reported 30 rape incidents involving British tourists. When such cases were investigated by insurance firms, it turned out that many of them were fraudulent and that although sex was consensual, rape charges were made for personal profit. Overall, the use of alcohol encourages many youngsters to violent behaviour, which may also include rape. The opportunity to make money by insurance claims is especially attractive to the poorer young tourists. There are also the cases where agents are also involved on this type of fraud. Insurance firms are currently scanning claim applications more thoroughly, including detailed examination of each case's specifics, but also the backgrounds of the persons involved.

# 4 Conclusions

The paper has examined the case of the fraud related with sex crimes. The insurance market is a market which deals with threats, risks and moral hazards. One sector where the insurance industry is vulnerable on cases of fraud is the tourist sector. Indeed, in many cases tourists are attempting to profit from their insurance by making fake claims for damages due of rape or other violent actions. The paper examined the case of Kavos in Corfu where there have been many cases of insurance frauds related with rape. Despite the fact that the insurance firms are not able to always correctly identify frauds, they are increasingly becoming more vigilant and thorough regarding holiday-related insurances claims. The implications of this type of fraudulent behaviour lends itself for highly relevant research; not only from the economic and insurance perspective, but also from a psychological and sociological perspective. The impact of such claims on destination image and reputation, as well as the implications for tourist health and safety-related research remain massively under-researched.

# References


Abbring, J., Chiappori, P. A., & Zavadil, T. (2008). *Better safe than sorry? Ex ante and ex post moral hazard in dynamic insurance data*. Discussion Paper 2008-77, Tilburg University, Center for Economic Research.

Alleyne, D., & Boxill, I. (2003). The impact of crime on tourist arrivals in Jamaica. *International Journal of Tourism Research, 5*, 381–391.

Arnott, R. (1992). Moral hazard and competitive insurance markets. In G. Dionne (Ed.), *Contributions to insurance economics* (pp. 325–358). Norwell, MA: Kluwer Academic Press.

Arnott, R., & Stiglitz, J. E. (1988). The basic analytics of moral hazard. *The Scandinavian Journal of Economics, 90*(3), 383–413.

Biagi, B., & Detotto, C. (2012). Crime as tourism externality. *Regional Studies, 48*(4), 693–709.

Biagi, B., Brandono, M. G., & Detotto, C. (2012). The effect of tourism on crime in Italy: A dynamic panel approach. *Economics – The Open-Access, Open Assessment E-Journal, Kiel Institute for the World Economy, 6*, 1–24.

Boyer, M., Dionne, G., & Kihlstrom, R. (1989). Insurance and the value of publicly available information. In *Studies in the Economics of Uncertainty* (pp. 137–155). New York, NY: Springer.

Chassagnon, A. (2005). *Heterogeneous risk in a moral hazard economy with adverse selection*. Mimeo, Paris School of Economics.

Chassagnon, A., & Chiappori, P. A. (2005). *Insurance under moral hazard and adverse selection: Efficiency and competition*. Mimeo.

Cohen, E. (1996). The sociology of tourism, approaches, issues and findings. In Y. Apostolopoulos, S. Leivadi, & A. Yiannakis (Eds.), *The sociology of tourism: Theoretical and empirical investigations* (Vol. 1, pp. 51–71). London: Routledge.

Gould, B., Weinberg, B., & Mustard, D. (2002). Crime rates and local labor market opportunities in the United States: 1979–1997. *Review of Economics and Statistics, 84*, 45–61.

Moira, P., Mylonopoulos, D., Vasilopoulou, P., & Kondoudaki, A. (2012). The management of delinquent behavior in Greek hotels. *e-Journal of Science and Technology (e-JST), 3*(8), 21–32.

Moira, P., Mylonopoulos, D., & Vasilopoulou, P. (2013). The different types of delinquent behavior in the hospitality industry. Case study from Greece. *International Journal of Management and Sustainability, 2*(11), 172–185.

Moufakkiv, O. (2005). An assessment of crime volume following casino gaming development in the city of Detroit. *Gaming Research and Review Journal, 9*, 15–28.

Rothschild, M., & Stiglitz, J. (1976). Equilibrium in competitive insurance markets: An essay on the economics of imperfect information. *The Quarterly Journal of Economics, 90*(4), 629–649.

Ryan, C. (1993). Crime, violence, terrorism and tourism: An accidental or intrinsic relationship. *Tourism Management, 14*, 173–183.

Walker, D. (2008). Do casinos really cause crime? *Econ Journal Watch*, 4–20.

# The Unethical Practice of Hotel Review Ghost-Writers

**Dimitrios Belias, Efstathios Velissariou, Alexandros Roditis, Michalis Chondrogiannis, Stavros Katsios, Dimitrios Kyriakou, Konstantinos Varsanis, and Athanasios Koustelios**

## 1 Introduction

Business ethics have increasingly attracted the attention of the business world over the last years. Notwithstanding, business ethics cannot be considered as to be a novel issue, since it has its theoretical roots in ancient times, where many philosophers and authors wrote about the business ethics. Today there are conflicting views related to the concept of business ethics, which have also stimulated many public discussions. Nevertheless, the numerous corporate scandals reported on a daily basis in the press, suggest that the need for ethical behaviour in business environment nowadays is as relevant as ever. Preventing unethical business behaviour is a complicated issue faced by business organisations today; and also a significant challenge for

D. Belias (✉) · E. Velissariou · A. Roditis
Department of Business Administration, Technological Educational Institute of Thessaly, Larissa, Greece
e-mail: dbelias@teilar.gr

M. Chondrogiannis · S. Katsios
Department of Foreign Languages, Translation and Interpreting, Laboratory for Geocultural Analyses, Ionian University, Corfu, Greece

D. Kyriakou
Department of Economic Sciences, Aristotle University of Thessaloniki, Thessaloniki, Greece

K. Varsanis
Department of Business Administration, Technological Educational Institute of Western Macedonia, Kozani, Greece

A. Koustelios
Department of Physical Education and Sport Science, University of Thessaly, Trikala, Greece



A. Papathanassis et al. (eds.), *Yellow Tourism*, Tourism, Hospitality & Event Management, https://doi.org/10.1007/978-3-319-94664-1_10

management, due to the fact that unethical business practices involve high cost for organizations, their stakeholders and the society in general (Bennett 2003).

The paper is going to examine the phenomenon of ghost-writers in the tourism industry. More recently, we have seen the phenomenon of 'water army' in the tourist community. The term 'water army refers to ghost-writers that get paid to post comments serving particular commercial or political interests. These comments reflect a hidden motive, which is usually to manipulate and mislead public opinion for the benefit of certain interest groups. Particularly, this is a problem when governments are attempting to code and understand public opinion; it is difficult for them to hear the real voices from their target electorate. The existence of 'water armies' has been a long-standing issue for tourism companies and the industry as a whole, where it is fairly easy and cheap to hire people who upload misleading and/or manipulated content. So, this is an under-researched field of tourism as scientific literature on the topic seems rather limited. The aim of this paper is to examine the existing literature on ghost-writing in the context of tourism. First, we introduce the concept of business ethics and their application in tourism; and subsequently we discuss their applicability/relevance in relation to social-media campaigns.

# 2 Literature Review

## *2.1 Business Ethics*

Business ethics is a field of applied ethics (Velasquez 1992) that examines ethical issues that arise in a business environment. According to De George (1987), business ethics entail five kinds of activity categories. The most dominant activity is the analysis of immorality incidents in business. The second type entails the empirical study of business practices while the third type consists of clarifying basic terms and revealing ethical business issues. The forth kind of activity concerns meta-ethical questions and a review of ethics theory. Finally, the fifth kind aims at the resolution of embedded problems.

## *2.2 The History of Business Ethics*

Business ethics are essentially the application of ethical rules and everyday morals to business practices (Bennett 2003). An example that comes into mind from the Bible, are the Ten Commandments, an ethics guide that is still adhered to by many people today. The applicable notion of stewardship in business, as well as other relevant ethical principles, can be found in Bible (De George 2005). Ancient texts, similar to the Ten Commandments, are also to be found also in other religions or traditions that seek to exercise an influence on and provide guidance for people's actions. Moving from religion to philosophy, there is also a long history related to ethics. Plato in 'the Republic', is known about his dialogues on the notion of justice, while Aristotle in his 'Politics', wrote about acquisition and trade as part of economic ethics. He also wrote about exchange, property, money and wealth and he made moral judgments connected to greed and the pursuit of wealth. Coming to the modern times, John Locke argued that defending private property constitutes a natural right, based on the labour one invests to secure/obtain the good in question. Adam Smith, before his most famous work The 'Wealth of Nations', wrote in the 'Theory of Moral Sentiments' about business ethics (Bennett 2003).

All these authors and many others have contributed to the historical development of ethics theory and their thoughts have become an integral part of the today's views on business ethics. The second half of the last century, was characterised by growing 'business ethics movement', originating from the US. This movement has spread from the US to other parts of the world, including Europe, where it has also become quite popular. According to Stieb (2009), business ethics in US has made great progress; both as an academic discipline and as a business practice over the last 40 years. The 1960s were known as the period of the rise of social issues in business, coinciding with the development of modern industries, the corresponding ecological problems caused, and growth of consumerism. Nevertheless, it was during the 1970s, when the rise of business ethics as a field of academic inquiry began. By the end of the decade, some central issues had emerged (like i.e. the moral status of the corporation, role responsibility in business, corporate disobedience) and many researchers turned their interest towards this new area (for instance Beauchamp, Bowie, Donaldson, Barry, De George, Velasquez). In the first half of 1980s, business ethics had become an academic field.

According to De George (2005), what differentiates the development of business ethics from the related isolated attempts until then, is the fact that business ethics became institutionalised. The business ethics field has developed alongside a growing a group of institutions, which were interested in its application and development. For the first time, it was also attempted to systematically study the entire range of moral issues in business as a whole. By the mid-1980s at least 500 courses in business ethics were attended by 40,000 students (De George 2005). In the earlier 2000s, a significant number of university courses in business ethics were in place; a small number of international journals were dedicated to this topic; and there were also many articles concerning business ethics in other academic journals (Hiironen 2004).

Nowadays, 'business ethics', as well as 'corporate social responsibility', are terms that are on everyone's lips in business. However, some people might think that business ethics is an oxymoron since "the mainsprings of business activity and the pursuit of profit preclude considerations of morality" (Barry 1997). Others may believe that business and ethics are complementary terms, since ethics is about the study of morality and there are plenty of moral issues that can arise in a business environment. Based on these conflicting views, one could say that business ethical issues actually reflect the interaction between profit maximizing behaviour and non-economic concerns.

## 2.3 Unethical Behaviour and Its Effects on Organisations

During the last decades, there is a growing crisis of confidence concerning corporate activity and also a strong belief that the business environment creates an atmosphere conducive to unethical behaviour. Besides, many researchers in the field of business ethics (e.g. Barry 1997), argue that the pursuit of profit precludes moral considerations. Thus, the goal of profit maximization, which according to Friedman (1970) and other theorists, is the only social responsibility of business, and thus compatible with unethical business behaviour. Nevertheless, unethical behaviour is one of the most corrosive and complex problems confronting business organisations today, becoming a critical field of research. Unethical issues can occur at any level—board of directors, executives, middle managers or staff—and within any operational area of the organization—production, accounting, finance, marketing, human resources (Collins 2011).

Examples of unethical business practices such as: bribery, illegal payments, kickbacks, improper accounting practices, employee discrimination, environmental pollution, insider trading etc. can be found in numerous corporate scandals, being reported on a daily basis by the media. Diverse terms have been adopted to describe employee misconduct in organisational settings such as: unethical behaviour, organizational misbehaviour, anti-social behaviour or deviant behaviour (Carvalho 2011). According to Badenhorst (1994), there are two types of unethical behaviour in organisations: unethical behaviour for personal gain and unethical behaviour that favours the organization. However, it appears that the latter type is more acceptable in the business community, as it is considered to be 'less ethical'; instead of 'unethical'. Furthermore, misbehaviour have been categorised as: extra-organizational and intra-organizational, depending where it occurs. Some authors also point out the difference between destructive deviant misbehaviour and unethical behaviour (Carvalho Wilks 2011). The former type is a set of intentional acts, conducted by employees that is against organisational norms and can harm the organization or its members, whereas the latter is "either illegal or morally unacceptable by the larger community" (Jones 1991).

There is a plethora of individual and situational factors that contribute to employees' decision on whether to behave ethically or unethically (Stead et al. 1990). There is little doubt that, personality, background, ethical decision history, as well as religious beliefs, age and quality of work experience, seem to all influence a person's ethical stance. Moreover, it is automatically assumed that unethical behaviour is the result of a person who has no value system; no clear distinction between right and wrong. Studies have shown that an individual's lack of moral values is not necessarily a cause for unethical behaviour. On the other hand, it appears that individuals with strong moral values do not maintain the same values in the business world, while they are often pressured to compromise their personal standards to achieve organisational goals (Carvalho Wilks 2011). Thus, we conclude that there is another set of factors within the organisational context, influencing individuals' propensity to engage in unethical behaviour. An organisational climate that encourages unethical decisions, managerial philosophy and behaviour, the behaviour of colleagues and the absence of an ethics policy, all appear to be related to unethical behaviour. Unethical behaviour has several diverse effects in organisations. Perhaps the most obvious effect is that moral disengagement in organizations can undermine the confidence and trust of its stakeholders. Organisations, however, rely on their ability to maintain the confidence of their stakeholders in order to ensure profitability. Unethical business practices can, directly or indirectly, have an impact on sales, since the loss of trust amongst customers can reduce their loyalty and motivate them to turn to competitors. Besides, research in consumer marketing has shown that, whether a firm acts ethically or not is an important consumer concern and that consumers are not merely interested about a firm's ethics; but they also adjust their purchase behaviour accordingly. In addition, unethical conduct may well adversely affect the stock performance of the organisation. It seems that shareholders punish unethical behaviour by driving down the value of the organisation's share price for a considerable period of time (Rao and Hamilton 1996). Unethical business practices are also associated with legal costs for the organization. Lawsuits and fines harm the organisation's reputation and can cost millions. According to Collins (2011), in a 2007 survey, 40% of the 250 largest U.S. corporations had at least one new lawsuit filed against them, amounting to a worth of 20 million dollars. Other less obvious costs are monitoring and recruiting costs. Organisations that employ or do business with unethical individuals, need to closely monitor them in order to prevent unethical behaviour. Thus, management often implement and maintain expensive control systems, which are likely to hinder a trust culture within organisations. Furthermore, unethical organisations incur additional costs for recruiting employees, customers, suppliers and investors, since they need to provide some premium in to order to offset their ethical deficiencies. Finally, policies that promote unethical behaviours in organisations, can often drive the most productive employees to ethically superior competitors and as result lead to higher turnover and the associated costs (Cialdini et al. 2004). In addition, moral employees, who are required to engage in immoral behaviours, tend to be less satisfied with their job and less committed to the organisation. This has a negative impact on their productivity. From all the above, it can be concluded that immoral business practices represent a key issue for business organisations. This may explain why, more recently, organisations have moved from a passive awareness/acknowledgement of the problem to more active approaches and policies.

## 2.4 Social Media in Tourism

Information and communication through the internet is nowadays a common tool for the destination choice of tourists everywhere. As stated by Xiang and Gretzel (2010), the number of potential travellers who inform themselves and book online has been constantly increasing. The report of the European Travel Commission (2010: 13), points out that leisure and business trips are planned by a majority (64–65%) over the

Internet, including booking tickets for air travel and hotel rooms. Until recently, the internet served to obtain information only through official web sites (websites) tourist agencies and measured tourism agencies that advertise specific countries and locations. Social media equip travellers with information sharing capabilities regarding holidays and business trips (Chan and Denizci Guillet 2011). This communication is both informative and entertaining. In our times, the degree of information-intensity on tourism products continues to grow, with social media gaining ground over conventional media such as television, radio and newspapers reduced (Mangold and Faulds 2009).

The great popularity of social media, according to many scholars, is attributed to the fact that users can create their own content, which is informative, fun and entertaining (for example, Leung et al. 2013). Instead, the 'traditional' information tools render users passive, since there is limited interaction and mostly a one-way communication (Bruhn et al. 2012). In tourism, social media have been embraced by internet users in their search for tourist destinations and their planning of holidays and business trips, while the feedback from other travellers, often strangers enables interaction through messages and comments, images, video and audio, but also through story-telling (Leung et al. 2013). This type of open communication is performed through multiple Internet platforms, such as social media (e.g., Facebook and Twitter), and the websites dedicated to travel and restaurants like TripAdvisor and Yelp, and personal blogs.

Sparks and Browning (2011) emphasise the importance of mouth-to-mouth communication, through the Internet, dissecting consumer relationship management from the providers of products and services worldwide. Internet users who wish to purchase a product or service can now, through social media, be informed by other users who have made purchases in the past and have made their own experiences (Sparks and Browning 2011). At the same time, communication takes place now, not only among family members, friends or even acquaintances, but also among people who have never met each other, from every corner of the world.

## *2.5 Ghost-Writing and Social Media*

The adoption and ubiquity of the internet and social media are as impressive as they are commonplace. Entrepreneurs in the hotel business enjoy international reach and can directly offer a variety of services to their visitors by communicating with the clients who are interested in booking their vacations at their establishments (Shleifer 2004). The right information at the right time, through the social media constitutes a significant advantage for tourism businesses. Guest reviews are a central influence on the decision-making processes of clients. Yet, there is a pending issue of credibility of such reviews, which are in many cases undermined by fact that a number of businesses create fake reviews for themselves or even for their competitors (Mayzlin et al. 2014). Consumer websites such as TripAdvisor are becoming increasingly popular today and have existed for a long time now. They contain more than 60 million of reviews concerning restaurants, attractions and hotels, which have a direct influence travellers' choices and ultimately bookings. As the popularity of sites such as TripAdvisor has increased, so have the fraudulent practice of fake reviews. These is considerable anecdotal evidence that this is a type of cheating has become an epidemic in tourism. Little is known about the economic incentives behind this. The distribution of star rating is being changed by the hotel owners and this observation is related to a broader body of literature referring to the distribution of opinions in user generated content (Shleifer 2004).

Fraud responds to economic incentives and is mainly driven by the hotel sector, who are prone to 'playing' the system, regardless the real opinions of visitors. Those incentives become higher during the summer period. In addition to leaving comments for themselves, hotels may insert fraudulent reviews with the aim of defaming/discrediting their competitors. Hotels tend to place or outsource the insertion of negative fake reviews, when faced with an increase in competition from independent small hotels that offer similar kind of services (Mayzlin et al. 2014).

## 2.6 *Ethics on Social Media: The Case of Ghost-Writers in Tourist Media*

Tourism services need proper information to promote their products through social media. The Internet, as it is today, is enabling the sale of several different tourist products, and therefore it is difficult for companies to achieve the diversification of their products (Yang and Wang 2015). Tourism in Greece has increased through the use of the social media and the Internet, while at the same time, the technological progress has made it necessary for the entrepreneurs to develop more intelligent methods for attracting tourists. Oftentimes, due to a short tourist season, and regional competition, tourism has resulted to the devastation of islands justified by the amount of money tourists spend during the summer period (Yang and Wang 2015). These risks can be addressed in many ways, but mainly through the use of controlled information technology. As internet use proliferates for the spreading of information, its proper utilisation becomes increasingly important (Middleton 1994). The internet has restructured the tourism sector, establishing itself as the main medium for the exchange of information and as a key means of customer contact.

E-commercial and social media are more or less independent from national or geographic boundaries. Therefore, any company that has an online presence/social media profile is capable of increasing its turnover and its establishing its reputation beyond local markets. The possibilities of managing and operating worldwide, 24 hours a day, without the requirement of physical presence in the country where the business is, are allowing entrepreneurs to grow and expand in a rate previously not imaginable. Companies who adopt new technologies are able to competitively adapt, utilising social media to gain an advantageous position by offering online content and up-to-date, on-demand on a hotel, country or destination. Given that in a few years all commercial activities will be operated through the social media, e-commerce is the biggest challenge for any company that wants to be innovative and competitive (Castells 2000).

It is well accepted that social media have dominated tourism more than may other sector in terms of customer decision-influencing. Until a few years ago, consumers would visit their local travel agent to make a booking. Today this is happening through social media and mostly through content brokers/aggregators such as tripadvisor.com and booking.com. A key determinant of the decision to make a booking or not, is the examination the corresponding reviews of other users, describing their experiences. This is the point where the challenges emerge. It is a common practice for many firms to use ghost-writers. Those are persons, often recruited online or from social media companies, who are paid so to write a positive review for the company or a negative review for a competitor. This turns to be a major inhibitor for the credibility and utilisation of social media for the tourism aggregators (Zeng and Gerritsen 2014). In many cases there are tourism companies, who are systematically using ghost-writers to, either to leverage their reviews when they have many negative ones, or to write a negative review for a competitor.

Actually, it seems that ghost-writing has become a rather popular job. A simple internet search reveals a large number of companies or freelancers offering this type of 'services'. There are also websites, providing review-manipulation hints and tips.[1] Surely, this corrodes the reliability and credibility of tourism companies and the sector as a whole. Many consumers cannot differentiate between real and fake reviews. This, in turn, affects their overall judgment and expectations of a hotel; and influence their decision to book or not. On this basis, one can assert that ghost-writing is a modern curse for the tourist industry (Kristensen 2013).

## 3 Discussion

Social media have dominated the world of tourism. Today, tourists use the social media to choose between destinations and holiday providers. For many, their holidays represent something sacred; after a long time, they will go somewhere to relax and spend some quality time. This means that they are seeking the best value for their financial possibilities. Therefore, they are likely to seek to read the reviews made from past users, hoping to make an informed and optimal choice. The fact that user reviews affect potential visitor choices, renders them a central issue for the industry. Some companies, take advantage of ghost-writers, who author fake reviews, especially on tripadvisor.com. To avoid and/or counter this phenomenon/practice some measures are possible. For example, booking.com requires that reviewers have actually booked a room and that the booking process done through

[1]For example: http://tripadvisor-warning.com/share/post-false-reviews-on-tripadvisor-free-and-easy

their website. There are having been many cases of ghost-writing, which have undermined the value of TripAdvisor and of other web sites. In some cases, the website has been forced to publicly apologise to their customer or the businesses affected from this kind of malpractice. However, it seems that there is no waterproof method against fake reviews. Customers are called to also pay attention and develop a filtering competence for processing online holiday reviews (Papathanassis and Knolle 2011).

Our research has shown that there is an extensive amount of systematic review fraud in online review platforms. Thus, it is important for platform designers to develop several safeguarding mechanisms against fraudulent misinformation. Yet, despite such mechanisms, there is no perfect mechanism for eliminating review frauds. There are fraud detection algorithms that can identify the fake reviews, allowing social/review platforms to filter out offending or misleading reviews, whilst reprimanding the businesses engaged in this kind of activity. The advantage of this process is that it is simple and cheap to implement. In any case, these algorithms seem to lack transparency and often contain bugs. Moreover, the review platforms can restrict reviews to verified purchases. While this can limit the extent of fake reviews, it may also lead to a reduction of legitimate content. On the other hand, by implementing limits, the process becomes costly for the businesses soliciting fake review providers. Platforms would also be well-advised to highlight the issue of ethics every time a person wants to author a review.

## 4 Conclusions

The paper has introduced the case of ghost-writing on the tourist industry. It seems that many businesses in this sector are recruiting ghost-writers to leverage their reviews, or to use them against their competitors. This practice undermines the credibility and existence of review and content platforms. Surely, this is a key challenge for the information-intensive tourism-sector. Overall, this is a practice, which has not been sufficiently examined in academic literature. Indeed, our literature search produced rather modest results, suggesting that there is research potential in this area.

## References


Badenhorst, J. (1994). Unethical behavior in procurement: A perspective on causes and solutions. *Journal of Business Ethics, 13*(9), 739–745.

Barry, N. (1997). *Business, ethics and modern economy*. The Sir Ronald Trotter Lecture, New Zealand Business Roundtable.

Bennett, C. (2003). *Ethics in business*. Mason, OH: South-Western.

Bruhn, M., Schoenmueller, V., & Schäfer, D. B. (2012). Are social media replacing traditional media in terms of brand equity creation? *Management Research Review, 35*(9), 770–790.

Carvalho Wilks, D. (2011). Attitudes towards unethical behaviours in organizational settings: An empirical study. *Ethics in Progress Quarterly, 2*(2), 9–22. Available online at www.ethicsinprogress.org
Castells, M. (2000). *The information society: The power of identity*. Oxford: Blackwell.
Chan, N. L., & Denizci Guillet, B. (2011). Investigation of social media marketing: How does the hotel industry in Hong Kong perform in marketing on social media websites? *Journal of Travel and Tourism Marketing, 28*(4), 345–368.
Cialdini, R., Petrova, P., & Goldstein, N. (2004). The hidden costs of organizational dishonesty. *MIT Sloan Management Review, 45*(3), 67–73.
Collins, D. (2011). *Business ethics: How to design and manage ethical organizations* (1st ed.). Wiley.
De George, R. (1987). The status of business ethics: Past and future. *Journal of Business Ethics, 6* (3), 201–211.
De George, R. (2005). *A history of business ethics*. Markkula Center for Applied Ethics. Scu, edu.
European Travel Commission. (2010). *Trends and prospects*. http://www.etc-corporate.org/?page=report&report_id=54
Friedman, M. (1970). The social responsibility of business is to increase its profits. *The New York Times Magazine*, (September 13), pp. 122–125.
Hiironen, A. (2004). *Adoption of codes of ethics by business organizations – The underlying reasons and aims*. Master thesis, Faculty of International Business, Helsinki School of Economics, Finland.
Jones, T. M. (1991). Ethical decision making by individuals in organizations: An issue Contingent model. *The Academy of Management Review, 16*(2), 366–395.
Kristensen, A. E. (2013). Travel and social media in china: From transit hubs to stardom. *Tourism Planning and Development, 10*(2), 169–177.
Leung, D., Law, R., van Hoof, H., & Buhalis, D. (2013). Social media in tourism and hospitality: A literature review. *Journal of Travel and Tourism Marketing, 30*(1–2), 3–22.
Mangold, W. G., & Faulds, D. J. (2009). Social media: The new hybrid element of the promotion mix. *Business Horizons, 52*(4), 357–365.
Mayzlin, D., Yaniv, D., & Chevalier, J. (2014). Promotional reviews: An empirical investigation of online review manipulation. *American Economic Review, 104*(8), 2421–2455.
Middleton, V. (1994). *Special characteristics of travel and tourism*. Oxford: Butterworth Heinemann.
Papathanassis, A., & Knolle, F. (2011). Exploring the adoption and processing of online holiday reviews: A grounded theory approach. *Tourism Management, 32*, 215–224.
Rao, S. M., & Hamilton, J. B., III. (1996). The effect of published reports of unethical conduct on stock prices. *Journal of Business Ethics, 15*(12), 1321–1330.
Shleifer, A. (2004). Does competition destroy ethical behavior? *American Economic Review, 94*(2), 414–418.
Sparks, B. A., & Browning, V. (2011). The impact of online reviews on hotel booking intentions and perception of trust. *Tourism Management, 32*(6), 1310–1323.
Stead, E., Worrell, D., & Stead, J. (1990). An integrative model for understanding and managing ethical behavior in business organizations. *Journal of Business Ethics, 9*, 233–242.
Stieb, J. (2009). Assessing Freeman's stakeholder theory. *Journal of Business Ethics, 87*(401–414), 1093–1102.
Velasquez, M. G. (1992). *Business ethics: Concepts and cases* (3rd ed.). New Jersey: Prentice Hall.
Xiang, Z., & Gretzel, U. (2010). Role of social media in online travel information search. *Tourism Management, 31*(2), 179–188.
Yang, X., & Wang, D. (2015). The exploration of social media marketing strategies of destination marketing organizations in China. *Journal of China Tourism Research, 11*(2), 166–185. https://doi.org/10.1080/19388160.2015.1017071
Zeng, B., & Gerritsen, R. (2014). What do we know about social media in tourism? A review. *Tourism Management Perspectives, 10*, 27–36.

# 'Sunbed Wars': A Holiday Nuisance and Its Impact on Holiday Satisfaction

**Stephanie Boecker and Alexis Papathanassis**

## 1 Introduction

Significant literature on the topics of customer satisfaction and service quality is available; yet the issue of 'sunbed wars' between vacationers is not addressed. In general, the phenomenon of sunbed wars is regarded as a typical German matter and it is amongst the most annoying holiday nuisances in hotel resorts and on cruise lines. The usual practice starts early in the morning. Vacationers 'reserve' sunbeds with their towels and other objects, to secure the most favourable places under the sun for the whole day. Other guests who have not been that 'proactive' arrive at the pool area and find all sunbeds already reserved. This is frequently results to frustration, verbal conflicts and even physical violence. Providers' attempts to regulate this kind of guest misconduct are often ignored and thus no further countermeasures are taken.

A survey undertaken in 2002 revealed that guests prefer using the hotel's facilities for relaxation and sunbathing (cf. Andriotis and Agiomirgianakis 2007, p. 3). People travel because of so-called 'push factors', which refer to the various motives for travel. People are in search of relaxation and want to escape from their routine day-to-day life (Costa et al. 2004, p. 120). Accordingly, people spend a lot of time in facilities such as the pools provided by hotels and cruise lines. As a result, the seemingly insignificant aspect of sunbed availability, may actually have a disproportionately negative influence customers' level of satisfaction.

S. Boecker (✉) · A. Papathanassis
Cruise Tourism Management, Bremerhaven University of Applied Sciences, Bremerhaven, Germany
e-mail: sboecker@studenten.hs-bremerhaven.de



A. Papathanassis et al. (eds.), *Yellow Tourism*, Tourism, Hospitality & Event Management, https://doi.org/10.1007/978-3-319-94664-1_11

### 1.1 Relevance

In relation to the above-mentioned concept of tourists' satisfaction, the relevance of this paper will be discussed. Accommodation represents the main element of the tourism value chain (cf. Devi Juwaheer 2004, p. 120) and accommodation providers face the challenge of constantly having to keep their guests 'happy'. Reaching and maintaining high levels of satisfaction has resulted to a fierce competitive landscape (Otto and Ritchie 1996 cited in Costa et al. 2004, p. 117). Furthermore, it is '*the key variable for gaining a competitive advantage*' (Honomichl 1993 cited in Kozak et al. 2008, p. 44). The quality of service, including a functional management of sunbeds, is supposed to result in customers' satisfaction. Customers' satisfaction is amongst the most important aspects when it comes to the hotel and cruise industry and should no longer be neglected (cf. Costa et al. 2004, p. 124). The present research aims at analysing vacationers' behavioural/perception-formation patterns related to the sunbed war phenomenon, whilst exploring its possible influence on customers' satisfaction level. Afterwards, the consequences for accommodation providers will be extracted to serve as further input for a possible counter-measures and strategies.

## 2 Research Methodology

Since there is no literature available touching on the sunbed war topic, an explorative—qualitative approach is adopted. More specifically, we opted for a Grounded-Theory approach. Grounded-Theory is based on '*generating theory and doing social research*' (Glaser 1987 cited in Strauss and Corbin 1994, p. 273). The main difference of Grounded Theory to other approaches is that the theory envelops during the actual process of data gathering and analysing (cf. Strauss and Corbin 1994, p. 274). As depicted in the following figure (see Fig. 1), the approach consists of three steps. During the first step, relevant data was collected. A total of 117 online content sources were mined and 28 unstructured interviews were completed; consisting of a diverse sample of German and foreign holidaymakers. Additionally, 14 online blogs/articles and the comments of 74 online users on online rating platforms like tripadvisor.de, etc. and forums like kreuzfahrten-treff.de, etc. were included for in the sample for subsequent coding. In the second step, the collected data was coded, interpreted and constantly compared to each other. Actually, the two processes of data collection, comparison and interpretation was carried out simultaneously and iteratively (cf. Charmaz and Belgrave 2002, p. 354).

The data collection and interpretation stopped once the saturation in qualitative data was observed (cf. ibid, p. 359). In the last step, a causality model, with implicit tentative hypotheses, was extracted. The data analysis during the first and in the second step were aimed at discovering categories. Subsequently, these categories were connected to each other in order to build up relationships among them, as to

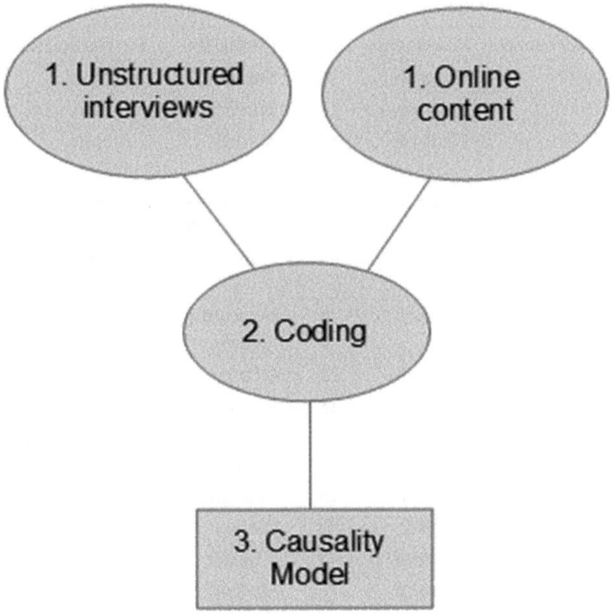


**Fig. 1** Research methodology

establish a pattern, a causality model (cf., ibid, p. 359), which could serve as input to further practically-relevant research on this particular topic (see Fig. 1).

## *2.1 Interviews: Overview*

Initially, 28 interviews were held and transcribed (see Table 1). The interviewees, that participated in this research, were of diverse demographic backgrounds and were purposively-chosen in order to examine the phenomenon in all its particulars and various angles. The age-range of the participants was supposed to cover as many age-groups as possible. As depicted in Fig. 2, the youngest interviewee is 15 and the oldest 83. Furthermore, the interviewees' occupational areas vary in terms of position, industry and salary classes; students but also housewives, teachers, a project manager, a parquet layer, etc. were surveyed. Additionally, the participants represented different nationalities: 22 Germans, one Polish, one Colombian, one Moroccan, one Greek, one French and one Indian. Moreover, 19 interviewees were in the position to provide first hand experiences, while 9 interviewees could report from second hand experiences (e.g. word-of-mouth, YouTube Videos), that was shown to give them an impression of this phenomenon (YouTube 2012). Another interesting observation was that 5 interviewees admitted openly their active involvement in sunbed wars, while all the rest (i.e. 23) denied any participation.

**Table 1** Interviews—Overview

| Interviewee | Nationality | Age | Profession | Participant | Experience |
|---|---|---|---|---|---|
| A | Deutsch | 26 | Student | Non | 1st hand experience |
| B | Deutsch | 28 | Student | Non | 2nd hand experience |
| C | Deutsch | 17 | Student | Non | 2nd hand experience/ YouTube video |
| CH | Deutsch | 28 | Social Insur-ance Clerk | Non | 1st hand experience |
| D | Deutsch | 54 | Guitar Teacher | Non | 2nd hand experience/ YouTube video |
| E | Deutsch | 28 | Forwarding Merchant | Non | 1st hand experience |
| F | Deutsch | 25 | Office Clerk | Non | 1st hand experience |
| E | Deutsch | 28 | Programmar | Non | 1st hand experience |
| H | Deutsch | 27 | Project Manager | Participant | 1st hand experience |
| I | Deutsch | 28 | Student | Non | 2nd hand experience |
| J | Deutsch | 50 | Parquet Layer | Non | 1st hand experience |
| K | Deutsch | 46 | Teacher | Non | 1st hand experience |
| L | Deutsch | 17 | Student | Non | 1st hand experience |
| U | Deutsch | 25 | Student | Participant | 1st hand experience |
| N | Polen | 21 | Student | Non | 2nd hand experience/ YouTube video |
| D | Deutsch | 65 | Teacher | Non | 1st hand experience |
| P | Deutsch | 29 | Housewife | Participant | 1st hand experience |
| Q | Deutsch | 15 | Student | Non | 2nd hand experience |
| R | Deutsch | 83 | Pensioner | Non | 2nd hand experience |
| S | French | 21 | Receptionist | Non | 2nd hand experience/ YouTube video |
| SCH | Deutsch | 21 | Receptionist | Non | 1st hand experience |
| T | Deutsch | 24 | Student | Non | 1st hand experience |
| U | Deutsch | 41 | Travel Agent | Non | 1st hand experience |
| V | Columbia | 31 | Chemical Engineer | Non | 2nd hand experience/ YouTube video |
| W | Deutsch | 59 | Manager | Non | 1st hand experience |
| X | Greek | 37 | System Architect | Participant | 1st hand experience |
| Y | India | 29 | System Architect | Non | 1st hand experience |
| Z | Marokko | 34 | Bricklayer | Participant | 1st hand experience |
| | | | | *(5) participants* | *(19) 1st hand experience* |
| | | | | *(23) non-panicipants* | *(9) 2nd hand experience* |
| | | | | | *(5) YouTube video* |

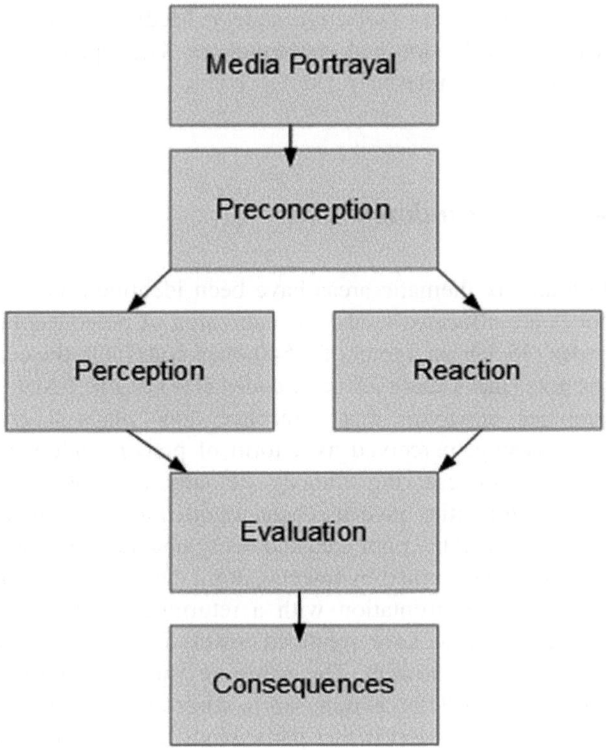


**Fig. 2** Causality model

## 3 Limitations

Grounded-Theory is a highly subjective approach to qualitative analysis (cf. Charmaz and Belgrave 2002, p. 359). Therefore, one has to have an open mind during the whole process of collecting and interpreting data as to not miss out any important points. Prejudices have to be kept at bay, staying clear from any influence and/or expectations regarding determinants. Another limitation is the relatively high proportion of German holidaymakers included in this research paper. Another critical point can be the scope of data collected, which is limited to sunbed wars in hotel pools. The dynamics and politics of sunbed allocation at public beaches were not examined and are potentially subject to higher complexity.

## 4 Coding Results: Categories

The coding process resulted in 1.519 open codes, which are allocated to 32 axial codes. Hereby, the open codes are considered as the essential properties of the axial codes (cf. Charmaz and Belgrave 2002, p. 359). The axial codes were grouped into six thematic areas (selective codes): Media portrayal, preconception, perception, reaction, evaluation and consequences. The Open-, Axial and Selective codes are illustrated in Table 2.

## 4.1 Key Findings

In total, six thematic areas have been identified. Obviously, the majority of open codes are allocated to the thematic area of preconception. It consists of 543 open codes (35.3%) in a total of 1.540 open codes. On the contrary, the category 'consequences' has s mere 15 open codes (1%) of the 1.519 total codes (see Table 2). It becomes apparent, that 'preconception' plays a critical role in that matter. Stereotyping, perceived as a form of preconception, causes vacationers to judge Germans for reserving sunbeds. Actually, it is not a German-specific phenomenon; other nationalities have also been reported to systematically reserve sunbeds. Guests arriving late at the pool area and being unable to find an available place (because all sunbeds are occupied by towels), don't dare removing towels, because of a potential unpleasant confrontation with a returning 'sunbed-blocker'. Nevertheless, some vacationers who have removed towels in the past, reported that confrontational-incidents were a rarity. The returning 'sunbed-blocker' accepted the situation and remained wordless; as opposed to confronting the guest who removed their towel. Another assumption is that participants involved, may tend to deny to reveal their sunbed-reservation behaviour during interviews. This assumption did not hold with our research, since interviewees openly admitted to having engaged in this type of behaviour in the past. The reservation happens, because of the biased belief, that all other guests will act similarly. The option of implementing counter-measures was met positively by the respondents, while the lack of intervention was associated as the underlying cause of complaints/grievances. Especially in forums, the vacationers of cruise lines seemed to regard a functional management concept for sunbeds an essential part of their pre-holiday research, potentially influencing their booking decision. Hotel guests tended to complain about the masses of German tourists, and therefore would avoid such resorts.

# 5 Causality Model of Sunbed Wars

On the background of the seven thematic areas, a causality model can be constructed, reviewing the variables and their interconnectedness (see Fig. 2). The relationships will be explained in depth in the following pages.

**Table 2** Coding results

| Open codes | References | Sources | Axial codes | References | Sources | Selective codes | References | Sources |
|---|---|---|---|---|---|---|---|---|
| Typical German | 14 | 9 | | | | | | |
| Discussion of worst nationality | 2 | 1 | | | | | | |
| Not only Germans | 1 | 1 | | | | | | |
| The British | 3 | 3 | | | | | | |
| Italians and the Spanish | 1 | 1 | | | | | | |
| German stereotype | 3 | 8 | Judged nationality | 30 | 13 | | | |
| Unused sunbeds | 10 | 3 | | | | | | |
| Early morning reservation | 5 | 4 | | | | | | |
| Return to bed | 3 | 3 | | | | | | |
| Before daily trip reservation | 1 | 1 | | | | | | |
| Fight for limited sunbeds | 1 | 1 | | | | | | |
| Running vacationer | 1 | 1 | | | | | | |
| Armed with towel | 1 | 1 | | | | | | |
| Discussing and violence | 3 | 2 | | | | | | |
| Place of Occurrence | 6 | 2 | Illustrated manner | 37 | 13 | | | |
| Typical do-nothing holiday | 1 | 1 | | | | | | |
| Sawing best places | 6 | 5 | | | | | | |
| Disadvantaged latecomer | 3 | 2 | | | | | | |
| Ignored regulations | 1 | 1 | | | | | | |
| Annoying custom | 9 | 6 | | | | | | |
| Declared battle zone | 3 | 3 | | | | | | |
| Ruined holidays | 1 | 1 | Prevailing opinions | 24 | 13 | | | |
| Frequent topic | 2 | 2 | | | | | | |
| Difficult separation | 2 | 1 | | | | | | |

(continued)

**Table 2** (continued)

| Open codes | References | Sources | Axial codes | References | Sources | Selective codes | References | Sources |
|---|---|---|---|---|---|---|---|---|
| Media exaggeration | 2 | 1 | | | | | | |
| Immediate evaluation | 1 | 1 | | | | | | |
| Increased phenomenon | 1 | 1 | | | | | | |
| Influential factor | 2 | 1 | | | | | | |
| Pre holiday worries | 1 | 1 | Influential factor | 12 | 4 | Media portrayal | 103 | 15 |
| Typical German | 7 | 5 | | | | | | |
| Judged German stereotype | 12 | 9 | | | | | | |
| The British | 2 | 1 | | | | | | |
| All nationalities | 12 | 11 | Accused nationality | 33 | 20 | | | |
| Limited sunbeds | 23 | 15 | | | | | | |
| Greed and egoism | 64 | 23 | | | | | | |
| Entitlement | 28 | 15 | | | | | | |
| Best places | 36 | 13 | | | | | | |
| Security and daily routine | 44 | 14 | | | | | | |
| Fear of failure | 22 | 10 | | | | | | |
| Convenience | 21 | 4 | | | | | | |
| Social status | 6 | 3 | Decisive motives | 251 | 50 | | | |
| Good course of holidays | 3 | 2 | | | | | | |
| Sunbed importance | 10 | 7 | | | | | | |
| Purpose of holidays | 14 | 6 | | | | | | |
| Pessimistic vacation | 3 | 2 | Holiday intentions and expectations | 30 | 9 | | | |
| Complaints about others | 3 | 3 | | | | | | |
| Considered inappropriate behavior | 6 | 3 | | | | | | |

| | | | | | | | | |
|---|---|---|---|---|---|---|---|---|
| Feelings of shame | 2 | 2 | | | | | | |
| No confession | 6 | 3 | Denied sunbed reservation | 17 | 7 | | | |
| Comparative thinking | 45 | 19 | | | | | | |
| Power games | 22 | 9 | | | | | | |
| Experienced vacationer | 2 | 1 | | | | | | |
| Provider's mismanagement | 20 | 12 | Inevitable participation | 89 | 27 | | | |
| Internal rule | 2 | 2 | | | | | | |
| Towel signals reservation | 4 | 2 | | | | | | |
| No permission | 1 | 1 | | | | | | |
| Permitted reservation | 5 | 3 | Erroneous pool regulations | 10 | 6 | | | |
| Undesired stress factor | 21 | 12 | | | | | | |
| Furious sunbed blocker | 10 | 7 | Anticipated consequences of towel removal | | | | | |
| Conflicts of all sets | 5 | 2 | | 36 | 16 | | | |
| Reservation practice | 26 | 21 | | | | | | |
| Reckless manner | 11 | 7 | | | | | | |
| Territorial behavior | 5 | 1 | | | | | | |
| Wasted sunbeds | 13 | 15 | Inappropriate reservation practice | 61 | 25 | | | |
| Corrupt employees | 3 | 3 | | | | | | |
| Corrupt room neighbors | 1 | 1 | | | | | | |
| Monetary means | 2 | 2 | | | | | | |
| Alternative means | 4 | 3 | Suspected bribery | 15 | 5 | Preconception | 542 | 64 |
| Typical German | 14 | 9 | | | | | | |
| Discussion of worst nationality | 2 | 1 | | | | | | |
| Not only Germans | 1 | 1 | | | | | | |
| The British | 3 | 3 | | | | | | |
| Italians and the Spanish | 1 | 1 | | | | | | |
| German stereotype | 9 | 8 | Judged nationality | 38 | 13 | | | |

(continued)

**Table 2** (continued)

| Open codes | References | Sources | Axial codes | References | Sources | Selective codes | References | Sources |
|---|---|---|---|---|---|---|---|---|
| Unused sunbeds | 10 | 8 | Illustrated manner | 37 | 13 | | | |
| Early morning reservation | 5 | 4 | | | | | | |
| Return to bed | 3 | 3 | | | | | | |
| Before daily trip reservation | 1 | 1 | | | | | | |
| Fight for limited sunbeds | 1 | 1 | | | | | | |
| Running vacationer | 1 | 1 | | | | | | |
| Armed with towel | 1 | 1 | | | | | | |
| Discussions and violence | 3 | 2 | | | | | | |
| Place of Occurrence | 6 | 2 | Illustrated manner | 37 | 13 | | | |
| Typical do-nothing holiday | 1 | 1 | | | | | | |
| Saving best places | 6 | 5 | | | | | | |
| Disadvantage latecomer | 3 | 2 | | | | | | |
| Ignored regulations | 1 | 1 | | | | | | |
| Annoying custom | 9 | 6 | | | | | | |
| Declared battle zone | 3 | 3 | | | | | | |
| Ruined holidays | 1 | 1 | Prevailing opinions | 24 | 13 | | | |
| Frequent topic | 2 | 2 | | | | | | |
| Difficult separation | 2 | 1 | | | | | | |
| Media exaggeration | 2 | 1 | | | | | | |
| Immediate evaluation | 1 | 1 | | | | | | |
| Increased phenomenon | 1 | 1 | | | | | | |
| Influential factor | 2 | 1 | | | | | | |
| Pre holiday worries | 1 | 1 | Influential factor | 12 | 4 | Media portrayal | 103 | 15 |
| Amusing entertainment | 19 | 11 | | | | | | |

| | | | | | | | | |
|---|---|---|---|---|---|---|---|---|
| Holiday nuisance | 59 | 31 | General evaluation | 102 | 44 | | | |
| Denied opportunity | 14 | 12 | | | | | | |
| Sunbed importance | 10 | 6 | | | | | | |
| Accepted situation | 9 | 7 | | | | | | |
| Irritated vacationer | 17 | 12 | | | | | | |
| Complaints | 31 | 22 | Level of nuisance | 81 | 30 | | | |
| Active countermeasures | 68 | 36 | | | | | | |
| Available sunbeds | 4 | 4 | | | | | | |
| Equal chances | 3 | 3 | Positive feedback | 75 | 41 | | | |
| Intervention required | 16 | 14 | | | | | | |
| Regulation required | 7 | 6 | | | | | | |
| More sunbeds required | 3 | 3 | Requirements | 25 | 20 | Evaluation | 259 | 82 |
| Sunbed taker's right | 9 | 4 | | | | | | |
| Unworried sunbed taker | 11 | 6 | | | | | | |
| Towel removal | 27 | 19 | | | | | | |
| Reaction of sunbed blocker | 25 | 14 | | | | | | |
| Support from hotel staff | 5 | 3 | | | | | | |
| Refused towel removal | 13 | 8 | | | | | | |
| Intended provocation | 7 | 3 | Sunbed takeover | 97 | 36 | | | |
| Participants' motives | 79 | 17 | | | | | | |
| Reservation practice | 27 | 11 | | | | | | |
| Adapted participants | 10 | 4 | Confessed participation | 116 | 19 | | | |
| Non-participants' motives | 17 | 10 | | | | | | |
| Search for free sunbed | 8 | 7 | | | | | | |
| Situational adaption | 6 | 6 | | | | | | |
| Search for alternative places and plans | 10 | 5 | | | | | | |
| Balcony | 4 | 4 | | | | | | |

(continued)

**Table 2** (continued)

| Open codes | References | Sources | Axial codes | References | Sources | Selective codes | References | Sources |
|---|---|---|---|---|---|---|---|---|
| No sunbed needed | 6 | 5 | | | | | | |
| Beach preference | 5 | 5 | Refused participation | 56 | 28 | | | |
| Derided seats | 6 | 2 | Tip money advantage | 6 | 2 | Reaction | 275 | 58 |
| Absent sunbed blocker | 34 | 18 | | | | | | |
| More towel than human | 23 | 14 | | | | | | |
| No return | 4 | 3 | | | | | | |
| Unused sunbed | 17 | 11 | Ineffective sun ted usage | 78 | 29 | | | |
| Server Occurrence | 21 | 14 | | | | | | |
| Mitigated Occurrence | 3 | 3 | Frequency of occurrence | 27 | 16 | | | |
| Germans | 5 | 4 | | | | | | |
| Majority of Germans | 9 | 5 | | | | | | |
| The British | 8 | 4 | | | | | | |
| The British and Russians | 2 | 2 | | | | | | |
| Greek | 1 | 1 | | | | | | |
| French | 1 | 1 | | | | | | |
| Nordic Countries | 1 | 1 | | | | | | |
| Americans | 1 | 1 | | | | | | |
| Appearance in masses | 2 | 2 | Practicing nationality | 32 | 15 | | | |
| Animal behavior | 1 | 1 | | | | | | |
| Running and pushing | 15 | 11 | | | | | | |
| Gathering before opening | 6 | 4 | | | | | | |
| Armed vacation | 2 | 2 | Perceived competition | 25 | 16 | | | |
| Discussions | 7 | 3 | | | | | | |
| Pushing each other | 3 | 3 | | | | | | |
| Aggressive sunbed blocker | 3 | 3 | Unpleasant confrontation | 13 | 9 | | | |
| Hotel owned towels | 3 | 3 | | | | | | |

| | | | | | | | | |
|---|---|---|---|---|---|---|---|---|
| Meaning of personal belongings | 3 | 3 | | | | | | |
| Modify sunbed | 1 | 1 | | | | | | |
| Occupied with towels | 21 | 12 | | | | | | |
| Occupied with personal belongings | 14 | 9 | | | | | | |
| Known towels | 1 | 1 | Marked territory | 43 | 19 | | | |
| Free sunbed | 21 | 13 | | | | | | |
| No available place | 29 | 20 | | | | | | |
| Challenging find a sunbed | 3 | 3 | | | | | | |
| Inconvenient pool area | 6 | 3 | Availability of sunbeds | 59 | 33 | | | |
| Before breakfast reservation | 16 | 12 | | | | | | |
| Whole day reservation | 7 | 7 | | | | | | |
| Before daily trip reservation | 1 | 1 | | | | | | |
| Double reservation | 3 | 3 | | | | | | |
| Reservation for others | 7 | 6 | | | | | | |
| Long discussion | 3 | 1 | Reservation practices | 37 | 26 | | | |
| Provider Ignorance | 1 | 1 | | | | | | |
| Lack of monitoring | 10 | 10 | Lack of Intervention | 11 | 11 | Perception | 325 | 67 |
| Decisive prebooking research | 5 | 4 | | | | | | |
| Influenced booking decision | 3 | 3 | Consequences for cruise operator | | | | | |
| Cruise-holiday avoidance | 2 | 2 | | 10 | 8 | | | |
| Unaffected booking behavior | 3 | 2 | | | | | | |
| Cheap-offer avoidance | 1 | 1 | Consequences for hotel operator | | | | | |
| German-holiday-resort avoidance | 1 | 1 | | 5 | 4 | Consequences | 15 | 11 |

## 5.1 Media Portrayal and Preconception

An obvious relationship can be established between the variables ‘media portrayal’ and ‘pre-conception’. In general, the ‘sunbed-war’ phenomenon is portrayed as being stereotypically German: German vacationers reserve the best places very early in the morning and then go back to bed or take a daily trip, before actually using the sunbed. Fights for a limited sunbed supply and vacationers who are racing against each other, armed with a towel, in order to get a sunbed, is a popular image, giving the impression, that a severe competition is taking place at pools. After the reservation is done, the sunbed remains empty, in some cases, for the rest of the day. According to media portrayals, late-comers, guests who haven’t been that proactive, have a considerable disadvantage in comparison to the early morning sunbed-blocker.

Moreover, media declare pool areas as primary holiday ‘battlefields’, because of the high occurrence of conflicts and violence, evoked by altercations about sunbeds. This mainly occurs in Spanish and Turkish holiday resorts and is a typical German-issue. Because of the media’s great influence, viewers may become influenced and biased, feeding their own prejedices and misconceptions, as stated by Interviewee T. More particularly, interviewee T revealed, that a holiday could start without being worried about getting a sunbed, and subsequently begin to worry about it once they hear about it.

## 5.2 Preconception, Perception and Reaction

The variable ‘preconception’ covers various prejudices towards the sunbed phenomenon. Preconceptions, amongst other biased opinions, include alleged motives, explaining the reasons behind vacationers’ early-morning reservation. Such motives are related to the provision of limited sunbeds, character traits such as egoism and greed, entitlement, the need for security and daily routine, feelings of fear of failure, the pursuit for convenience and the demonstration of social status. Moreover, a sunbed is deemed to be of utmost importance for every vacationer. They just want to spend their time relaxing at the pool area and it seems as if they don’t have other holiday interests. Because of the previously-mentioned motives and the assumed holiday intentions, the biased vacationer presumes that all other vacationers are going to get up early, rendering a competition in sunbed-reservations inevitable. This means that non-participants may be disadvantaged, when arriving later at the pool area. This assumption does not only impact on perceptions, but also stimulates behaviour and reactions.

### 5.2.1 The Prejudiced Opinion May Influence Vacationer's Perception

According to the biased presumption, that all vacationers react in the same manner and are going to reserve sunbeds early in the morning, it is believed that sunbeds will be blocked, to keep the '*open possibility*' (Interviewee K), denying other vacationers the opportunity to have a sunbed (cf. Interviewee S). This may cause vacationers to perceive the sunbeds as unused, but nonetheless blocked. Furthermore, sunbeds are believed to be limited and 29 open codes are suggesting that vacationers couldn't find any available sunbed. On the contrary, 21 open codes revealed vacationers' perception of sufficient free sunbeds. They could find a sunbed, but their demands regarding the particular spot, were low in comparison to other vacationers' demands towards their sunbed, was mentioned by Wendy, online user. In comparison to the contention, that a competition is happening at the pool area, vacationers perceived other holidaymakers as if they were running for the best places and pushing each other. They further witnessed discussions related to sunbeds. Mainly, the phenomenon is perceived as endemic to all-inclusive holidays, offered in the Turkish Riviera and Mallorca. Referring to the bias related to nationality, the reservation practice is regarded as being typically German, but also other nationalities are mentioned. The Germans are perceived to appear in masses and but other nationalities such as: French, Greek and the British, have also been reported reserving sunbeds. Another bias is reflected by the assumption, that people 'behave like animals' and that their behaviour is the equivalent animal territorial behaviour. Animals mark their territory with urine (cf. Merkur 2015) and vacationers' with towels. Indeed, the vacationers' behaviour was described as an animal behaviour by online user Mendacium, and the sunbeds are perceived as marked with towels and personal belongings, according to 43 open codes. Furthermore, another preconception accuses the provider, for not having a functional management concept. Hence, particular vacationers may attribute the problem to the provider's lack of intervention.

### 5.2.2 The Prejudiced Opinion May Influence Vacationer's Reaction

Actually, it is assumed that every single vacationer is participating in the sunbed-war phenomenon, leading to the bias that active involvement in this misbehaviour is inevitable. Vacationers are going to imitate the expected behaviour of other vacationers, waking up in the break of dawn to reserve a sunbed before anyone else can, in order to achieve their personal goal of getting a sunbed. The reaction is stimulated by the motive, that everyone else is going to do the same (as stated by Interviewee Z). This means that non-participants may be disadvantaged, when arriving later at the pool area. On the contrary, prejudice can cause other vacationers to avoid the participation in the sunbed-war phenomenon altogether. They would rather prefer to take the least favourable places or to search for alternative places at the beach, than to participate in such a petty activity, and in the worst case, let their holidays get spoilt by the accompanying stress. On the expectation of unnecessary stress and fuelled by the media image of a pool area as a battlefield, some vacationers will refrain from removing towels of unused sunbeds, because they fear the confrontation risk with furious sunbed-blocker, more than the risk of not getting a suitable sunbed. Moreover, bias refers to the prevalence of erroneous pool regulations. An informal rule amongst vacationers is that a towel may signal a reservation and that it cannot be removed. Nevertheless, some vacationers who removed towels, did not experience any drawbacks. Rarely, did a confrontation take place, was argued by interviewee CH. In case the sunbed-blocker became aggressive, the hotel staff would be asked to mediate. The hotel staff would then decide on behalf of the towel-remover (online user of Discuss). Both variables, 'perception' and 'reaction' can be further linked to 'evaluation'.

## 5.3 Perception, Reaction and Evaluation

In accordance to the constructed causality model, 'perceptions' and 'reactions' related to the sunbed-war phenomenon discussed here. Thereby, the vacationers' general opinion can be categorised between seeing it as a holiday nuisance or as simply amusing entertainment. On the one hand, the perception of and the reaction to the reservation of sunbeds may lead vacationers to evaluate the phenomenon as holiday nuisance as stated in 59 open codes. Accordingly, the unavailability of sunbed stimulates various forms of nuisance. Sunbeds are perceived as being unused, resulting in a limited availability of sunbeds. Mentioned as really annoying, is the blocking practice of people who tend to be absent for long periods of time. This is encountered with frustrations by vacationers who are in search of a free sunbed. Furthermore, they get upset and state that their opportunities of enjoying their holiday is impaired, due to the unavailability of sunbeds (cf. Interviewee CH). On the contrary, some vacationers seem to accept the situation as given, and don't want their holidays to be spoilt by participating in the 'sunbed-wars' (cf. Interviewee O).

A travel agent (interviewee U) stated that, the sunbed-war is not regarded as a criterion, that would lead a vacationer to avoid a particular hotel. Those holiday-makers would rather tend to complain about other guests' behaviour and the mass tourism in general, than file complaints addressing directly the sunbed reservation phenomenon. On the other hand, this phenomenon is regarded as amusing/entertaining in 19 open codes. Some vacationers make a fun out of the phenomenon and this somewhat, presumably, enriches their holiday experience. Interviewee G confessed that altercations, due to a towel removal are, from his point of view, an extremely positive holiday-highlight. Other vacationers declared, that the phenomenon offers them a great entertainment while on vacation (cf. Interviewee K).

Furthermore, counter-measures are considered as positive interventions by the accommodation provider; giving equal chances to everyone. Counter-measures such as a 'towel police' and the removal of unattended things by an employee are considered positive. It is argued, that these counter-measures inhibit sunbed reservations, because if the things are removed, it becomes pointless to block any sunbed (cf. Interviewee SCH). As a result, vacationers do not have to worry anymore, because every customer is treated equally and fairly. Participants don't have to wake up in the break of dawn, can sleep longer, and non-participants are also capable of getting a sunbed.

### *5.4 Evaluation and Consequences*

The consequences for cruise operators seem to be significantly higher than hotel operators. This may be due to the differences between hotels and cruise ships. On board a cruise ship one cannot escape the masses, while during hotel stays one has the alternative of going to the beach as stated by an online user Marthamuse. Absent counter-measures cause online users to write negative comments on forums and that in turn, may influence other potential vacationers, having a huge impact on booking behaviour. Moreover, some potential customers would avoid holidays on cruise ships altogether.

## 6 Tentative Hypotheses

On the basis of the causality model, tentative hypotheses can be derived. The following four tentative hypotheses will be detailed with the aid of academic literature.

- Hypothesis: Media portrayals are generating biased preconceptions.
- Hypothesis: The generated preconception stimulates vacationers to perceive sunbed shortages and an ongoing competition at hotel pools.
- Hypothesis: Due to the formed preconceptions, vacationers are reserving sunbeds.
- Hypothesis: The absence of counter-measures drives online users to write negative comments on forums and this may in turn influence booking decisions.

### *6.1 Hypothesis: Media Portrayals Are Generating Biased Preconceptions*

The sunbed reservation phenomenon is a frequent topic of media coverage in television, articles and the social media, conveying and reinforcing stereotypes (cf. Dovidio et al. 2010, p. 8). These stereotypes '*are socially supported, continually revived and hammered in, by our media of mass communication–by novels, short stories, newspaper items, movies, stage, radio, and television*' (Allport 1954 cited in Mutz and Goldman 2010, p. 1). Stereotypes evolve over time and result to human beings immediately assessing related information individually, and using those *collected beliefs* at a later point in time for the interpretation of social and emotional signals (cf. Nelson 2004, p. 4). Furthermore, people have the tendency to evaluate the received information by television as *real-world* and *first-hand* experience. The experience, watched on television is almost similar to an experienced event that has happened in real life (cf. Mutz and Goldman 2010, p. 11). A large television screen for example, supports the broadcast to remain longer in one's memory. The greater the pictures the closer and more real is it perceived by its receiver (cf. ibid 2010, p. 12). One reason for the popularity of television is that the information can be received considerably easier than print (cf. Krendl 1986; Salomon 1983b, 1984; Salomon and Leigh 1984 cited in Cennamo 1993, p. 35). This is due to the oral language used by television, which is complemented by lifelike illustrations (cf. Cennamo 1993, p. 35). These illustrations are generating pictures in our minds (cf. Lippmann 1922 cited in Mutz and Goldman 2010, p. 11).

Moreover, it doesn't require a high level of intellectual effort (cf. Ibid 1993, p. 36); compared to print media that provide *only text and still pictures* (Ibid 1993, p. 35). Therefore, if the media portrays the hotel pool environment as discussed above, it may stay in the memories of human beings and generate pre- and during-holiday biases and/or negative expectations. Interviewee T stated: 'Media has a great influential role, and a holiday could begin without being worried if a sunbed would be available.' Therefore, vacationers are subjected and reinforce stereotypes, which is regarded as a form of preconception (cf. Dovidio et al. 2010, p. 5).

## 6.2 Hypothesis: The Generated Preconception Stimulates Vacationers to Perceive Sunbed Shortages and an Ongoing Competition at Hotel Pools

Stereotyping, and all other forms of pre-conception, is a mechanism helping human beings to put different kinds of information and events that they constantly encounter in their daily lives into categories (Nelson 2004, p. 4). '*We cannot possibly avoid this process*' (Allport 1954 cited in Nelson 2004, p. 5). Vacationers are doing the same: organising information and first hand-experience into categories. These categories are generating *beliefs* and *expectations* (ibid 2004, p. 4). In the case of sunbed-wars, vacationers develop personal opinions, including beliefs and expectations, towards their holiday experience. Furthermore, *stereotypes guide our social behaviour and often govern what information we seek, heed and remember* (Fiske 1988 cited in Nelson 2004, p. 4). That gives rise to an individual evaluation system, in which unrelated variables are forced to a relationship (cf. Ibid 2006, p. 26). This is decisive in terms of guiding individuals on how to perceive people and other happenings in their environment; based on their previously established characteristics which are fitting to their individual developed categories (Nelson 2004, p. 5). *In general, stereotypes produce a readiness to perceive behaviours or characteristics that are consistent with the stereotype* (Dovidio et al. 2010, p. 7). Human beings tend to quickly apply those characteristics at the first phases of their individual perception and the impact is regarded as purposeful (cf. Dovidio et al. 2010, p. 7). Hence, stereotypes are pictures in one's mind, which are guiding their individual perception. If vacationers are bombarded over and over again with the 'battlefield' image of pool areas, as presented by media, where sunbeds are limited and an intense competition for the best places under the sun is taking place, they will most likely perceive the illustrated behaviour more intensely while on vacation than a vacationer who hasn't been prejudiced by media. According to the coding results in the category 'perception', 29 open codes were connected with the instance of vacationers not being able to find a sunbed, while 21 open codes revealed that sufficient sunbeds were free. This coding result could support the idea, that vacationers tend to perceive things rather selectively, depending to their media-exposure.

## 6.3 Hypothesis: Due to the Formed Preconceptions, Vacationers Are Reserving Sunbeds

*Preconceptions are biased opinions that are subjective in nature. Cognitive biases are subjective or predisposed opinions that may emanate from specific heuristics* (Bazerman 1990; Busenitz and Lau 1996 cited in Simon et al. 2000, p. 115). Furthermore, such biases are considered as erroneous and rigid *generalisations* (Allport 1954 cited in Dovidio et al. 2010, p. 5). Referring to biases, it is already stated that it they have a huge influence on an individual's perception. Therefore, its great influence on a person's behaviour should not be underestimated. Accordingly, people actions are based on their biased opinion (cf. Schwenk 1986, cited in Simon et al. 2000, p. 127). Moreover, such biased opinions are considered as erroneous and rigid *generalisations* (Allport 1954 cited in Dovidio et al. 2010, p. 5). As a result, the decisions of vacationers are less *rational* (cf. Barnes 1984 cited in Simon et al. 2000, p. 115). This causes a negative attitude and a derived negative behaviour towards a particular target group (Dovidio et al. 2010, p. 5). In this case, the target group consists of all other vacationers, who are concurrently at the same holiday destination. The perceived competition as discussed previously, is the decisive reason that reinforces the development and reinforcement of biased opinions (cf. ibid 2010, p. 5). In other words, the prejudice that a competition is occurring at hotel pools, causes vacationers to act competitively. Moreover, such biased opinions stimulate vacationers to anticipate problems and an impaired holiday experience (cf. Barnes 1984; Hogarth 1980; Schwenk 1984 cited in Simon et al. 2000, p. 117). Referring to sunbed wars, vacationers fear not getting a sunbed if they don't participate in the reservation practice. Conclusively, they engage in this practice, believing that everybody is doing it. They seem to feel in competition with all other vacationers, contributing to negative attitudes and behaviour towards other holidaymakers.

### 6.4 Hypothesis: The Absence of Counter-Measures Drives Online Users to Write Negative Comments on Forums and This May Influence Other Potential Vacationer's Booking Decision

The internet is a powerful medium as it is used constantly by billions of people, enabling online word-of-mouth communication between online users. Unlimited *communicative space* is provided to write about each and every topic (cf. Sun et al. 2006, p. 1105). Opinions concerning diverse topics are discussed or shared with other people, who are not physically present (cf. Dennis et al. 1998; Ridings and Gefen 2004 cited in Sun et al. 2006, p. 1106). Even topics such as 'sunbed-war' are discussed online and have been included in this research. There are numerous relevant comments found online in online forums and on rating platforms. Due to impersonal communication, people are encouraged to write honest opinions without being afraid of facing other persons' reactions (cf. Roed 2003 cited in Sun et al. 2006, p. 1105). Furthermore, these opinions are more *influential* than a usual conversation between a limited number of participants. One online comment can reach high numbers of readers in a very short time (cf. Phelps et al. 2004 cited in Sun et al. 2006, p. 1106). More specifically, online users are in search for advice on unknown-to-them topics, such as the sunbed provision in hotel resorts, and on cruise ships for example. Online opinions are very influential here, because inexperienced online users tend to solely base their decision on others', rather than their own; experiences (Murray 1991; Ohanian 1990; Rodgers and Chen 2005 cited in Sun et al. 2006, p. 1105). Therefore, potential vacationers' decision to book a holiday could be aborted, if they happen to encounter criticism and/or negative information. If they find out, for example, that sunbeds are blocked and that the responsible staff is not intervening, they would probably look for alternatives. As previously-mentioned, in the online forum Kreuzfahrten-Treff, experienced online users are recommending cruise lines on which a functional sunbed management concept is implemented.

## 7 Conclusion

The first objective of this paper was to gain an understanding of the behavioural/ perception-formation aspects of the sunbed-war phenomenon, from a vacationers' perspective. In total and following a coding process, six thematic areas could be identified, reflecting different determinants. The highest percentage of codes corresponded to 'preconceptions', also known as prejudgements. In general, the sunbed-war phenomenon is presented on numerous media channels and thus viewers/listeners are frequently confronted with this topic. Particularly, television is using real images, that remain like pictures in one's mind, shaping stereotypes. This stereotype, which is indeed a form of preconception, may influence vacationers' prejudices, perception and reaction. Eventually, their overall holiday evaluation will be based on their biased experience. Among these stereotypes, is also the one of 'the German holidaymaker', who is supposed to be the sun-bed blocking nationality number one. But our research reveals that other nationalities are doing the same.

Allegedly, it is believed that among other reasons, the limited provision of sunbeds, character traits such as egoism and greed, entitlement, the need for security and daily routine, feelings of fear of failure, the pursuit for convenience and the demonstration of social status, all stimulate other vacationers to reserve sunbeds early in the morning and keep them for the whole day, regardless their actual use. Involvement in this type of misbehaviour seems to be inevitable, because it is believed that every vacationer is doing so. Based on this prejudice, other vacationers tend to imitate such behaviours. Accordingly, they reserve sunbeds early in the morning or already in the previous evening, blocking more than one sunbed, for group and family members. Afterwards, they leave the sunbed, and sometimes the bed stays empty for the rest of the day. Other vacationers, who haven't been that 'proactive' and refrain from participating in sunbed wars, arrive later at the pool area to find all sunbeds reserved. They hesitate removing the towels, of unused sunbeds in the fear of a confrontation with a furious sunbed-blocker, who could return and reclaim their 'reservation'. This is accompanied with a feeling frustration, because they cannot find any available place. Alternatively, the 'courageous ones' remove the towels, stating that just on rare occasions someone confronted them directly. The level of nuisance differs amongst vacationers. Some vacationers are annoyed and upset by this practice, and immediately look for alternatives. Other guests are entertained by it, seeing their holiday enriched by the excitement of a confrontation. The second objective of this paper was to determine possible strategies for accommodation providers, to ensure the guest's level of satisfaction. One the one hand, counter-measures were evaluated positively, because they give equal chances to all vacationers and ultimately results to always available sunbeds. On the flipside, the lack of intervention leads to complaint; especially in forums, where the vacationers of cruise lines seem to regard a functional sunbed management concept a key question of their pre-holiday research and booking decision. As a consequence, customers may avoid booking a holiday with a specific holiday-provider. Hotel guests would rather complain about the masses of German tourists, and avoid such resorts altogether. Therefore, this paper proposes that accommodation providers should not ignore the issue, and they are urged to apply practicable counter-measures. As discussed in the beginning of this paper, customer satisfaction is a competitive advantage. Counter-measures for holiday-nuisances, such as 'sunbed-wards', are directly connected to vacationers' level of satisfaction. If countermeasures are adapted properly, guest satisfaction would increase, resulting in positive word-of-mouth recommendations.

## 8 Topics for Further Research

This research is the basis for further quantitative research, in which the tentative hypotheses can be tested. Furthermore, it offers a plethora of unexplored topics, as for example, that the Germans generalise, attributing particular negative character traits and holiday-behaviour to their own nationality. This piece of research challenges such stereotypes, showing that it is not only Germans who are reserving sunbeds. The interesting questions here is: To what extent does tourist misconduct and misbehaviour is affected by (and affects) cultural stereotypes?

Furthermore, the underlying behavioural pattern of the sun-bed wars phenomenon is not merely applicable for sun-beds, but also for a variety of other holiday-encounters as: buffets, bus excursions, airport check-in areas and gates, etc.

## References

Andriotis, K., & Agiomirgianakis, G. M. (2007). Tourist vacation preferences: The case of mass tourists to Crete. *Tourism Analysis, 12*(1/2), 51–63.

Cennamo, K. (1993). Learning from video: Factors influencing learners' preconceptions and invested mental effort. *Educational Technology Research and Development, 41*(3), 33–45.

Charmaz, K., & Belgrave, L. (2002). Qualitative interviewing and grounded theory analysis. In J. F. Gubrium, J. A. Holstein, A. B. Marvasti, & K. D. McKinney (Eds.), *The SAGE handbook of interview research: The complexity of the craft* (2nd ed.). London: Sage.

Costa, G., Glinia, E., Goudas, M., & Antoniou, P. (2004). Recreational services in resort hotels: Customer satisfaction aspects. *Journal of Sport and Tourism, 9*, 117–126.

Devi Juwaheer, T. (2004). Exploring international tourists' perceptions of hotel operations by using a modified SERVQUAL approach – A case study of Mauritius. *Managing Service Quality, 14* (5), 350–364. https://doi.org/10.1108/09604520410557967

Dovidio, J. F., Hewstone, M., Glick, P., & Esses, V. (2010). Prejudice, stereotyping and discrimination: Theoretical and empirical overview. In J. F. Dovidio, M. Hewstone, P. Glick, & V. M. Esses (Eds.), *The SAGE handbook of prejudice, stereotyping and discrimination* (pp. 3–29). London: Sage.

Kozak, M., Bigné, E., & Andreu, L. (2008). Satisfaction and destination loyalty. *Journal of Quality Assurance in Hospitality and Tourism, 5*(1), 43–59. https://doi.org/10.1300/J162v05n01_04

Merkur. (2015). *Tierisches Verhalten. Warum im Urlaub der Handtuch-Kampf beginnt*. Retrieved July 18, 2017, from https://www.merkur.de/reise/sonnenliege-handtuch-pool-reservieren-woher-kommt-verhalten-zr-3747667.html

Mutz, D. C., & Goldman, S. K. (2010). Mass media. In J. F. Dovidio, M. Hewstone, P. Glick, & V. M. Esses (Eds.), *The Sage handbook of prejudice, stereotyping and discrimination*. London: Sage.

Nelson, T. D. (2004). *Ageism: Stereotyping and prejudice against older persons*. Cambridge, MA: MIT Press.

Simon, M., Houghton, S. M., & Aquino, K. (2000). Cognitive biases, risk perception, and venture formation: How individuals decide to start companies. *Journal of Business Venturing, 15*(2), 113–134.

Strauss, A., & Corbin, J. (1994). Grounded theory methodology. *Handbook of Qualitative Research, 17*, 273–285.

Sun, T., Youn, S., Wu, G., & Kuntaraporn, M. (2006). Online word-of-mouth (or mouse): An exploration of its antecedents and consequences. *Journal of Computer-Mediated Communication, 11*(4), 1104–1127.

YouTube. (2012). *Flamingo oasis sun lounger dash.* Retrieved July 18, 2017, from https://www.youtube.com/watch?v=HKijUh_LQWs

[illegible]

# Part III
# Systemic Governance and Institutions

# Informal Tourism Economy and EU Funding: The Case of Romania

**Dragoş Dumitru Jaliu and Anamaria Sidonia Răvar**

## 1 Introduction

Situated at the border between formal, modern economy on one hand and underground economy on the other hand, the informal economy comprises a wide array of market behaviours, entities, products and services. A broad definition of the concept is provided by the European Commission (2017), which describes informal economy as encompassing enterprises, jobs, and workers that are not regulated or protected by the state.

Lack of regulation may in fact be regarded as the fundamental feature of the informal economy. Thus, the activities encompassed by this sector are not illegal, but rather remain uncovered by the national legal framework; where comprehensive regulations do exist, informal businesses fail to comply with requirements to register, pay taxes, obtain certifications/authorisations required by law, or provide certain benefits to their workers (Keen 2015). Thus, the informal economy includes activities that do not fall under the remit of the law either because regulations do not apply, or because they are weakly enforced and easily evaded (Sinha and Kanbur 2012). According to Keen (2015), three types of informal entities may be distinguished:

- Evaders—are covered by the law but do not comply with it;
- Avoiders—adjust their activity so as to fall outside the purview of official regulation;
- Outsiders—are not covered by the existing legal framework.

D. D. Jaliu (✉)
National School of Political Studies and Public Administration, Bucharest, Romania
e-mail: jaliud@fonduri-structurale.ro

A. S. Răvar
Centre for a Sustainable Society Association, Bucharest, Romania



A. Papathanassis et al. (eds.), *Yellow Tourism*, Tourism, Hospitality & Event Management, https://doi.org/10.1007/978-3-319-94664-1_12

The informal economy functions in close interaction with formal businesses. In some cases, the latter resort to including informal businesses into their own supply chains (European Commission 2017). In other cases, formally registered enterprises may choose to pay workers (at least partially) cash-in-hand. Consequently, there is no clear divide between the formal and informal economy, which makes the latter hard to measure (Kraemer-Mbula and Wunsch-Vioncent 2017, in Boyd 2017).

According to ILO (2015), over 90% of all SMEs worldwide carry out some informal activity, absorbing more than half of the workforce at global level. It has the biggest expansion in Sub-Saharan Africa, South Asia and Latin America, but it is also present in developed countries. Moreover, the informal economy has experienced a continuous growth during the last decades, both in rural and in urban areas (Brown and McGranahan 2016).

In most cases, the informal economy leads to informal employment, since workers do not pay taxes, do not enjoy social protection and are often exposed to compulsory overtime, lay-offs without notice, and unsafe working conditions. Due to this, the informal economy is often perceived as offering low-quality jobs, addressed to workers who are excluded from opportunities in the formal sector, such as women, migrants and other vulnerable groups (ILO 2015). The informal economy's impact on employment is indeed significant, since it accounts for over 80% of non-agricultural employment in South Asia and approximately two-thirds in Sub-Saharan Africa and East and South-East Asia respectively (Vanek et al. 2014).

Not surprisingly, the informal sector is generally associated, by policymakers, with low productivity and poverty. Despite its continuous growth and large share in employment, it is believed that the informal sector contributes between 25% and 50% of non-agricultural GDP (Charmes 2012, in Brown and McGranahan 2016). The informal economy is also linked with other 'dangers', such as distortion of competition, since informal businesses have a cost advantage over formal businesses and prevent the latter from gaining market share (Farrel 2004).

However, some researchers, development experts and policy-makers, believe that informal economy may also be associated with positive effects on entrepreneurship, flexibility and resilience (IIED 2017), acting as a 'necessary evil' of the overall development process. A variety of arguments have been brought forward to support this idea: informality provides employment to people who have no other alternative (Farrel 2004) and provides pathways to the reduction of poverty and inequality (Chen 2016). Moreover, recent research has shown that the informal sector also shows signs of innovation, as informal enterprises are more inclined to strive for creative solutions to reduce costs and bring value to the market using the available resources (Boyd 2017). As the debate over the positive and negative effects of informal economy progresses, what becomes obvious is the need to gain a profound and comprehensive understanding of what the informal economy is and how it manifests itself (IIED 2017), and what efforts should be taken to further the development of businesses and communities through policies tackling the downfalls of informality.

Formalisation of businesses is also regarded by many policymakers as a solution to increasing productivity, ensuring decent work and achieving inclusive development.

In this respect, the ILO (2015) adopted Recommendation 204 concerning the transition from the informal to the formal economy. Chen (2016) however, advocates for an alternative approach, of neoliberal persuasion, in which the informal economy functions alongside the formal economy in a hybrid, inclusive system. Rather than spending resources on stimulating or even enforcing formalisation, the author recommends policymakers to focus on extending social protection to informal workers and creating an enabling environment that would ultimately lead to an increase in the productivity of informal enterprises. This neoliberal approach, views informal enterprises as start-ups that have a potential to bring added-value to society and even become formal over time if they are offered tax forgiveness (provided they reinvest more of their profits in their business) and if proper support services are put in place to encourage their entrepreneurial spirit (Neuwirth 2012).

This neo-liberal deregulatory perspective is challenged by some more recent research. A study built on cross-national comparative data from the 27 member states of the European Union concludes that, lower levels of state intervention are correlated with larger—and not smaller—informal economies (Williams 2013). Thus, the solution might be more, rather than less, regulation of the economy. On the other hand, the Deputy Director of the Fiscal Affairs Department in the IMF, Michael Keen (2015), argues that a higher level of regulation does not necessarily bring a lower level of informality, but rather affects the structure of the informal sector. Thus, the adoption of additional regulations may motivate outsiders to become avoiders, but will rarely lead to better compliance with regulations. Hence, the effectiveness of regulation remains questionable.

A concept closely related to that of the informal economy is the 'shadow' or 'unofficial' economy, which is regarded as encompassing activities that fall under two categories: undeclared work—which includes wages that are not declared by either businesses or workers so as to avoid taxation, bureaucracy or loss of social benefits, and underreporting—when businesses report only part of their income to avoid taxation (AT Kearney 2013). Overall, the shadow economy includes informal business activities, aimed at generating benefits in natural or monetary form (Mróz 2002 in Schneider et al. 2015), which are often performed by registered businesses alongside formal activities. Hence, the transactions being part of the shadow economy are not accounted for in the calculation of the GDP (Din et al. 2016).

Another similar concept is that of the 'non-observed economy', which is defined by the European Commission (2010) as comprising: (1) illegal activities where the parties are willing partners in economic transactions, (2) hidden and underground activities where the transactions themselves are not against the law, but are unreported to avoid official scrutiny, and (3) informal activities where typically no records are kept. Thus, the non-observed economy includes transactions made by both unregistered and registered entities.

Although the factors that facilitate and enhance the presence of shadow economy (e.g. predominance of cash transactions, lack of transparency surrounding transactions, limited enforcement) still persist in Europe, the shadow economy has been registering a continuous decrease in recent years (AT Kearney 2013). In 2014, the shadow economy accounted for more than 18% of all economic activity in the EU

(Schneider et al. 2015).[1] Over 60% of the overall shadow economy in Europe is concentrated in EU's five largest economic powers: Germany, France, Italy, Spain, and the United Kingdom (AT Kearney 2013). Still, the shadow economy's share in GDP (computed based on 2014 data) is the largest in East European countries and Baltic states: 23.5% in Poland, 25% in Latvia, 27% in Estonia and Lithuania, 28% Croatia and Romania, 31% in Bulgaria (Schneider et al. 2015). Despite its relatively large share in GDP, shadow economy has registered a constant decrease in recent years, a trend that seems to be correlated with shrinking income tax rates and with a decline in cash payments. The correlation between the size of the shadow economy and the volume of cash payments has also been demonstrated by more recent studies. Thus, the majority of East European countries with a large shadow economy are also characterised by a relatively small number of cards per capita, a small number of terminals, and a modest share of card transaction value in the overall GDP as compared with countries in Western and Northern Europe (EY 2016).

Despite of the fact that entrepreneurs engaging in informal activities are exposed to potential negative consequences, such as paying fines or having their activity suspended, the shadow economy is still perceived by many businesses as advantageous as compared to, alternatively, complying to regulations. This is due to several reasons. Firstly, by not paying taxes, both entrepreneurs, as well as workers, are able to make some savings. In the case of businesses, these savings could be further used for investments, for expanding the business or for increasing shareholder's profits. Secondly, the shadow economy is often perceived as a normal part of doing business and since most businesses formally report at least some of their activity, entrepreneurs and business owners are not affected by a 'guilty conscience' (AT Kearney 2013). Thirdly, due to lack of enforcement, informal activities may be perceived as easy to carry out and hard to detect, which lowers the opportunity cost of engaging in shadow economy.

Whatever advantages shadow economy may bring to individual entrepreneurs, those are significantly outweighed by the negative consequences at societal level. These include lost government revenue (due to unreported transactions and tax evasion, which leads to a reduced tax base), lower quantity and quality of public goods (due to limited resources available for public investments), distortions in competition (companies engaging in informal activities have lower operating costs), and an overall degradation in economic and social institutions (EY 2016).

A multitude of potential measures have been put forward with the aim of reducing the shadow economy and hence its adverse effects, with the majority of them targeting the decrease of cash payments, through obligations to make electronic payments of wages, salaries and social security benefits, thresholds for consumer cash payments, obligation to operate POS terminals and tax incentives (EY 2016). Even if stronger regulations are put in place and enforced, the shadow economy will

[1]Study based on data from 31 European countries, including EU-28, Norway, Switzerland and Turkey.

most likely persist even in the most advanced economies, as it is a natural element of the economic or social life (Schneider et al. 2015).

## 2 Informal Economy and EU Funding in Tourism: The Case of Romania

Tourism is widely recognised as a sector in which informal (household or family labour) or even illegal labour is often used and in which formal suppliers co-exist alongside informal businesses (UNWTO and ILO 2014). According to UNCTAD (2013), the majority of tourism-related businesses in developing countries tend to be SMEs, many of which are operating in the informal economy. However, in spite of the existence of real-life evidence supporting the widespread expansion of informal economy in the tourism sector, there have been few attempts to measure its size and overall effects (Kesar and Čuić 2017). According to a report by AT Kearney (2013), hotels and restaurants represent one sector category with the highest share of shadow economy, amounting to approximately 19% of the total GDP produced in this sector at EU level (AT Kearney 2013); this level is exceeded by construction (31%) and retail (20%). Although tourism is not limited to the activity of hotels and restaurants, this figure suggests the large scale and potentially significant impact of informality in this particular sector.

In spite of the large share of informal activities, tourism has long been viewed as an instrument for poverty reduction in developing countries (Mitchell 2010; Rogerson 2014), contributing to an increase in wealth and to the creation of employment and business opportunities (Din et al. 2016). The concept of 'pro-poor tourism' emerged, representing an approach to tourism development in which the private and public sectors, including development agencies and NGOs, collaborate to ensure that tourism generates significant tangible benefits for the poor (Rogerson 2014); these benefits may be of economic, but also of social, cultural and environmental nature (Dao Truong 2017).

According to the World Travel and Tourism Council (WTTC 2017), in 2016, tourism accounted for a share of 10.2% in the global GDP and of 10% in the worldwide employment. Moreover, tourism contributed to 6.6% of the total global exports and to almost 30% of the total global service exports. Also, the annual growth rate of the tourism sector (3.1%) outpaced that of the global economy (2.5%), and the WTTC (2017) estimated that tourism "will continue to be at the forefront of wealth and employment creation in the global economy" in the upcoming period. Apart from its contribution to economic growth and job creation, tourism also exerts a leverage effect on other industries, since the provision of tourism services involves a variety of related industries, such as public utilities, agriculture, telecommunication, manufacturing, retail, cultural, personal, security and health services (Din et al. 2016). In fact, it is estimated that one job in the core tourism industry creates about 1.5 additional or indirect jobs in related industries (UNCTAD 2013). Moreover, tourism is a people-driven industry and has the potential to absorb a high number of semi-skilled and even unskilled workers (Saner et al. 2015).

However, the prevalence of informal or shadow economy in tourism may lead to a halt in the industry's development (Smith 2011), through a number of mechanisms, including, but not being limited to the following (Din et al. 2016):

- Distorting competition and progress, by allowing businesses with informal activities and lower operating costs to compete against formal businesses that comply with general and industry regulation, and eventually even drive them out of the market;
- Loss of revenue due to tax evasion, and consequently to a decrease in public investments, with a negative impact on the development and maintenance of infrastructure (including public utilities, transport services, tourism information services etc.);
- Avoiding labour and health regulations, which leads to businesses using untrained staff, working in inappropriate conditions and without social security.
- Therefore, informal economy in tourism may be regarded as deteriorating to all stakeholders in the sector, including customers, employees, companies, and governmental bodies (Kesar and Čuić 2017).

Ultimately, informal economy may lead to a decrease in the quality of tourism services and to the deterioration of the overall image of tourism destinations (Pavičević 2014, in Badariah et al. 2015). Although data regarding the impact of the shadow economy on tourism development is still scarce, there is empirical evidence supporting a better mitigation of uncontrolled informal activities. Thus, a study by Din et al. (2016) using data on 149 countries for the period 1995–2008 indicates a positive correlation between tourism receipts and several governance indicators, such as regulatory quality and control of corruption. Hence, it may be assumed that a better enforcement of regulations leads to a decrease in the shadow economy and in the long run to an increase in tourism receipts.

In Romania, the informal sector represents almost one third of the total GDP (Schneider et al. 2015). Tourism is believed to bring a significant contribution to the informal sector, although the actual size and scope of this contribution had not been formally measured or determined. Overall, informality in the Romanian tourism sector stems from two types of activities:

- Un-authorised business activities performed by entities which are either not formally registered as a legal person, or by formal entities which do not hold the authorisations, licenses or certificates required by law for the provision of specific services (e.g. accommodation);
- Official business activities which are not reported or underreported so as to avoid paying taxes.

A series of measures have been taken in 2016 and 2017 against economic operators in order to ensure compliance with the legislation; these included imposing sanctions under the form of fines, suspending the licenses of companies that have undertaken informal activities, and publishing lists of economic operators who do not hold the certificates and licenses required by law (Ministry of Tourism 2016). Therefore, the enforcement policy is focused on control rather than prevention.

The main type of companies targeted by government control measures and sanctions are travel agencies, either retailers or tour-operators, who are required by law to apply for and obtain a specific license (Government of Romania 1999). In the first 10 months of 2017 alone, the Ministry of Tourism suspended the licenses of over 80 travel agencies in Romania (Buican 2017). Moreover, the sanctions applicable to travel agencies operating without a license or whose insurance policy had expired, increased after a change in the legislation regulating the sale of tourism services (Government of Romania 2017). Furthermore, starting with 2017, travel agencies are required to regularly report information to the Ministry of Tourism regarding their commercial activity (e.g. no. of contracts, total value of contracts, no. of cancelled contracts) so as to allow a more closely monitoring of the industry.

However, travel agencies are not the only tourism operators practicing informal activities. Informality also affects other actors in the tourism supply chain, such as tour guides or accommodation providers. In fact, according to the president of the National Association of Travel Agencies (2016), over 20% of all accommodation services available at the Romanian sea-side are sold 'underground'.

One determinant of un-authorised business activities is the cost of obtaining authorisation, licenses and certifications, which act as an entry barrier, especially for SMEs. Thus, obtaining a license by a travel agency is dependent on holding an insurance for insolvency, whose costs are sometimes difficult to cover by new entrants. Moreover, accommodation structures are legally bound to hold a classification certificate issued by the Ministry of Tourism, which is dependent on complying with a series of norms regarding amenities and services provided by the respective structure (National Tourism Authority 2013). However, an interview-based research carried out by Răvar (2015), indicated that economic operators in the tourism industry tend to believe that some of these norms are restrictive, since they oblige accommodation structures to make investments which bring little value added to the final consumer (e.g. ensuring a television set in common spaces for bed and breakfast facilities). Last but not least, tourism operators incur significant costs with the training and certification of professionals employed on certain positions (e.g. managers of travel agencies, travel guides), since the current legislation does not allow for the recognition and validation of skills obtained through informal education or on-the-job training.

The interview-based research conducted by Răvar (2015) also revealed that, in some cases, external funding available for business creation and development acts as an incentive to formalise previous informal activities carried out by entrepreneurs in the tourism sector. This is largely due to the fact that externally-financed projects in general, and EU-funded projects in particular, provide entities (physical and legal persons) with the funding necessary to obtain authorisation, licenses and certifications, which they would have otherwise been unable to obtain due to lack of financial resources. On the other hand, the implementation of EU-funded projects implies a tighter control of activities and budget execution by the relevant public authorities,

**Table 1** Measures financed from European structural and investment funds in tourism and tourism-related sectors

| 2007–2013 financial exercise | 2014–2020 financial exercise |
|---|---|
| • Regional Operational Programme (REGIO), financed under ERDF:<br>– Rehabilitation of cultural heritage sites<br>– Creation, development and modernization of tourism infrastructure<br>– Promotion of the tourism potential and development of the destination management/ marketing infrastructure<br>• Human Resource Development Sectorial Operational Programme, financed under the ESF:<br>– Romania Start-Up *(creation and development of start-ups in high value-added industries, such as creative industries and tourism)*<br>• National Programme for Rural Development, financed under EARDF:<br>– Development of tourism activities *(investments in tourism accommodation, entertainment activities and information facilities in the rural area)* | • Regional Operational Programme (POR), financed under ERDF:<br>– Rehabilitation of cultural heritage sites<br>– Diversifying local economies through the sustainable development of tourism<br>• Human Capital Operational Programme, financed under the ESF:<br>– Romania Start-Up Plus *(creation and development of start-ups—not limited to the tourism industry)*<br>– Diaspora Start-Up *(creation and development of start-ups by Romanians formerly living/working abroad—not limited to the tourism industry)*<br>• National Programme for Rural Development, financed under EARDF:<br>– Support for the creation of non-agricultural activities in the rural area<br>– Support for investments in the creation and development in non-agricultural activities |

not only during the project's implementation, but also during the project's sustainability period.

The main source of European financing for investment projects in the tourism sector is the European Regional Development Fund (ERDF), which finances, on one hand, infrastructure projects—including tourism infrastructure projects—with the aim of reducing development differences among EU regions and states, and on the other hand supports direct investments in private companies, particularly in SMEs (Jaliu and Răvar 2012). In Romania, there have been a number of financing measures funded through the European Regional Development Fund, but also under the European Social Fund or the European Agricultural and Rural Development Fund, supporting investments in tourism or in tourism-related areas, such as the rehabilitation of the natural or/and cultural heritage, both in the 2007–2013, as well as in the 2014–2020 financial exercises. As revealed in Table 1, while some measures target exclusively tourism and tourism-related investments, others support the overall development of infrastructure or the economy, financing investments in various sectors, including but not being limited to tourism.

Other financing sources for projects in the field of tourism or in related industries/ fields include the European Economic Area (EEA) programmes (e.g. the "Conservation and Rehabilitation of the Natural and Cultural Heritage" Programme), the Swiss-Romanian Cooperation Mechanism (previous projects funded under this programme include, for example, the creation of bicycle trails), and national funding schemes for SMEs (e.g. Start-Up Nation national programme).

An analysis of the implementation of the Regional Operational Programme 2007–2013 in Romania showed that, the contracting rate for the priority axis dedicated to tourism development and promotion (PA 5—Sustainable development and promotion of tourism) exceeded 90% one year ahead of the end of the financial exercise, which is indicative for a high interest of potential beneficiaries for projects targeting the tourism sector. Still, public entities remain the main beneficiaries of these funds, with 50% of funds assigned through the programme being contracted by local and central public authorities. By contrast, 37% of the allocation was contracted by NGOs, with the rest of 13% being contracted by private for-profit organisations (Jaliu and Răvar 2012).

## 2.1 *Methodology*

The analysis above, reveals that informal activities are indeed present in the tourism sector, although their scale and impact has not been yet determined. One factor that facilitates the emergence and persistence of informal activities in the sector are the perceived entry barriers on the market. Data collected through direct qualitative research, although not representative for the entire population, indicates that the implementation of EU-funded projects may stimulate business owners in the tourism sector to make the necessary investments, in order to comply with existing regulations and thus formalize previously informal business activities. In this respect, the following hypotheses have been formulated:

- H1: Entry barriers for tourism enterprises are perceived as being too high in the formal economy
- H2: EU-funded projects exert a positive impact on decreasing informal economy, by bringing tourism activities from the informal to the formal sector

A qualitative research was conducted, consisting of structured interviews with representatives of organizations (NGOs and SMEs) carrying out tourism-related activities. Overall, 10 interviews were carried out in the first quarter of 2017, five of which with beneficiaries of external funding, and five with non-beneficiaries of external funding. Out of the five subjects representing organisations who had previously implemented externally-funded projects, four were beneficiaries of EU-funding, through the National Programme for Rural Development (two subjects) and the Human Resource Development Sectorial Operational Programme—“Romania Start-Up” (two subjects). Another subject had been a beneficiary of a project financed through the European Economic Area Programme.

The research was exploratory, in the sense that it was not aimed at testing the two hypotheses formulated above, but rather to determine their plausibility and set the basis for further research into the subject.

Overall, the interview guide focused on the following themes/subjects:

- The main behaviours associated to informal economy in tourism;
- The motivations to engage in informal business activities;

- The entrepreneurs' propensity to 'formalise' their activity following the implementation of an externally-funded project;
- The degree to which entrepreneurs who have already benefitted from external funding reduced their informal activities as a result of the project.

A secondary aim of the research was to identify possible characteristics of enterprises carrying out informal activities in Romania, in view of obtaining a better image of the informal sector. A profile of the 'informal entrepreneur' in tourism may be further defined through more comprehensive studies that can provide statistically representative results, and hence would allow policy makers to design more effective measures to regulate and manage informal activities.

The interviews were conducted face-to-face. Judgement sampling was used, the authors contacting individuals with appropriate characteristics required for the sample (person with a decision function in an NGO or for-profit enterprise providing tourism services, formally and/or informally in Romania). The selection of subjects was also facilitated by one of the authors having previous knowledge of entrepreneurs carrying out informal activities in the tourism sector, as a result of a series of interviews conducted in 2015 as part of her PhD research.

## 3 Results and Discussion

The data collected during the interviews were compiled and subsequently coded (i.e. content analysis). All subjects included in the research represent persons with managerial positions in formally-established organisations, either in SMEs or NGOs with economic activity, which provide tourism services: in urban areas (three subjects) or in rural areas (seven subjects). A common characteristic of the organisations is their relatively small size (1–10 employees/permanent collaborators), and the fact that they have been on the market for maximum 5 years. Out of the 10 organisations represented by the subjects, 5 provide guided tours, 3 provide accommodation facilities and dining, and 2 provide more complex services, including accommodation, dining, and guided tours in the surrounding area.

Although engaging in informal activities was not a criterion in the selection of subjects, the data collected from the interviews shows that all investigated entities have engaged to a certain degree in informal activities. Overall, subjects were open to discuss about undeclared activities, but not about underreporting. This is not surprising since the interviewees' responses indicate that undeclared activities are not perceived as being associated with unethical behaviour. Hence, entrepreneurs tend to have a more relaxed view towards undeclared activities as compared to underreporting, the latter being generally associated with tax evasion and widely recognised as an illegal and anti-competitive practice. In fact, the majority of the interviewed subjects expressed their belief that the informal business activities they are currently carrying out represent only a transition stage in the organisation's development process, and that in the long-term such activities will be gradually formalised, authorised and declared. Moreover, informal activities are not viewed as an option or choice of the entrepreneur, but rather as a necessity; according to the answers provided by the subjects, the alternative would be, in most cases, to go out of business.

The data collected through the interviews shows that in all investigated cases, informality stems from providing services without holding the licenses and certificates required by law or by holding only some of these licenses/certificates. Thus, only two of the entities organising guided tours hold a license issued by the Ministry of Tourism (alternatively, by the National Tourism Authority for licenses issued prior to 2017). Out of the two organisations holding a license, only one had a tour-operator license, while the other one held a license valid only for retail travel agencies (although the services it provides are typical to tour-operators). Furthermore, only two of the subjects providing guided tours worked with certified tour guides. Four of the organisations providing accommodation and dining services only held a classification certificate for bed and breakfast, despite also providing other meals, either on request or on a regular basis. In fact, one of these facilities is actually well-known in the local market for its fine cuisine and for organising banquets. Another organisation was, at the time of the interview, in the process of obtaining the classification certificate as a bed and breakfast facility; however, the subject acknowledged that the facility provided accommodation services for several months prior to applying for the classification certificate.

The interviews revealed that the most common informal activities carried out by the subjects' organisations include:

- Organising guided tours without holding a tour-operator license;
- Organising guided tours by entities that only hold a license for retail travel agencies;
- Providing accommodation in spaces that are not yet authorised as accommodation facilities;
- Providing lunch and dinner in spaces that are only authorised as bed and breakfast facilities;
- Working with personnel that does not hold a certificate for performing certain activities (e.g. tour guides).

With regard to the motivations for engaging in informal activities, the majority of subjects providing guided tours cited the lack of financial resources necessary for covering the expenses related to the authorisation process (i.e. the insolvency insurance required for obtaining the tour-operator license). Moreover, since the guided tours organised by the studied entities are only provided on a seasonal basis, for a limited number of customers, the costs are disproportionate in relation to the relatively small scale of activities performed. A similar motivation was expressed by the representatives of bed and breakfast facilities. Thus, since some services (organising lunches and dinners for small groups, organising banquets for private and corporate events) are only provided on occasional basis, the subjects' perception was that the costs incurred by obtaining the necessary authorisations/

classification certificates are substantially higher than the benefits. Moreover, the entrepreneurs felt that holding a classification certificate for a restaurant facility (instead of a facility offering solely breakfast) would oblige them to comply with even more regulations, e.g. by preventing them from sourcing food products from local, small-scale producers.

The interviewees, also mentioned difficulties related to finding qualified personnel (e.g. certified tour guides) and higher costs associated to employing such personnel as being among the motives behind engaging in undeclared activities. According to the subjects, most small-scale providers of tourism services prefer to work with people from the local community, who have an extensive knowledge of the area and its resources despite not holding a certification.

The data collected through the interviews also show that the subjects' organisations are often confronted with bureaucracy and a lack of understanding of the legal framework. These factors have been associated particularly with the activity of NGOs. According to one representative of an NGO providing cultural tours, in order to obtain the tourism license, the organisation needs to bring modifications to its statute, which takes a significant amount of time and requires significant expenses (e.g. with lawyer fees). Moreover, the legislation regulating the provision of tourism services by NGOs is perceived as vague and organisations lacking legal expertise have difficulties in interpreting it. The fact that the current legislation does not allow for the validation of competences obtained through non-formal education or on-the-job training was also mentioned as a factor hindering the formalisation of activities. Hence, persons that already have extensive practical experience in the field are still required to attend the same courses as those without prior experience; there is no possibility to take an exam for the validation of competences (e.g. for tour guides).

Last but not least, according to the interview subjects, the seasonal character of tourism activities and the relatively high fixed costs incurred by organizations often force them to cut down on administrative and legal costs, even if this means not being compliant with the legal provisions. In other words, not formalising one's activity is in some cases a survival strategy for many organisations, especially for those whose activity is small-scale and seasonal.

The perception of subjects representing entities that have not yet benefitted from external funding is that EU-funded projects indeed represent an incentive for them to authorise and declare previous informal activities. In fact, two of the subjects interviewed expressed their intention to apply for EU funding explicitly for the development and formalisation/authorisation of some activities which they are already providing informally.

The interviews revealed that the implementation of externally-funded projects did determine changes in what regard the 'formalisation' of project beneficiaries' activity. Out of the five organisations which have benefitted from funding, two provide guided tours, while the other three are bed and breakfast facilities; all five provided these services informally prior to their projects' implementation. The two entities offering guided tours both obtained a tourism license as a result of the project's implementation (as costs with the insurance policy were covered through the project). Still, only one of these organisations was working with certified tour guides at the time of the interview. Moreover, all three accommodation facilities obtained their classification certificate after having implemented a project financed from structural funds or under the EEA mechanism. However, all three are only authorised for bed and breakfast, although they occasionally provide other services for which they still do not hold authorisation (guided tours in the proximity of the facility, lunches and dinners).

## 4 Limits and Conclusions

The results of the research are particularly relevant for undeclared work, but the analysis does not tackle the issue of underreporting, which remains an important component of the informal economy. Moreover, since the research was strictly interview-based, the results reflect the subjective opinions and beliefs of a limited number of subjects. For a higher relevance of results, the qualitative research should be followed by quantitative research based on a statistically representative sample of respondents. Although all the subjects interviewed had previously engaged in some kind of informal activity, one cannot generalise by concluding that tourism enterprises in Romania are all characterised by this level of informality. For example, the tour-operators interviewed are small organisations, which provide guided tours in small communities, and their activity is largely seasonal; it is hard to believe that informal activities are as prevalent in larger organisations with more and better resources at their disposal.

Our research indicates that obtaining the licenses and certificates required by law and employing certified personnel, both represent major issues in the transition from informal to formal economy in the tourism sector. As initially presumed, the subjects taking part in the research generally believe that the costs of formalisation often exceed the benefits, and that the entry barriers on the formal market are particularly high for small organisations. Overall, results indicate that EU funding does exert an impact on the reduction of informal economy in tourism, providing incentives and resources for obtaining authorisation/certification. However, externally funded projects are not sufficient to ensure compliance with the current legal framework; although the analysed organisations did formalise part of the previous informal activities, they continued to provide other services informally. Other measures, such as fiscal incentives for SMEs and NGOs, simplification of the legal framework or reduction of bureaucracy in the authorisation process may be needed to ensure long-term compliance.

## References

AT Kearney. (2013). *The shadow economy in Europe, 2013*. Available at https://www.atkearney.com/documents/10192/1743816/The+Shadow+Economy+in+Europe+2013.pdf

Badariah, H. D., Habibullah, M. S., & Baharom, A. H. (2015). Does the shadow economy matter for tourism? International evidence. *Taylor's Business Review, 5*(1), 1–9.

Boyd, T. (2017). The informal economy in developing nations: A hidden engine of growth. *WIPO Magazine, 3*, 30–36.

Brown, D., & McGranahan, G. (2016). The urban informal economy, local inclusion and achieving a global green transformation. *Habitat International, 53*, 97–105.

Buican, A. (2017). *Statements of the Minister of Tourism regarding amendments of government ordinance regulating the sale of tourism services packages*. Available at http://www.capital.ro/dobre-agentiile-de-turism-nu-vor-mai-putea-vinde-pachete-turistice-mai-devreme-de-12-luni-de-la-data-plecarii.html

Chen, M. A. (2016). The informal economy: Recent trends, future directions. *New Solutions, 26*(2), 155–172.

Dao Truong, V. (2017). Tourism, poverty alleviation, and the informal economy: The street vendors of Hanoi, Vietnam. *Tourism Recreation Research, 43*(1), 52–67.

Din, B. H., Habibullah, M. S., Baharom, A. H., & Saari, M. D. (2016). Are shadow economy and tourism related? International evidence. *Procedia Economics and Finance, 35*, 173–178.

European Commission. (2010). *Annex A to the Proposal for a Regulation of the European Parliament and of the Council on the European System of national and regional accounts in the European Union*. Available at http://ec.europa.eu/transparency/regdoc/rep/1/2010/EN/1-2010-774-EN-F1-11-ANNEX-8.Pdf

European Commission. (2017). *Informal economy*. Available at https://ec.europa.eu/europeaid/sectors/human-development/social-inclusion/informal-economy_en

EY. (2016). *Reducing the shadow economy through electronic payments*. Available at www.ey.com/Publication/vwLUAssets/Report_Shadow_Economy/$FILE/REPORT_ShadowEconomy_FINAL_17.pdf

Farrel, D. (2004). The hidden dangers of the informal economy. *McKinsey Quarterly*. Available at https://www.mckinsey.com/global-themes/employment-and-growth/the-hidden-dangers-of-the-informal-economy

Government of Romania. (1999). *Government ordinance no. 107/1999 regulating the sale of tourism service packages*.

Government of Romania. (2017). *Ordinance no. 26/2017 for changing government ordinance no. 107/1999 regulating the sale of tourism service packages*.

International Institute for Environment and Development – IIED. (2017). *The informal economy and sustainable development*. Available at www.iied.org/informal-economy-sustainable-development

International Labour Organization. (2015). *Recommendation no. 204 concerning the transition from the informal to the formal economy: Text of the recommendation adopted by the conference at its 104th session in Geneva, on 12 June 2015*. Available at http://www.ilo.org/ilc/ILCSessions/104/texts-adopted/WCMS_377774/lang--en/index.htm

Jaliu, D. D., & Răvar, A. S. (2012). *Consideration on the financing of tourism development and promotion strategies in Romania*. "Ovidius" University Annals, Economic Sciences Series, Volume XII, Special Issue, pp. 87–92.

Keen. (2015). Why we need to rethink the informal economy. *World Economic Forum*. Available at https://www.weforum.org/agenda/2015/06/why-we-need-to-rethink-the-informal-economy

Kesar, O., & Čuić, K. (2017). Shadow economy in tourism: Some conceptual considerations from Croatia. *Zagreb International Review of Economics and Business, 20*(2), 65–86.

Ministry of Tourism in Romania. (2016). *List of travel agencies whose license has been suspended at their own request or by decision of the Ministry*. Available at http://turism.gov.ro/autorizare-turism/lista-agentiilor-de-tur-cu-licenta-radiata-la-cerere-sau-retrasa-2016/

Mitchell, J. (2010). *An unconventional but essential marriage: Pro-poor tourism and the mainstream industry*. London: Overseas Development Institute.

National Tourism Authority in Romania. (2013). *Order of the President of the National Tourism Authority no. 65/2015 for approving the methodological norms for the issue of classification certificates of tourism accommodation facilities and public eating establishment, of tourism licensed and tourism certificates*. Available at http://turism.gov.ro/wp-content/uploads/2013/05/Ordin1.pdf

Neuwirth, R. (2012). How the informal economy could help save the rest of it. *Harvard Business Review*. Available at https://hbr.org/2012/01/the-candy-man-in-america

President of the National Association of Travel Agencies. (2016). *Approximately 30.000 tourists are accommodated underground on the sea-side*. Press declarations. Available at http://adevarul.ro/economie/stiri-economice/aproximativ-30000-turisti-cazati-negru-litoral-1_57b1b2d05ab6550cb8c7ca38/index.html

Răvar, A. (2015). *Innovation and creativity in the sustainable development of cultural tourism destinations*. PhD thesis. Bucharest University of Economic Studies.

Rogerson, C. M. (2014). Informal sector business tourism and pro-poor tourism: Africa's migrant entrepreneurs. *Mediterranean Journal of Social Sciences, 5*(16), 153–161.

Saner, R., Yiu, L., & Filadoro, M. (2015). Tourism development in least developed countries: Challenges and opportunities. In A. A. Camillo (Ed.), *Handbook of research on global hospitality and tourism management* (pp. 234–261). Hershey: IGI Global.

Schneider, F., Rackowski, K., & Mroz, B. (2015). Shadow economy and tax evasion in the EU. *Journal of Money Laundering Control, 18*(1), 34–51.

Sinha, A., & Kanbur, R. (2012). Introduction: Informality—Concepts, facts and models. *Margin: The Journal of Applied Economic Research, 6*, 91–102.

Smith, A. (2011). Obstacles to the growth of alternative tourism in Greece. *African Journal of Hospitality, Tourism and Leisure, 1*(3), 1–8.

United Nations Conference on Trade and Development. (2013). *Sustainable tourism: Contribution to economic growth and sustainable development: Issues note prepared by the UNCTAD secretariat*. Available at http://unctad.org/meetings/en/SessionalDocuments/ciem5d2_en.pdf

Vanek, J., Chen, M., Heintz, J., & Hussmanns, R. (2014). *Statistics on the informal economy: Definitions, regional estimates and challenges. Women in informal employment*. Cambridge, MA: Globalizing and Organizing.

Williams, C. (2013). Tackling Europe's informal economy: A critical evaluation of the neo-liberal de-regulatory perspective. *Journal of Contemporary European Research, 9*(2), 261–278.

World Tourism Organization (UNWTO) and International Labour Organization. (2014). *Measuring employment in the tourism industries – Guide with best practices*. Available at https://www.e-unwto.org/doi/pdf/10.18111/9789284416158

World Travel and Tourism Council. (2017). *Travel and tourism: Economic impact 2017*. Available at www.wttc.org/-/media/files/reports/economic-impact-research/regions-2017/world2017.pdf

# Tourism in 'Yellow Times': The De-formalisation of the Greek Economy and Its Impact on Tourism

**Stavros Katsios**

## 1 Introduction

While over the last decades public and private entities worldwide have taken initiatives. or were forced to take measures, to combat economic crime (like corruption) as a real and acute threat to the national economies and democratic institutions, the current economic crisis, and particularly in countries more severely hit, like Greece, has taken priority over compliance and implementation needs in the sense of consistent application of regulations and norms. It's a development, which jeopardizes the prospect for economic and social inclusiveness in an environment having the potential to annotate the development goals urgently needed for economic recovery particularly in times of economic uncertainty and instability. In that framework, one of the most important challenges faced by national economic systems is the problem "unreported economic activities" (UEA), "informal economic activities" (IEA), the "informal economy" (IE), "underground economy" (UE) or "shadow economy" (SE). The "informal economy" consists of criminal activity, such as drug sales, smuggling, prostitution, bookmaking, gambling and other unlawful enterprises, as well as otherwise legal transactions that are mainly conducted in cash and unreported to fiscal or other competent authorities; this part of the shadow economy is also known as the "parallel economy". The level of the informal economy is indicative for the degree to which the economy is formalised, and to whether there is a significant level of informal economic activity in the country. Because of various conditions in a country, including low regulatory and law enforcement capacity, limited economic regulation or overregulation, high levels of social exclusion, and/or tax considerations, some economic activities may remain or become unregistered and informal. Such activities may, or may not, be illegal in their own right. Generally, no records are kept of informal economic activities, making it difficult

S. Katsios (✉)
Geolab Institute, Ionian University, Corfu, Greece
e-mail: skatsios@ionio.gr



A. Papathanassis et al. (eds.), *Yellow Tourism*, Tourism, Hospitality & Event Management, https://doi.org/10.1007/978-3-319-94664-1_13

for law enforcement authorities to access transaction and client information. Informal/unregistered economic activities pose challenges for law enforcement agencies when they investigate and attempt to prosecute economic offenses and trace proceeds of crime. The larger the informal economy, the lower the level of formalisation of the economy. Regarding the tourism industry as part of the wider service sector it is obvious that, the international tourism community's systematic efforts during the past decade has contributed in increasing awareness of corruption and other financial crimes, providing an effective legal framework for combating it.

Given its significance for national economies, for both corporations and national/local governments, tourism is especially vulnerable to crime and simultaneously providing a battleground for possible responses to it. Accordingly, the conceptual interplay between tourism and illicit revenues focuses on 'risk' and security following the growing tendency for contemporary social life to be organised around attempts to predict and prevent future threats and harms, rather than simply to detect and punish past wrongs. Risk in the context of tourism is clearly of primary concern, with a focus upon effective risk management, exploring the role of the tourism-crime nexus in researching the ways in which 'risk' "regulates" the organisation of contemporary economic and social life; such an approach has primarily to do with the problem of the availability of reliable data on corruption. Corruption is part of everyday life, and not only of the everyday life in bureaucracies, but also of the one in institutions, in groups, in human relations in general, regardless whether these are public or private. It is a phenomenon emerging, whenever formal or informal networks are formed. Corruption arises independently of whether these networks are embedded in a definite organisational culture, in various administrative systems, in weak or strong state structures or in transnational organisations and businesses (Haler and Shore 2005).

## 2 Tourism Industry as an Economic and Social Incubator

During the last two decades the tourism industry has developed to becoming one of the most important attributors to the economic growth and development of many countries across the planet. In 2006, international tourism generated over USD 682.7 billion in revenue (compared to only USD2.1 billion in 1950). In 2017, international tourism outpaced the global economy (for the seventh successive year) with a direct growth of 4.6%, making up 10.4% of the global total GDP (USD8272.3 billion), 9.8% of total employment (313,221,000 jobs), 6.5% of world exports, 4.5% of world investment (USD882.4 billion) and visitor exports generated USD1494.2 billion (6.5% of total exports globally). In 2018, this is expected to grow by 3.9%, and the world is expected to attract 1,395,660,000 international tourist arrivals. By 2028, international tourist arrivals are forecasted to a total of 2,094,210,000 generating expenditure of USD2311.4 billion, an increase of 4.1% pa.

Europe had a particularly strong year in 2017 with arrival numbers rising by 8.0%, buoyed by strong growth in Southern European Mediterranean destinations, which enjoyed particularly strong visitor exports growth in 2017 after declines in recent years, including Greece (9.5%), Italy (6.5%), Portugal (16.3%) and Spain (10.3%). In 2017, the long-haul segment of demand recovered strongly and was accompanied by robust inter-regional travel, thanks to the strength of the European economy. In 2016 Greek tourism made up 18.6% of the country's total GDP, 23.4% of total employment (860,315), with a market share of 2% of the total global tourism market and 3.1% of the European tourism market (WTTC 2018).[1] According to the Bank of Greece (2016), Greek tourism revenues (cruises not included) amounted a total of 12.7 billion euros.

Due to the expansion of the tourism industry and the growing dependence of many countries on tourism as a major source of investment and revenue, it is essential to assess the environment regarding the threats and the vulnerabilities of a competitive tourism industry. Such an environment has a lot to do with the formalisation of the economy, meaning the degree to which the economy is formalised and whether there is significant level of informal economic activity in the country. Due to its inter-sectoral character, the economic impact of tourism goes beyond businesses that directly provide tourists with services and products, involving a number of diverse tourism-related industries as well. The tourism value chain incorporates many sectors of the economy through both the backward and forward linkages. Tourism depends on the development of basic infrastructural services such as energy, telecommunications and environmental services; agriculture, manufacturing and other support services; and the tourists require services from the financial, telecommunications, retail, recreational, cultural, personal, hospitality, security and health services, among others (UNEP 2013). Nevertheless, the prevalence of the informal economy can be an obstacle that can limit and disrupt the development of the tourism industry, as a part of the wider service sector. Such complex and highly fragmented economic structure, in which the provision of services significantly prevails, triggers the emergence of the informal economy, with all its positive and negative implications (Kesar and Čuić 2017).

## 3 Tourism, Crime and the Informal Economy

In general, tourism competitiveness is determined by the relationship between the country's tourism environment and its overall business environment. Accordingly, the degree to which corruption plays a role in the business and economic environment has yet to be considered as a relevant determinant of tourism competitiveness. Tanzi (1998) defines corrupt practices as activities that are considered to be illegal, unethical and dishonest business practices carried out by a bureaucracy or by political leadership, and Transparency International (2018) defines corruption as the 'misuse of entrusted power for private gain'. Undoubtedly, corruption is one of

[1] All values are in constant 2017 prices and exchange rates.

the greatest obstacles in economic and social development, as it weakens the institutional foundations of nations, distorts the rule of law and erodes trust amongst its citizens, and pollutes the social and cultural image of a country (World Bank 2008). Furthermore, corruption affects a country's business and economic conditions negatively and hampers its ability to compete in the global economy (Kehoe 1998; Lambsdorff 2003). Given that corruption plays a significant role in creating and defining a country's business and economic environment, as well as its overall image, it is logical to conclude that the level of corruption present in a country will affect its tourism competitiveness (Das and DiRienzo 2010).

The broad definition of the informal economy would include both legal and illegal market activities, monetary and non-monetary transactions, which are not included in the calculation of the gross domestic product. Studies have indicated that the existence of the shadow economy has been a major obstacle for the development of the tourism sector. Terrorism, organised crime, illegal market activities, have all been linked to the informal economy (Schneider and Enste 2000). Shadow economic activities have been associated with tourism-related activities and facilities such as: wholesale and retail, hotels and restaurants, transportation and communication industries. Schneider (2013) reports that in Turkey, Spain, Italy, Greece Germany and Poland; the shadow economy comprises 25–35% of the tourism-related industries—wholesale and retail, hotels and restaurants, transportation and communication industries. On the other hand, the shadow economy in the Greek tourism sector is 22% of the official economy (Schneider 2009). On another note, organised crime also plays a part in the tourism industry; tourism is appealing to organised crime, offering low and medium-risk opportunities to invest illegally-gained money into hotels and other tourism related facilities and activities (Badariah H. Din et al. 2016). Thus, investing criminal proceeds into tourist infrastructure and services is one method to launder illicit funds.

As pointed out by Webb et al. (2013), the informal economy affects competition and progress in the tourism sector.

- Loss of revenue due to tax evasion: is prevalent in the informal economy and funds cannot be injected back into the tourism sector, impairing the industry's growth potential and development.
- Avoiding labour, health and environmental regulations: untrained staff without any social security and with working conditions that do not follow any health and safety regulations.
- Using harmful fuels, chemicals and other raw materials: creating negative externalities to the environment and local communities.
- Unfair competition: due to tax evading activities, potentially affecting serious businesses' possibilities to stay on the right side of the law and consequently the tax morale in the industry and in the country.

Furthermore, less investment and new talent could then speed up the downward spiral of the tourism industry (Armbrecht and Carback 2011).

In Greece, as the result of various conditions including low regulatory and law enforcement capacity, high levels of social exclusion, and/or tax considerations, some economic activities may remain or become unregistered and informal. Such activities may, or may not, be illegal in their own accord. Generally, records of informal economic activities are not kept, rendering it difficult for law enforcement authorities to access transaction and client information. Informal/unregistered economic activities pose challenges for law enforcement agencies when they investigate and attempt to prosecute tax offenses and trace proceeds of crime. As in every industry, the global competitiveness is a critical determinant on how well the sector performs and of its resulting global market share. Consequently, the factors that drive an industry's competitiveness directly affect the overall (Greek) tourism performance.

As the number of tourist arrivals is affected by the level of safety and security of the destination countries, developing countries and particularly the least developed countries suffer from law and order problems and pose therefore a risk to potential tourists (Moyo and Ziramba 2013). Countries with high crime rates, terrorism and combat incidents, human rights violations and a bad heritage management record, will be visited by fewer foreign visitors. These consequences can prove devastating for the local societies as the majority of tourism-related business in developing countries, particularly in least developed countries (LDCs), tends to be small, medium-sized and micro enterprises, many of which are operating in the informal economy (UNCTAD Secretariat 2013). Beside the national (internal) economic and social factors influencing the size and impacts of the informal economy, these issues are magnified with the explosion of international free trade and economic integrations throughout the world, which call for international harmonisation and the introduction of strategic global law enforcement policies to combat them (Katsios 2006).

## 4 Level of Formalisation of the Greek Economy

The informal economy consists of criminal activity, such as drug sales, smuggling, prostitution, bookmaking, gambling and other unlawful enterprises, as well as otherwise legal transactions that are mainly conducted in cash and unreported to fiscal or other authorities. This part of the shadow economy is also known as the "parallel economy" or, in a pragmatic approach to the question of definitions, as simply "unreported economic activities".

The level of the informal economy in Greece is linked to the underground economic activities, which are generated by the determinants of the economy, the tax and national insurance burdens and the intensity of the relevant national regulations. Greece shows profound signs of a transition country in terms of the high levels of regulation, leading to a high incidence of bribery and a large shadow economy. In these terms, the informal economy is the total value of transactions by businesses and individuals occurring 'off the books'. In other words, this could be anything from paying a tradesman or a babysitter in undeclared cash to the illegal wildlife trade, counterfeiting and money laundering.[2] Consequently the informal economy, defined as all 'off-the-books' and unregulated activity, is considered as one of the main negative effects derived from the serious structural problems of the Greek economy. "Economic activities, whether legal or illegal, which are required by law to be fully reported to the tax administration but which are not reported and which therefore go untaxed unlike activities which are so reported" (OECD 2017).

While the informal economy is a long-standing problem, over the last decade Greek tax administrations have strengthened their efforts to identify and tackle its different aspects with some success. Though consideration was taken till today to the 2012 Information Note (OECD 2012) stressing the importance of tax administrations having multi-faceted strategies covering a wide range of informal economic activity, the informal economy in Greece is constantly changing and adapting to recent changes in ways of working and business models. The growth of the digital economy and wider social changes are facilitating a new informal economy. In turn, this can create new societal problems and potentially further undermine tax compliance.

The gross domestic product (GDP) measures of national income and output for a given country's economy. The gross domestic product (GDP) is equal to the total expenditures for all final goods and services produced within the country in a stipulated period of time. Untaxed and unrecorded economic activity boomed during the global financial crisis and sustained a significant growth until today. Greek GDP actual data, historical chart and calendar of releases, were last updated in October 2017. The Gross Domestic Product (GDP) of Greece was worth USD194.56 billion in 2016. The GDP value of Greece represents 0.31% of the world economy. GDP in Greece averaged USD110.34 billion from 1960 until 2016, reaching an all-time high of USD354.46 billion in 2008 and a record low of USD4.45 billion in 1960.

The severe economic crisis beginning in 2008 led the Greek economy to a prolonged recession. The informal economy although a reality for all the countries, finds its manifestation in the economies of Greece, Portugal, Italy and Spain, which were unable to refinance their government debt or to bail out over-indebted banks on their own during the recent global debt crisis. The estimates of the size of the informal economy are based on a combination of the cash (currency/demand) approach with the Multiple Indicators Multiple Causes (MIMIC) method (Schneider and Enste 2013; Schneider et al. 2011; Dell'Anno et al. 2006). The German IAW in Tubingen argues that among the OECD countries, Greece was holding the first place in terms of the level of its underground economy in 2015, reaching the impressive 22.4% of GDP, namely almost one quarter of the Greek economic activity. Italy followed closely with 20.1% while the Spanish black economy is 18.2% and the Portuguese 17.6%.

According to recent estimates (Schneider 2013), prolonged economic crisis in Greece has somehow reduced the phenomenon of the informal economy, and more

---

[2]Although a number of scholars exclude activities like money laundering from the informal economy filed.

specifically, the recession in the formal economy is so strong and also reductions in the income of citizens so great, having vertically further decrease even the demand for the activities of the informal work (e.g. house-keepers etc.). As a result, the informal sector in Greece has declined substantially, accounting in 2013 for 23.6% of the GDP, compared to 24% in 2012, 25.1% in the pre-crisis 2007 and 28.2% in 2003. Meanwhile, the fight against tax evasion in Greece has begun, to some extent, paying off. More specifically, the amount of tax evasion related to indirect taxes and self-employment in Greece decreased to 4% of GDP in 2010 from 5.6% in 2009. In the years 2012 and 2013, the informal economy has decreased in most of the 38 countries of the OECD, compared to 2008. However, contrary to other countries, the reason of the reduction in Greece was the prolonged economic crisis and not a structural change.

Concerning the most critical factors that matter the most to the creation of the informal economy in 38 OECD countries for the period 1999–2010, indirect taxation ranks first (average 29.4%) and self-employment second (22.2%), while in Greece this figure is reversed. Specifically, in Greece self-employment plays by far the most crucial role in the size and growth of the informal economy (37.6%), followed by indirect taxation (21.8%). In Greece, among the 38 countries of the OECD, unemployment ranks third in the list of factors with the greatest impact on the size and growth of the informal economy, with a share 'contribution' of 18%, due to the fact that lack of work often incites the unemployed towards informal economic activity as to ensure their living. In Greece, the most affected country by the crisis in the Eurozone, illegal activity accounts for over 20% of national income (IAW 2017).

Overall, Greece ranked high among the 27 EU Member States, in terms of the informal economy, significantly exceeding the EU average. According to Schneider (2013), the breakdown of the informal economy into economic and service sectors in Greece shows that the largest shadow economy sector is tourism (service sector incl. hotels, restaurants, catering, etc.) with 22% and a size of 14.19 billion euros (National Statistical Service of Greece 2017),[3] followed by the entertainment and leisure sector of 21% a value of 13.55 billion euros in 2008/2009. Then the household shadow economy sector has a magnitude of 18% (out of 100% total shadow economy) and a value of 11.61 billion euros (Fig. 1).

GDP in the Euro Area went up to USD11,885.66 billion in 2016 from USD11,616.14 billion in 2015. Greek GDP declined to USD194.56 billion in 2016 from USD194.86 billion in 2015. The Current Account to GDP in the Euro Area went up to 3.3% in 2016 from 3.2% in 2015. Greece's Current Account to GDP

[3]GDP from Services in Greece increased to 9663.65 million euros in the second quarter of 2017 from 7545.09 million euros in the first quarter of 2017. GDP from Services in Greece averaged 10,937.84 million euros from 1995 until 2017, reaching an all-time high of 17,098.90 million euros in the third quarter of 2008 and a record low of 6942.63 million euros in the first quarter of 1995. Labour costs in Greece increased to 89.50 Index Points in the second quarter of 2017 from 88.80 Index Points in the first quarter of 2017. Labour costs in Greece averaged 80.38 Index Points from 1995 until 2017, reaching an all-time high of 107.40 Index Points in the fourth quarter of 2009 and a record low of 48.50 Index Points in the first quarter of 1995.

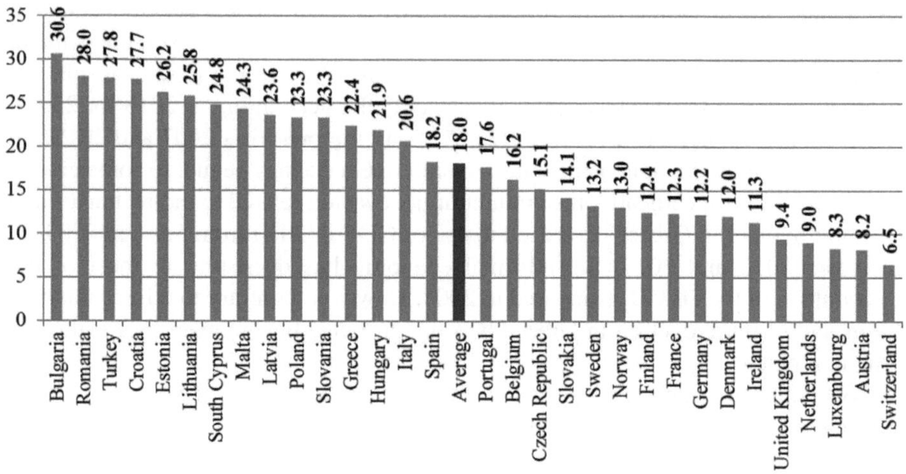


**Fig. 1** Size of the informal economy of 31 European Countries in 2015 (in % of GDP). Source: Schneider (2015)

declined to −0.6% in 2016 from 0.1% in 2015. The GDP Annual Growth Rate in the Euro Area went up to 2.3% in Q2 2017 from 2% in Q1 2017. Greece's GDP Annual Growth Rate rose to 0.8% in Q2 2017 from 0.4% in Q1 2017. GDP Growth Rate in the Euro Area went up to 0.6% in Q2 2017 from 0.5% in Q1 2017. Greece's GDP Growth Rate was reported at 0.5% in Q2 2017 (National Statistical Service of Greece 2017). Unemployment Rate in the Euro Area was last registered at 9.1% in Aug 2017. According to the National Statistical Service of Greece (2017), Greece's Unemployment Rate declined to 21% in July 2017 from 21.3% in June 2017.[4]

From a governmental policy perspective, knowing the size of the informal economy is less important than knowing who is operating there and how. The overall degree of state intervention measured by the number of laws and regulations, including their constant amendments is sufficient, but nevertheless, problematic. In Greece, the laws, reforms and regulations are numerous and often contradicting, which combined with the degree of their intensity, lead Greek citizens straight to the informal economy.[5] Thus, the unemployed are a double burden for the state, as they

[4]Greece unemployed persons rose to 965.98 thousand in July 2017 from 960.96 thousand in June 2017. Greece Employed Persons rose to 3843.19 thousand in July 2017 from 3834.81 thousand in June 2017.

[5]This is directly related to the burden of social security contributions as regulations lead to an increase in labor costs in the formal sector which in turn leads to an increase in unemployment (as occurs in many OECD countries). All of the above provide an incentive for workers to be used in the shadow economy, especially when labor costs are passed on to the same.

continue to receive social benefits and if their activities, undertaken in the informal economy, became official then employers and employees would have paid less tax (Eurostat 2017).[6]

There is a general rule that the greater the number of rules and regulations in an economy, the greater share of total GDP is occupied by the informal sector. Indeed, an increase of government regulations is related with an increase to that share. Therefore, many studies suggest that the Greek government should give more emphasis on the enforcement of laws and regulations rather than increasing their number. It is widely accepted that weak policy enforcement, high taxes, and a preference for informal labor lead to increased participation in informal economic activities and amplify the fluctuations of the official economy in output and consumption.

## 5 Determinants of the Greek Informal Economy

The use of cash can be considered as a decisive factor for the size and sustainability of the Greek informal economy[7] and especially in the tourism branch. According to ECB (2017) study on the use of cash, cards and other payment instruments used at points of sale (POS) by euro area consumers in 2016 in the European Union cash was least used in the Netherlands, Estonia and Finland, where its share in the number of transactions range between 45% and 54%. In terms of value, the share of cash was highest in Greece, Cyprus and Malta (above 70%), while it was lowest in the Benelux countries, Estonia, France and Finland (at, or below, 33%). Furthermore, in some countries, such as Greece and Italy, there are still a considerable number of people below the age of 55 without internet access or who do not use the internet frequently. Thus, internet panels used in these countries do not include this part of the population. Since people with internet access are more likely to adopt new means of payment more quickly, card use in these countries may be over-estimated to some extent.[8] In Cyprus, Malta and Greece the share of cash in value of payments was the highest, ranging from 72% to 75%. In Lithuania, Slovakia, Austria, Spain, Italy and

---

[6]Of course, according to Eurostat the percentage change in real labor cost per unit were −2.9% in 2011, −7.4% in 2012 and −1.1% in 2013. This decrease reflects the significant decline in turnover in almost all sectors of the Greek economy and the existence of significant employment rate in informal or unofficial forms of employment. There was also a reduction in the average gross earnings in the whole economy by 4.6% in 2010, 1.7% in 2011, 6.6% in 2012 and 7.7% in 2013 as the efforts made by the government under the agreed memorandum for the country's exit from the crisis intensify.

[7]By other payment instruments at POS we refer to the use of cheques, direct debit, credit transfers and mobile payments, among others. We have grouped them into one category given their relatively small market share compared with cash and cards. The use of virtual currencies was not within the scope of this study.

[8]Because of the introduction of capital controls in Greece in 2015, it is difficult to compare the relevant payment statistics data with the survey results. In terms of value of payments made at POS, in all countries the share of cash was much lower than in terms of number of payments.

Slovenia the share ranged from 62% to 68%. Italy, Spain and Greece were the countries where consumers made the highest number of cash payments per day, with 1.7 transactions per day, i.e. nearly 12 per week.

The share of cash payments above 100 euros in the total value of cash payments at the POS was 26% in Greece. The use of cash for recurrent payments includes, for some countries, payments made at a POS, which, in other countries, would be typically done via remote payment methods such as credit transfers or direct debits. These are mainly recurrent payments, such as rent, utilities, telephone subscriptions and insurance, but also payments for the home delivery of oil or gas, or medical services. As seen in the following chart, in some countries it is usual to pay these recurrent expenses in cash. On average 26% of all rent in Greece said to be paid in cash.[9] In addition, utility bills were frequently paid in cash—for example, 56% of the respondents in Greece said they paid their electricity bill in cash. Also, 9% of respondents indicated that they paid their taxes mainly in cash and 10% stated that they paid their insurance mainly in cash. Furthermore, on average almost one out of three respondents indicated that they paid their medical bills mainly in cash.

On acquiring cash—referring to any cash withdrawals from an ATM or bank counter during the day of the diary survey or any other cash obtained from other sources, such as from cash reserves at home—17% reported having withdrawn cash or obtained cash from other sources during the day like ATM (39%) or received it from other people such as family, friends or colleagues (19%). In 14% of the cases, respondents used cash reserves kept at home. In 6% of cases the consumers obtained their cash via cashback in a shop,[10] the same result as for bank counter cash withdrawals (6%).

In Greece people do not only hold cash for their purchases, but they also keep cash as a store of value, keeping precautionary cash reserves outside bank accounts. Despite the banking crisis in Greece, resulting to a significant increase of cash withdrawals, on average only 22% of Greek respondents said that they kept cash as a precautionary reserve. Finally, as indicated in the following chart, in Greece, a large share of respondents stated that they prefer using cash to cashless means of payment.

Focusing on the determinants of the Greek economy, the tax and national insurance burdens and the intensity of the relevant regulations in Greece, one might conclude that Greece shows profound signs of a transition country in terms of the high level of regulation leading to a large shadow economy. The taxation problems arising from high administrative-compliance costs and bribery indicate the

---

[9]See L. 446/2016 (A 240) on the obligation for accepting card payments. According to a 2016 survey of Public Issue Agency on behalf of the Hellenic Confederation of Commerce and Entrepreneurship (ESEE) 68% of Greeks use frequently plastic money: 61% use debit cards, 21% use credit cards and 6% prepaid cards.

[10]Cashback is a transaction in which a card-holder asks a retailer to add an amount to the total purchase paid by debit or credit card in order to receive that amount in cash along with the purchase. In 2016 cashback was offered in Belgium, Germany, Estonia, Ireland, Greece, Lithuania, the Netherlands, Austria, Portugal, Slovakia and Finland. In some of these countries it is offered only on a very limited scale.

urgent need for tax reforms designed to simplify the regulation framework. Improvement of the quality of Greek institutions and the rationalisation of administrative-compliance costs are a prerequisite for successful and urgently needed tax reforms in terms of reducing the overall Greek shadow economy, through the simplification of the regulatory framework.

Overall the studies exploring the Greek informal economy[11] during the economic depression era imply that, since it is heavily influenced by economic conditions (unemployment) and policies (fiscal austerity and tax increases), the informal economic activities take place in the sense of economic survival (among others Schneider and Buehn 2012).

The comparatively large size of the informal economy in some high-income countries, such as Greece—whose levels of corruption are also comparatively high according to Transparency International's Corruption Perceptions Index (CPI) (Transparency International 2018)—indicates that the country's income level is not a sufficient indicator of institutional quality. As a result, the effect of corruption on the informal economy should not be linked with a country's income level and ought to be assessed by indicators, which are more representative of institutional quality, such as bureaucratic structures (Echazu and Pinaki 2008). The agents in countries with a large informal economy rely on shadow economic activities and bribe bureaucrats in order to avoid detection. The subsequent decrease in tax revenues reduces the quality of public services, infrastructure, and the incentives to remain in the official economy (Buehn and Schneider 2011). Thus, the relationship between corruption and institutional ineffectiveness is the primary indicator for the existence of a complementary relationship between the size of the informal economy and corruption. In conclusion, not only the shadow economy grows primarily due to weak institutions and rule of law (Singh et al. 2012), but institutional quality is also responsible for the levels of corruption (Dreher et al. 2009). Looking at the estimates regarding the size of the Greek shadow economy, it is important to consider the significance of its determinants. An early study concerning the determinants of tax evasion in Greece concludes that widespread tax evasion is largely due to the historical mistrust between the Greek state and its citizens (Ballas and Tsoukas 1998). Over a decade later, and despite the positive externalities of the euro experience (prior depression), low tax morale, influenced by distrust, both in the government or state institutions and in other taxpayers, remains a major cause for the inability of fiscal authorities to meet the projected tax receipt goals (Kaplanoglou and Rapanos 2013). Taking into account World Bank (2015) and OECD (2015) it seems that it is not the size of the tax burden per se that influences the size of the shadow economy; rather, it is the institutional quality and reciprocity reflected

[11]The first is undeclared work, which accounts for roughly two-thirds of the shadow economy. It includes wages that workers and businesses do not declare to the government to avoid taxes or documentation. Undeclared work is widespread in construction, agriculture, and household services (such as cleaning, babysitting, elderly care, and tutoring). The other one-third comes from underreporting, which is when businesses—primarily those that deal heavily in cash, such as small shops, bars, and taxis—report only part of their income to avoid some of the tax burden.

through the tax burden.[12] Moreover, another dimension of tax morale in Greece, not related to trust in public institutions, is frequently termed by the Greek media as the 'sport of tax evasion', refers to the norm of evading taxes for personal gain, and can be understood as the absence of a 'social norm' of tax compliance (Alm and Torgler 2011).

Tax evasion is a serious cause for large public deficits by provoking lack of financial sources thus, making the state unable to cover its costs. This leads the Greek government to increased external and internal borrowing. The first means less independence and freedom of economic and other options for the country, but also an increase in government debt due to higher interest rates of foreign borrowing. The second is an increase in interest rates in order to attract private capital to meet the public deficit, but this deteriorates the circulation of money in the market and captures large private funds, resulting in the reduction of private investments, which is absolutely necessary for the development of economy. The overall result is economic stagnation and loss of competitiveness, a critical and long lasting drawback of the Greek economy. Even more, tax evasion means creating disparities among citizens, since some professions can evade taxes and some not, which not only creates inequality of the burden on taxpayers, but also taxes become onerous for non-tax evaders because of government revenue lag, which is usually covered by the burden of those who already pay taxes. Another negative consequence of tax evasion is that companies are discouraged from new investments and risk-taking as to increase their profitability, since this can be accomplished much easier by not paying taxes. Tax evasion means wasting resources in unproductive activities as it creates high transaction costs for tax evaders. It also entails high administration and transaction costs for the government, as it has to establish and maintain an effective control mechanism that is essential for purposes of mitigation of tax evasion. On the other hand because of the informal economy, whose main part and cause is tax-evasion, many private incomes remain outside official statistics and calculations as e.g. GDP and are not properly reflected to the real economic situation. Therefore, the governments do not have an accurate picture of the situation and are likely to take wrong decisions in relation to the economy and the creation of revenues, thereby imposing additional burdens on consistent and law-abiding taxpayers. Furthermore, if we take into account that the activities of tax evaders are paid in cash, tax evasion reduces the elasticity of cash demand to changes in public interest rates, which in turn means more difficulties in implementing monetary policy.

[12]Data from OECD (2015) and the World Bank (2015) ("average personal income tax and social security contribution rates on gross labor income for the average wage earner" while "total business tax rate as a percentage of commercial profits") reveal that, although the tax burden in Greece has increased since 2010 (when the first bailout occurred), it is still lower than that of the eurozone's core countries such as France and Germany.

## 6 Deficiencies and Room for Improvement

In sum, the regulation of most West European labor markets and the high tax and social security contribution burdens seem to be the two most important causes of the relatively large informal economy in Greece (like in the most European OECD countries). For the informal economy to exist, the following two conditions must be met:

- those involved in the informal economy must have an incentive in order to decide to take action in this area. In other words, the benefits they expect from expanding their activities in the informal sector have to be larger than the suspected cost of their revelation.
- the adequate opportunities should be provided, i.e. there exist employment opportunities in the informal economy.

From time to time, several measures have been proposed by the Greek governments in order to find appropriate ways to deal with the phenomenon of the informal economy. Some of these propositions are in place, but even more are 'frozen', without a hope to ever be implemented. The most significant of these measures, as well as new ones, are summarised below:

- Incentives for voluntary compliance achieving a gradual reduction of the cost of the tax audit and also violations and irregularities that have been committed will be revealed by the taxpayers themselves;
- Regulations for young entrepreneurs creating a climate of mutual trust with taxpayers and especially with young entrepreneurs who are new comers on the market;
- Incentives for disclosure of violating behavior concerning tax issues disclosing cases for which there should be elements that have actually taken place, since that in these cases the taxpayers will be exempt from fines and other kind of penalties;
- Expenditure discounts of the tax payers' income revealing whatever legitimate deductions or exemptions are provided by law for the taxpayers, not to be hidden, but to be given so as to allow taxpayers and state to build a mutual trust;
- Fair tax burden to develop a fair taxation system and the tax burden to meet and be consistent with the real conditions of the economy;
- Control mechanisms & frequent checks;
- Education expanding the citizens' knowledge on taxation principles and issues;
- Legislation simplification and codification should be a priority, so as to enable citizens and companies to know in a clear way, what are their tax obligations and the perspective of a stable and safe economic environment;
- Improvement of the public sector productivity transparency and quality;
- Rigorous registration of foreigners-immigrants, as it is generally accepted that the largest proportion of workers employed without insurance are immigrants, especially nowadays that the migration flows from Syria and Africa have become a scourge and threaten the whole socioeconomic structure of Greece.

## 7 Conclusions and Recommendations

Taking into account the available data there are two big policy challenges for Greek tourism and indeed for the Greek economy[13]: The first is to undertake incentive-oriented policy measures in order to make work less attractive in the informal economy. The second is to have policy institutions, which work efficiently and as a constraint for administration and politicians (Vousinas 2017). Measures that should be implemented, in order to reduce the informal economy in Greece and increase the growth rate, are mainly related to consistent and fair taxation practices. It is also considered important to reduce the restrictions on product and labour markets (over-regulation) as to ease access to the formal economy, and, finally, to place regular checks and sanctions where necessary to achieve compliance. It is the only way to start reducing the corruption of public servants and citizens, too.

Last but not least, related inquires must be performed so as to identify why Greek citizens evade taxes and what they would like to receive as goods and services in exchange for preferring the formal economy. It would also be useful to consider what is it for which citizens would be willing to comply in order to establish an honest relationship with the state.

In conclusion, the measures to tackle tax evasion and the underground economy in Greece are almost identical to the measures for addressing the effects of the debt crisis, which still plagues the country. The economic crisis has hit Greece hard and it seems that no sector or policy of the Greek state remains unaffected. Greece's possible responses can either be portrayed in a more compliant Greece preserving its political autonomy in the international arena and seeking to bridge the divide with the rest of the European Union, or in a more or less static country, with no dramatic changes, as long as the badly needed reforms stagnate and with them the Greek society and the country's role in the region and in the European Union. In this sense, the development and competitiveness of the Greek tourism industry can be part of the solution, as well as part of the problem. If one assumes that two thirds of all activities in the informal economy complement those in the official sector, the development of the informal economy can lead to higher value-added figures. Hence, it is necessary to choose those economic and fiscal measures that strongly increase incentives to move the production from the informal economy sector to the formal economy. Only then will the decline of the informal economy be a blessing and an accelerator for the tourism industry.

Several questions accordingly arise with regard to the compliance abilities of Greece's institutional and entrepreneurship arsenal at such a time of economic and social difficulties. One of the key points of the debate remains on whether the country will fall victim to the crisis, or will the crisis energise its assertiveness through compliance? The compliance issue could prove more important than a mere governance issue. Taking into account the study of Das and DiRienzo (2010) and

[13]Katsios, Stavros (2006) "The shadow economy and corruption in Greece." South-Eastern Europe Journal of Economics 1.2006: 61–80.

given its developed country characteristics, Greece's marginal gain in tourism competitiveness from a reduction in corruption levels will rather be limited. Besides numbers, the question on the future of Greek tourism—like the question on the future of Greek Economy—will be decided primarily in terms of public governance: economic freedom and a stable, functioning and accountable democratic state guarantying the rule of law.

Although compliance with international standards has been seen as extremely effective in circumventing structural difficulties of decision-making processes in international organisations, even when international standards are adopted and reflect current 'best practice', country compliance is often poor and the international mechanisms for promoting compliance are weak. In this sense, the question on how compliance relates to the concept of convergence remains unanswered.

What is with cases like Greece then? Does compliance also mean implementation? Experience answers this question with a clear "no" and indeed most of the literature distinguishes between implementation and compliance (Raustiala and Slaughter 2002).

Implementation occurs when states adopt international standards in domestic legislation; however, such implementation may not prevent bureaucratic and private sector behavior that is inconsistent with these standards. Compliance and implementation are unquestionably connected with reforming governance and particularly in the case of Greece, as governance reform is viewed as the condition sine qua non for the formalisation of the economy and the further development of the tourism industry. How can such a transformation be achieved, changing established practices and habits, and to what extend is it possible to make realistic assumptions about the predictability of relationships between policies, actions and their consequences? And finally how can we assess the suitability of reformed policies, institutions and processes as forms of intervention to national capacities?

There is an urgent need to correspond to a minimum level of regulatory initiatives, which transcend national economic, social and political structures in an overall effort to reduce the Greek informal economy.

Under the tourism industry perspective, crucial parameters of good governance remain those maintaining effective market structures, drastically reducing bureaucratic procedures, reducing state activities to sectors that can guarantee cheaper and better services and goods and ensuring economic and human development. Although the strategy may differ from country to country it is certain that the urgently needed 'good governance practices' characterise every successful state without acknowledging good governance as a 'luxury' (Kaufmann and Kraay 2002). Thus, the effectiveness of national institutions and policies remain critical for securing the sound governance of the Greek tourism industry.

## References


Alm, J., & Torgler, B. (2011). Do ethics matter? Tax compliance and morality. *Journal of Business Ethics, 101*(4), 635–651.

Armbrecht, J., & Carlback, M. (2011). The shadow economy: Its effects on the competition in the Swedish restaurant industry. In R. Andriotis, A. Theocharous, & F. Kotsi (Eds.), *Proceedings of the International Conference on Tourism (ICOT 2011): Tourism in the era of uncertainty* (pp. 28–47). Greece: International Association for Tourism Policy.

Ballas, A., & Tsoukas, H. (1998). Consequences of distrust: The vicious circle of tax evasion in Greece. *Journal of Accounting, Ethics & Public Policy, 1*(4), 572–596.

Bank of Greece. (2016). Retrieved from https://www.bankofgreece.gr

Buehn, A., & Schneider, F. (2011). Corruption and the shadow economy: Like oil and vinegar, like water and fire? *International Tax and Public Finance, 19*(1), 172–194.

Das, J., & DiRienzo, C. (2010). Tourism competitiveness and corruption: A cross-country analysis. *Tourism Economics, 16*(3), 477–492.

Dell'Anno, R., Gómez-Antonio, M., & Pardo, A. (2006). The shadow economy in three Mediterranean countries: France, Spain and Greece. A MIMIC approach. *Empirical Economics, 33*(1), 51–84.

Din, B. H., et al. (2016). Are shadow economy and tourism related? International evidence. *Procedia Economics and Finance, 35*, 173–178.

Dreher, A., Kotsogiannis, C., & McCorriston, S. (2009). How do institutions affect corruption and the shadow economy? *International Tax and Public Finance, 16*(6), 773–796.

ECB – European Central Bank. (2017). *The use of cash, cards and other payment instruments used at points of sale (POS) by euro area consumers in 2016*. ECB Occasional Papers No 201. Retrieved from https://www.ecb.europa.eu/pub/pdf/scpops/ecb.op201.en.pdf

Echazu, L., & Pinaki, B. (2008). Corruption, centralization, and the shadow economy. *Southern Economic Journal, 75*(2), 524–537.

Eurostat. (2017). Retrieved from http://ec.europa.eu/eurostat/statistics-explained/index.php/Europe_2020_indicators_-_Greece

Haler, D., & Shore, C. (2005). Introduction-sharp practice: Anthropology and the study of corruption. In D. Haler & C. Shore (Eds.), *Corruption – Anthropological perspectives*. London: Pluto Press.

IAW. (2017). Institute for Applied Economic Research, University of Tübingen, Germany.

Kaplanoglou, G., & Rapanos, V. (2013). Tax and trust: The fiscal crisis in Greece. *South European Society and Politics, 18*(3), 283–304.

Katsios, S. (2006). The shadow economy and corruption in Greece. *South-Eastern Europe Journal of Economics, 1*, 61–80.

Kaufmann, D., & Kraay, A. (2002). Growth without governance. *Economia, 3*(1), 169–229 Retrieved from http://www.worldbank.org/wbi/governance/pubs/growthgov.htm

Kehoe, W. J. (1998). The environment of ethics in global business. *Journal of Business and Behavioral Science, 2*, 47–56.

Kesar, O., & Čuić, K. (2017). Shadow economy in Tourism: Some conceptual considerations from Croatia. *Zagreb International Review of Economics and Business, 20*(2), 65–86.

Lambsdorff, J. G. (2003). KYKLOS, Vol. 56–2003, Fasc. 4, pp. 457–474.

Moyo, B., & Ziramba, E. (2013). The impact of crime on inbound tourism to South Africa. *African Security Review, 22*(1), 4–18.

National Statistical Service of Greece. (2017). Retrieved from https://tradingeconomics.com and https://statistics.gr

OECD. (2012). Retrieved from http://www.oecd.org/tax/forum-on-tax-administration/publications-and-products/49428209.pdf

OECD. (2015). Retrieved from http://stats.oecd.org/

OECD. (2017). Retrieved from https://www.oecd.org/tax/administration/shining-light-on-the-shadow-economy-opportunities-and-threats.htm

Raustiala, K., & Slaughter, A.-M. (2002). International law, international relations and compliance. In W. Carlnaes, T. Risse, & B. Simmons (Eds.), *The handbook of international relations* (p. 539) (Princeton Law & Public Affairs Paper No. 02-2). London: Sage.

Schneider, F. (2009). Size and development of the shadow economy in Germany, Austria and other OECD countries: Some preliminary findings. *Revue Economique, 60*, 1079–1116.

Schneider, F. (2013). *Size and development of the shadow economy of 31 European and 5 other OECD countries from 2003 to 2013: A further decline*. Johannes Kepler University, Linz.

Schneider, F. (2015). Size and development of the shadow economy of 31 European and 5 other OECD countries from 2003 to 2015: Different developments. *Journal of Self-Governance and Management Economics, 3*(4/2015), 7–29.

Schneider, F., & Buehn, A. (2012). *Shadow economies in highly developed OECD countries: What are the driving forces?* (IZA Discussion Paper no. 6891).

Schneider, F., Buehn, A., & Montenegro, C. E. (2011). Shadow economies all over the world: New estimates for 162 countries from 1999 to 2007. In F. Schneider (Ed.), *Handbook on the shadow economy* (pp. 9–77). Cheltenham: Edward Elgar.

Schneider, F., & Enste, D. H. (2000). Shadow economies: Size, causes, and consequences. *Journal of Economic Literature, XXXVIII*(March 2000), 77–114.

Schneider, F., & Enste, D. H. (2013). *The shadow economy: An international survey*. Cambridge: Cambridge University Press.

Singh, A., Sonali, J.-C., & Adil, M. (2012). *Inclusive growth, institutions, and the underground economy* (IMF Working Paper No. WP/12/47). Washington, DC: International Monetary Fund.

Tanzi, V. (1998). *Corruption around the world: Causes, consequences, scope and cures* (IMF staff papers).

Transparency International. (2018). Retrieved from https://www.transparency.org/country/GRC

UNCTAD Secretariat. (2013). Retrieved from http://unctad.org/en/PublicationsLibrary/tdr2013_en.pdf

UNEP. (2013). *United Nations Environment Program*. Retrieved from http://web.unep.org/

Vousinas, G. (2017). Shadow economy and tax evasion. The Achilles heel of Greek economy. Determinants, effects and policy proposals. *Journal of Money Laundering Control, 20*(4), 386–404.

Webb, D., et al. (2013). Self-determination theory and consumer behavioral change: Evidence from a household energy-saving behavior study. *Journal of Environmental Psychology, 35*, 59–66.

World Bank Annual Report. (2008). p. 23. Retrieved from http://siteresources.worldbank.org/EXTANNREP2K8/Resources/YR00_Year_in_Review_English.pdf

World Bank. (2015). Retrieved from http://data.worldbank.org/indicator/IC.TAX.TOTL.CP.ZS?page=1

WTTC. (2018). *The economic impact of travel and tourism*.

[illegible]

# Responsibility Vs. Star-Related CSR in the Hungarian Hotel Sector

Gyöngyi Kovács

## 1 Introduction and Literature Review

The hotel industry, which is also called the 'queen' of tourism, plays a significant role within an economy; in terms of employment and revenue generation. Besides its positive effects, however, it has become clear that hotel operations could have some negative environmental and social consequences as well. This occurs especially where mass tourism is flourishing, or where the natural environment or social structure are highly fragile (Puczkó and Rátz 2002). The idea of sustainability has quickly spilled-over in the hotel industry. Thus, decades of Hungarian and international precedents show, that the tourism sector has been trying to remedy those negative effects, which are often caused by itself (Dávid et al. 2012).

Nowadays, environmental protection, eco-friendly operational practices and awareness have almost mutated to a requirement and guest expectation; constituting way more than a mere marketing ploy. Most of these practices entail economic benefits as well. Positive actions related to society and its stakeholders (including employees, residents of the destination, groups of poor people, and people in need from remote areas) and their well-being are defined as Corporate Social Responsibility' (CSR) (Tóth 2007). Though it is based on fairness and low-abiding operation, it is mostly voluntary.

In order to foster sustainability, holistic thinking is needed in all industries, including tourism. This thinking method treats business interests, environmental protection (or recovery), and the well-being of all stakeholders equally (Kun 2009). Together with various 'green' programs, such as green hotel classification and environmental management systems, CSR programs are slowly integrated into daily practices. Although Hungary lags behind the Western countries, promoting

G. Kovács (✉)
Eszterházy Károly University, Eger, Hungary
e-mail: kovacs.gyongyi@uni-eszterhazy.hu

 
A. Papathanassis et al. (eds.), *Yellow Tourism*, Tourism, Hospitality & Event Management, https://doi.org/10.1007/978-3-319-94664-1_14

economic legality within the industry, stabilising employment, creating fair working conditions, supporting local people, and donating money is becoming increasingly systematic (Csáfor 2009). It is important to highlight, that actions should not be superficial or campaign-like, for merely promotional purposes.

On the other hand, publicising ones SCR activities is essential as it may set a good example for others to follow. Generally, CSR studies examine the actions of large multinational enterprises which have extensive supply chains. Despite the fact that the vast majority of tourism activities are performed by small and medium-sized enterprises, we can find larger international actors as well. Additionally, this sector represents an increasingly considerable economic power worldwide. Therefore, the author should ask the following questions: What do the actors and decision-makers of tourism do to protect the environment they live in, and the society, which keeps fuels and supports it? How do they relate? What example do they set for competitors, for guests and possibly for other economic sectors?

## 2 Materials and Methods

For this study, both primary and secondary data were used. The statistical analysis was based on three major databases, and the relevant literature was studied and extracted by the author. The population concerned was based on the data series of the Hungarian Central Statistical Office (Központi Statisztikai Hivatal, KSH). In the study, the group of relevant service providers was made up of those hospitality units,[1] which belong to the 'Hotel' category, according to Governmental Decree 239/2009 (X. 20.).[2] Thus, this work excludes pensions, campsites, holiday homes and other types of accommodation. The second database is a list of classified hotels by the organization called 'Hotelstars Union'. This institution was established in 2009 and it is currently active in 16 European countries.[3] The third database contains the member hotels of the 'Hungarian Hotel & Restaurant Association' (HHRA). With the help of the organisation, the full list of members was made available for this research on the 13th of September, 2016. Since the length of membership is one year, and the turnover rates are lower, the above mentioned list is more reliable than the list of the hotels classified by Hotelstars Union.

The first step of the analysis was to exactly define the sets, since neither the Hotelstars Union's classification, nor the membership to the hotel association is compulsory. Accordingly, 'hotel' is an exact economic unit. Unfortunately, the data from Hungarian Central Statistical Office (Központi Statisztikai Hivatal, KSH) are

[1]"The type of accommodation, which was established to provide accommodation services exclusively. In addition to accommodation, other services are also provided. At least eleven rooms shall be utilized and the number of beds shall be at least twenty-one"

[2]http://net.jogtar.hu/jr/gen/getdoc2.cgi?dbnum=1&docid=A0900239.KOR

[3]http://www.hotelstars.hu/Default.aspx?tabid=211 downloaded: 11.11.2016

published rather late, so they could only be used to represent scales, instead of making accurate comparative statistics. Member hotels of the HHRA (Hungarian Hotel & Restaurant Association) have been examined from multiple aspects, since they are basically divided into two major categories by the association: 'member of a hotel chain', 'not belonging to a hotel chain'. Classification is only applicable to those seven hotel chains which are registered members of the hotel association. Subsequently, the almost 100 hotel units of Accent Hotel Management, Accor Hospitality, Danubius Hotel and Spa Private Company Limited by Shares, Hunguest Hotels Zrt., Mellow Mood Hotels, SCH Szállodalánc és Üdülőszövetkezet and Service 4 You Hotel Management belong to hotel chains. However, the hotels of Hilton International, Boscolo Hotels, Kempinski Hotels, Iberostar Hotel & Resorts, and the Abbazia Group should be treated as a single unit. The list of hotel chains and groups appearing in Hungary is extensive. These aforementioned hotels cannot be compared with smaller and independent units, since they are strictly-regulated by international standards, including environmental protection measures and CSR. As a result, it is difficult to represent sustainability strategies in this research. Hotels are not categorised by the Hotelstars Union's classification system; they are just listed on the basis of the number of stars (actually there are 10 different levels from 1* to 5* superior categories).

Besides statistical analysis and evaluation, the author also constructed a pilot version of a structured questionnaire, which was completed by the hotel managers. The majority of the questions were the same, but a distinction had to be made between classified and non-classified hotels. Large hotel chains with environmental program and CSR documentation needed to be highlighted, and it was also necessary to separate hotels which have won a Green Hotel Award. Though responses are unsuitable for statistical analysis, conclusions can be still be drawn, and they clearly indicate the sustainability-related problems and tendencies. The answers can be utilised to guide further research in this area.

## 3 Results and Discussion

Based on the Hungarian Central Statistical Office's (Központi Statisztikai Hivatal, KSH) data for July 2016, there were a total of 1064 active hotels in 2015[4] in Hungary, where potential guests could choose from a total of 60,297 rooms to book. By 2016, the number of rooms increased by 1.8% so in the given period, the sample could be compared to 61,369 rooms (MSZÉSZ Trend Riport 2016). In 2016 HHRA counted 393 member hotels (with 34,512 rooms), 60% of which were classified. According to these facts, only 36% of Hungarian hotels belong to the hotel association. Based on the methodology, the sample was completed with those hotels which do not belong to a hotel association, but obtained the Hotelstars

[4]https://www.ksh.hu/docs/hun/xstadat/xstadat_eves/i_oga001.html

Union's classification. This means another 88 units with 4271 rooms. The subject-matter of the examination included 481 hotels with a total of 38,783 rooms. This covers 45% of the Hungarian hotels, but nearly 65% of the rooms. It can be safely assumed that the majority of hotels with large capacities and a lot of rooms are association members and/or classified units.

During the study period, 326 of the 481 hotel units had obtained a classification, which is illustrated by Fig. 1. In both cases it can be stated that only a few lower category hotels (from 1* to 2* superior) are not willing to undergo a classification procedure.

The study also included Green Hotels, which have been, so far, classified in Hungary, since they have exhibited more environmental responsibility than the average hotel. There are 56 awarded hotels (Green Hotel, special award or Ever-Green Awards), of course some of them have won these awards several times. The study, based on press reviews and content analysis of hotel websites shows, that despite of the importance and responsibility of the environment, only 32% (18 units) of the Green Hotels use their title as a marketing tool. Table 1 summarizes the

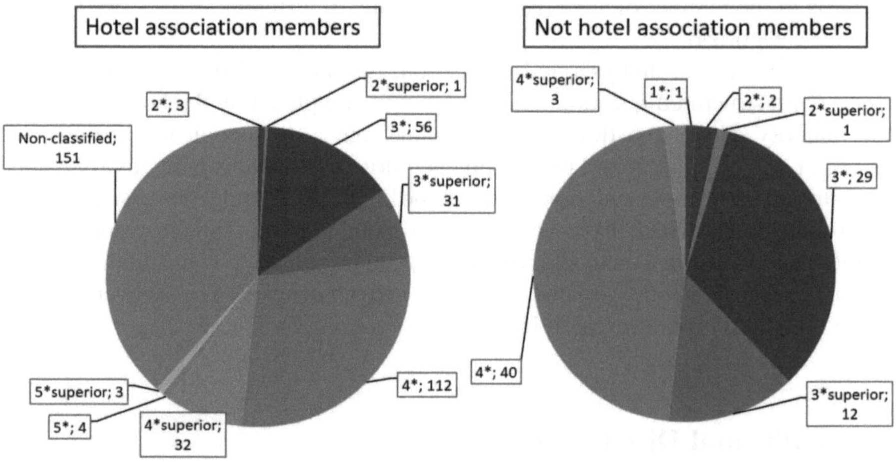


**Fig. 1** Partition of the hotel's star rating. Source: Author

**Table 1** Communication of the stars and the union's membership

| | Hotel association members (unrated: 151!!!) (n = 392) | Not hotel association members (n = 88) |
|---|---|---|
| Using "stars" | 299 hotels | 75 hotels |
| Hotelstars Union's classification and/or logo | 78 hotels | 31 hotels |
| Communication of hotel association membership | 32 hotels | Not relevant |

Source: created by the author

number of hotels, which use the Hotelstars classification and hotel association membership in their marketing communications.

The criteria and the consequences of the use of stars for hotels without Hotelstars Union's classification was the most problematic situation in 2016. According to previous regulations, non-classified hotels are not allowed to use stars. However, contrary to the Hotelstars logo, stars are not protected with trademark. Up to this point, nobody has been punished for the use of the stars. The Hungarian Authority for Consumer Protection (Nemzeti Fogyasztóvédelmi Hatóság) declares in its statement: '*...after the expiry of transitional arrangements and the elimination of old standards and classification systems, those accommodation service providers who do not wish to join the new trademark system, have to provide guests with quality information in other ways...*'.[5] In the spring of 2016, a large-scale inspection was carried out. The authorities warned or punished those who did not comply with regulations (violation of price indication or franchising regulations), but it did not sanction the illicit use of stars.[6] In case of a smaller hotel, the classification procedure for 1* costs 66,000 HUF+VAT (220€ if 1 €=300 HUF), but for a large hotel 4* superior or higher classification it can cost as much as 377,000 HUF+VAT (1257 €). This may be a considerable expenditure for some hotels. The table indicates, that despite of having a right to use the trademark, only 33% of the classified units used Hotelstars logo. The communication of HHRA membership is even worse. Only 8% of the hotels communicated their membership online, although it costs tens of thousands of Forints annually.

The environmental and social activities of international hotel chains are mostly represented on their website, and relevant press reviews can also be considered effective. Despite the fact that many of its members are Green Hotel Award winners, those hotel chains traditionally called Hungarian (Danubius Hotel and Spa Private Company Limited by Shares and Hunguest Hotels Zrt.) are communicating ineffectively, regardless who their owners or operators are. This suggests that the management decisions of international chains are centralised. In Hungary, hotel managers have greater decision freedom in these kinds of actions (which is partly or completely disregarded by the central marketing). The examination of independent hotels showed, that 10–15% of the units have been communicating environmental protection actions, often as a result of a European Union tender or development. Less than 10 hotels emphasised and actively communicated the importance of sustainable operations. The situation is even worse with CSR activities. Less than 30 hotels have been leading local communities or initiatives, or have done something which is visually beneficial for their employees (Table 2).

Amongst the respondents of the structured pilot questionnaire, 16 respondents were finally evaluated carefully, to represent the whole sample. Accordingly, all categories from 2* superior to 5* were represented in the study; as well as 4 non-classified hotels. The author could include hotels from Budapest, as well as

[5]http://www.hotelstars.hu/Default.aspx?tabid=215

[6]http://www.nfh.hu/node/14690

**Table 2** Respondents of the structured questionnaire. Source: created by the author

| Hotelstars union's classification | Locations | Rooms | Hotel chains |
|---|---|---|---|
| 3* | Gosztola | 28 | No |
| 3* | Leányfalu | 15 | No |
| 3* superior | Gyöngyös | 35 | No |
| 3* superior | Martfű | 44 | No |
| **4*** | **Budapest** | 227 | Accor hospitality |
| **4* superior** | **Vecsés** | 75 | No |
| **4* superior** | **Visegrád** | 174 | No |
| 5* superior | Sárvár | 271 | No |
| Non-classified | Baja | 48 | No |
| Non-classified | Parádfürdő | 99 | No |
| Non-classified | Sopron | 78 | No |
| Non-classified | Budapest | 97 | No (TFE hotels) |
| **3*** | **Budapest** | 28 | HOTUSA hotels |
| 2* superior | Eger | 19 | No |
| 3* | Mezőkövesd | 54 | No |
| 4* | Sárvár | 20 | No |

from bigger and smaller towns in the countryside. The questionnaire consisted of 7–9 open points, all of which were answered by senior executives. The number of questions administered was dependent on whether the respondent hotel was:

- a hotel association member (in 12 cases) or not (in 4 cases),
- it received a green hotel award (in 4 cases, indicated by a bold face) or not,
- it was rated (in 12 cases) or not.

The questions focused on the reasons why these decisions were taken, but these are irrelevant for the scope of this study. Other questions in some cases had surprising results. These were directed to sustainable operation, environmental protection and social responsibility. None of the respondents complied to the ISO 14001 standard or any other environmental management systems. Four of them considered environmental protection unnecessary and a waste of time. However, other respondents thought it is important, and five hotel managers consider themselves and their operation committed to it. Sixteen respondents had rather 'colourful' and diverse sustainable and CSR activities. These are summarised in the following list (numbers in parenthesis are indicating the frequency of the answer).

- Tender specifications (2)
- Locally organized festivals, and supported local events (2)
- They (should) naturally do selective waste collection, use energy saving light bulbs, change towels, use frying oils, produce compost, use recycled toilet paper, use room cards etc. (8)
- Purchasing from local producers (2), charity campaigns for the local population in need (2)

- Employing and training local people with other profession (1), discounts for pensioners (therapy) (1), creating a vegetable garden (1)
- Spending large amounts of money on energy saving measures (4)
- City cleaning actions, Earth Day and World Water Day events (1), employee trainings (about sustainability) (1), local student trainings (1), Red Cross campaigns, blood donations (1) Using geothermal energy with heat pumps (1), Biios building monitoring system (1)

## 4 Summary and Conclusions

Comparing the result of the structured questionnaire and the online communication it is observed, that there is a strong willingness to adopt sustainability in hotel operations, but this is not considered to be a marketing activity. This could be explained by a form of 'modesty' and/or the underestimation of its marketing impact. In order to make these actions a practice, good examples should be introduced to the competitors and the guests as well.

In sum, it can be concluded, that in Hungary there are several good ideas and initiatives to adopt environmental and corporate social responsibility, but unfortunately these are often temporary and stay in the background. Smaller units do not adopt international examples, and they do not care much about voluntary actions or the creation of a long-term sustainability strategy.

## References

239/2009. (X. 20.). *Korm. rendelet a szálláshely-szolgáltatási tevékenység folytatásának részletes feltételeiről és a szálláshely-üzemeltetési engedély kiadásának rendjéről*. Downloaded November 11, 2016, from http://net.jogtar.hu/jr/gen/getdoc2.cgi?dbnum=1&docid=A0900239.KOR

Csáfor, H. (2009). A Kárpátok eurorégió országainak CSR-gyakorlata. In: J. Szlávik (szerk.). *Vállalatok társadalmi felelősségvállalása*. Budapest: Complex Kiadó

Dávid L., Vargáné Csobán K., Kovács G., & Vasa L. (szerk.) (2012). *TURIZMUSÖKOLÓGIA Zöldülő turizmus—Fenntartható turizmusfejlesztés*. Budapest: Szaktudás Kiadó Ház

Hotelstars Union adatbázisa. Downloaded November 11, 2016, from http://www.hotelstars.hu/Default.aspx?tabid=211

Kun, A. (2009). *A multinacionális vállalatok szociális felelőssége. CSR-alapú önszabályozás kontra (munka)jogi szabályozás*. Budapest: Ad Librum Kft

Magyar Szállodák és Éttermek Szövetsége: Trend Riport 2016. (2016). *A hazai és a nemzetközi szállodaipar teljesítményéről*, 2016 július. Downloaded October 13, 2016, from http://www.hah.hu/files/3814/7436/6564/Trend_riport_2016_jan.-jl..pdf

Puczkó, L., & Rátz, T. (2002). *A turizmus hatásai*. Budapest: Aula Kiadó.

Tóth, G. (2007). *A Valóban Felelős Vállalat. A fenntarthatatlan fejlődésről, a vállalatok társadalmi felelősségének (CSR) eszközeiről és a mélyebb stratégiai megközelítésről*. Környezettudatos Vállalatirányítási egyesület (KÖVET). http://www.otlethid.hu/doc/VFV.pdf

# Reputation Management in the Tourism Industry

**Michalis Chondrogiannis, Stavros Katsios, Dimitrios Belias, Efstathios Velissariou, Ioannis Papadimopoulos, and Athanasios Koustelios**

> *When a management with a reputation for brilliance tackles a business with a reputation for bad economics, it is the reputation of the business that remains intact.*
>
> Warren Buffett

## 1 Introduction

Management theorists seem to agree that identity is a unique part of corporate entity (Rose and Thomsen 2004). Managers of large companies devote a significant part of resources and their efforts to maintain and improve corporate identity, which is important for the success and survival of their companies. Indeed, a good corporate identity and reputation provides a company with competitive advantage and influences customer buying behaviour (Nguyen and Leblanc 2001). Especially in the case of services such as the hospitality and tourism, consumers cannot test the quality of services prior to purchase. In this case, a strong one corporate identity can be an indicator of the expected quality of the services and goods offered. However, corporate reputation does not only affect customers and all other stakeholders. An organisation or business entity, which is perceived in a favourable way, has the ability to: attract investors and competent employees, motivate suppliers and to be positively addressed by regulators (Bennett and Kottasz 2000). It is implied,

M. Chondrogiannis (✉) · S. Katsios
Department of Foreign Languages, Translation and Interpreting, Laboratory for Geocultural Analyses, Ionian University, Corfu, Greece
e-mail: f15chon@ionio.gr

D. Belias · E. Velissariou · I. Papadimopoulos
Department of Business Administration, Technological Educational Institute of Thessaly, Larissa, Greece

A. Koustelios
Department of Physical Education and Sport Science, University of Thessaly, Trikala, Greece

 
A. Papathanassis et al. (eds.), *Yellow Tourism*, Tourism, Hospitality & Event Management, https://doi.org/10.1007/978-3-319-94664-1_15

from above, that corporate reputation ultimately affects corporate finance performance.

However, despite the growing number of studies that underline the interest of organisations and the advantages of managing corporate identity, research on how to actually deal with corporate identity problems is limited (Ruth and York 2004). A particularly neglected field of research concerns the role and activities of the public-relations function in large organisations. This is in itself a cause for concern, as corporate reputation has clearly and directly been linked to the effective use of public relations (Hutton et al. 2001). A limited number of previous studies have attempted to quantify the involvement of companies with corporate communication and identity. However, most studies have remained at the theoretical and conceptual level (e.g., Davies and Miles 1998; Hutton et al. 2001) and are more focused on generic issues with no differentiation on particular market segments and no specification on risk management implications. For this reason, this paper attempts to fill in the gap in the related literature, by emphasising on the hotel sector and its approach on risk management.

Referring to hospitality sector, the majority of leading organisations, and especially 5-star hotels, offer high quality services and facilities. For this reason, these features cannot be readily used as a basis for differentiation (Morgan et al. 2003). Hence, the need for big companies to promote a unique identity is more important than ever. Even for tourists who have never before visited a hotel, a destination or even a country, corporate identity forms their first impression and can strongly influence their purchasing intentions. In this sense, the corporate reputation emerges as an important element determining the success of an organisation. Nevertheless, although corporate reputation emerges as a very important corporate element, the concept has not received enough attention from researchers in the field of tourism and hospitality. Although relevant studies have attempted to explore the concept, most discussions have rotated around the related notion of 'destination image' (Hosany et al. 2007). Therefore, there is a need of research emphasising on company-level reputation; especially in today's digital environment, where the tourist companies are operating mostly on the internet and more particularly on social media.

Our work here, reflects a literature review relying on academic sources, retrieved from online search engines and databases such as ESBCO and science direct. Our search revealed a number of papers and other references, helping us to present the basic theories on the topic and subsequently to proceed with suggestions for future research.

## 2 Literature Review

### 2.1 *The Need for Reputation Management*

Several scholars argue that corporate identity management, including reputation management, is a substantial administrative process of powerful companies. A strong corporate identity can: make a company stand out from its competitors (Dolphin 2004), boost it financially (Cooper 1999), influence the purchasing behaviour of its clients (Nguyen and Leblanc 2001), and have a strong impact on stakeholder loyalty (Balmer 1995). However, while there is a large amount of evidence that agencies are increasingly interested in the benefits of corporate management identity (Van Riel 1995), many ambiguities exist, as to how to practically implement it (Ruth and York 2004). An area of ambiguity is related to the way an organisation communicates its identity and more specifically the role of the public relations function. Indeed, this is surprisingly absent from relevant discussions and it has not been a major aspect of the research examining the way in which companies adopt corporate identity management as a distinct and an important aspect of public relations (Hutton et al. 2001).

Previous studies have attempted to provide data on the ways in which companies can manage their identity reach to their target audience, through public relations, but most of the discussions have remained at a theoretical level (e.g., Davies and Miles 1998; Hutton et al. 2001). In tourism and hospitality management, corporate reputation is considered vital to the success of an organisation. Nowadays, leading organisations offer excellent services and thus differentiation is more difficult to achieve (Morgan et al. 2003). As a result, the need to portray a unique identity is more necessary than ever. As Nguyen (2006) argues, even for a tourist who has never visited a hotel, a specific place or even a whole country, the organisations identity forms their first impression can have a great impact on their purchasing intentions. However, although the identity emerges as an undoubtedly dominant corporate component, it does not emerge frequently in hospitality research. It is worth mentioning that, despite the availability of numerous papers addressing the concept of identity, most of the corresponding discussions have been focused on the concept of the image; focusing mainly at the destination- rather than on the corporate level (Hosany et al. 2007). It appears that tourism and hospitality research is characterised by an absence of systematic efforts to understand the issues related to how organisations communicate their corporate identity (Public Relations). This absence has not gone unnoticed. Indeed, Oh et al. (2004) highlight the lack of studies in the field of public relations, stating that from the total results in hotel marketing surveys between 2002 and 2003, only 2.1% was related to public relations. The authors argued that corporate identity did not appear to be a systematic research aspect in the studies they examined.

## 2.2 Reputational Risk

Up to this point, we have discussed the positive effects reputation has on tourist companies. Indeed, it can become a powerful public relations tool and it can allow holiday brands to leverage their performance by using their reputation as a central marketing instrument. However, reputation management is subject to a significant influence; the company and its brand are overexposed to the dynamics of their markets and the perceptions of their consumers (Payne et al. 2009). This means that if consumers are brand-aware, they will also be sensitised to negative news/information regarding it. 'Reputational risk' means that there is a high risk of damages on the firm's reputation, including loss of revenues, destruction of shareholder value and even potential criminal prosecution during a serious crisis. In order to avoid this, a company must look after issues such as: ethics, security, sustainability and quality control. It is also important to work fostering a culture that promotes fairness and the prevention of damage (Oh et al. 2004).

Fitzpatrick (2000) and Wang et al. (2010) have states that risk management has an important impact on tourism and refer to reputational risk as follows:

1. Tourism is a 'fragile social institution': Its course is affected and is formed through a series of immeasurable factors such an economic crisis, terrorist acts, ecological disasters, war situations that can be created at any time, an unstable political climate that can characterise a country. All these create uncertainty and concern for prospective travellers. In these cases, the work of the public relations department/function is particularly challenging and important, and should aim at formulating strategies in order to deal with the impending crises.
2. The 'distant' and 'unknown' of the product: The holiday package booked months ago, concerns a place unknown and usually distant to the final consumer. At this point, the role of public relations is decisive, since it ought to bridge the distance between the prospective consumer and the tourist destination.
3. The employee turnover and employment of unskilled staff in the marketing department is a negative factor for business: In traditional organisational charts, reputation management is depicted at board/management levels. The responsibilities of the marketing team broadly extend within the entire width and depth of organisational structure, function and actions of an organisation; inward and outward.
4. The subjectivity of moods in tourism: The way in which the tourist product is perceived and in general the holiday business, depends on the unpredictable moods of tourist and the public. Economic-, social-, cultural-, was well as individual/psychological-factors such as: personality, mood, perception, are only some determinants of the tourists' moods. Public Relations require good knowledge of the socio-demographic and psychographic characteristics of of their target audiences.

## 2.3 *The Risk of Having the Customer as a Co-Value Producer: Reputation Management in the Digital Era*

In 2000, the social web was introduced and developed forming what is collectively known as Web 2.0. Hoyer et al. (2010) found that by searching and sharing opinions, information and experiences with others, social media has not only become a common resource for consumers, but also majorly affects the reputation of companies. At present, consumers plan vacation tours with the aid of web 2.0 online sources such as personal blogs and communities of virtual tourists. This information is combined with the content provided by tourism and hospitality providers and/or destination-marketing organisations (DMOs). The hospitality industry is significantly influenced by social networking, mainly by frequent travellers, posting reviews online. These reviews are perceived as being more valid and useful than those of the official rating agencies. The importance of online reviews can be asserted based on the Nielson Company's (Wilson et al. 2009) research; 90% of the participants trusted the recommendations posted by other users who they know personally, while 70% trust the recommendation of other users with whom they are not acquainted. This shows that the consumers' role is crucial, as it affects the purchasing decisions of others based on the content that they as users generate. The review by Banks and Humphreys (2008) concludes that the social media's participatory architecture permits tourists to post their knowledge, evaluations and experiences regarding particular destinations and brands. This tends to inspire others. Certainly, several tourism and hospitality firms utilise social media platforms as part of their marketing strategy, involving consumers in the promotion and distribution of their product/service. For example, they may hire professional bloggers, sponsor blog posts, or facilitate online discussions in forums. In addition, the user-generated content has the potential to offer market research data; enabling tourism and hospitality organisations to extract/mine consumer attitudes towards destinations and products (Schmallegger and Carson 2008). Therefore, participation and collaboration in social media platforms, allow consumers to create value for the tourism and hospitality providers. The social media user has been empowered to access and participate in the process of developing value, co-existing with tourism and hospitality organisations (Hoyer et al. 2010).

Eventually the consumer's online communication might progress into a process of innovative networking and social interaction (Potts et al. 2008), binding the opportunities with the benefits of social production. Conversely, tourism and hospitality require destinations and providers to adjust and co-exist with a web-enabled, socially-networked consumer base (Banks and Humphreys 2008). Banks and Humphreys (2008) discovered that such an evolving co-creation could not be directed in the same way as employees can; if an organisation increases the degree of control they exercise on the online community, there would be a risk of losing creativity. Nonetheless, tourism and hospitality organisations are required to develop new competencies in social media, in order to enable co-work between their employees and their co-creating consumers.

Payne et al. (2009) proposed that social media strategies could be integrated into the process of new product development. This might elevate the ability of tourism and hospitality organisations to create value for, and together with, their consumers. Firms can become involved with their customers by interacting more frequently, by seeking opportunities to develop new technologies (such as the development of social media) and by utilising user-generated content. Piller et al. (2012) refer to the idea that improvements in effectiveness and efficiency can be led by social media. The cost of interacting with the participants can be lowered and their contribution and numbers can be significantly higher. In addition, the knowledge possessed by individuals is enhanced by the heterogeneous nature of groups, which, in terms of innovation management, is viewed as a critical success factor. According to Kohler et al. (2011), a lot of advancements have been made over the last years in three different areas: graphics, bandwidth volume and network connectivity. All these support the emergence of virtual communities by making it more attractive to the users. The role of customers has been altered by the advent of social media. Customers have also gained a massive amount of power, resulting by their relative public influence enabled by web 2.0; there is more control exercised by the users and less by the firms. From the initial process of search until the final sales process, this influence can be exercised at different degrees. As consumers connect to the web more frequently, five different powers have been identified: "a global view, experimentation, information access, activism and networking" (Kohler et al. 2011).

Potentially, more influence is exercised when consumers are enabled by these powers in order to gain more information about a particular company, product or service, either internationally or locally where individuals form groups. Piller et al. (2012) suggests that the relationship between the customer and the firm has an impact on social media. Nevertheless, the above example shows that the primary relationship is between the customers themselves. The large scale capability of altering the relationship between market actors and market structures, is preserved by the social media and the real co-design processes. Piller et al. (2012) also reported that tasks, such as distribution and marketing, are easily and more effective for the customers who utilise social media. The travel and leisure industry is often characterised by the need to communicate and market to a large mass of potential customers. This can draw a natural fit to the use of the Internet and to social media along with the suitability of social media as a channel for cost-effective mass communication (Deloitte and Touche 2015).

Online tools and social media platforms can be conveniently and readily used to present a positive company image to the consumers. This also has a direct positive impact on sales. Sites like Twitter and Facebook have also been used as a way to communicate feedback and complaints to the hotels. The communication process initiated in this manner is a dialogue between consumers and management. Thus, social media serves as one of the most effective platforms of co-creating with the customer, as the levels of engagement and participation are higher. Online interpersonal influence is an important area to explore because consumer behaviour can be highly dependent on it. Hence it is important that marketers learn to moderate and facilitate this kind of online dialogue. Mowat (2010) proposed that the opportunities made possible by the adoption of social media, should be correctly used by hotel managers because social media tools have enabled and encouraged guests to give their feedback about the services. The same is true for value co-creation; hotels can utilise social networking for gathering valuable feedback and responses. This requires a highly effective content strategy so that the mined data used in the formulation, development, modification, improvement and expansion of the products and services.

Web technologies have significantly impacted on marketing over the past decade, rendering 'branding' a domain where online management communication and feedback loops need to be understood and addressed; otherwise ineffective branding could result to image and reputation damages. Marketers are often the individuals managing the brands online and controlling the communication with the outside sources. The management of websites as brand communication vehicles, enables businesses to make, check and maintain the customer relationship in a more advantageous, easy-to-understand way. The web has intensified the velocity and the geographic spread of all sorts of data. Using social networking, individuals can influence a company's business with incorrect information and other fabricated news. Nevertheless, it can also turn into an organisation's best accomplice, as organizations can utilise social networking to screen and control 'unfriendly data' appearing in those online discussions. Careful observation is a necessary measure in order to avert 'online defamation crusades'. Organisations can likewise exploit these devices by being actively involved in online discussions, enhancing the image of the business, as it permits the business to directly react to faultfinders, to repudiate data or to add a fair remark around a negative instance. Demonstrating openness and honesty, companies can publicly react to individuals' comments and reassure them that they are genuinely listening.

## 3 Discussion

Tourism and hospitality organisations can obtain a great deal of content and value from co-creation. Yet, Potts et al. (2008) has addressed the challenges facing organisations in terms of the corresponding effect on reputation. By integrating the co-creator with the internal team, executives are forced to manage the organisation by means of new mechanisms that require controlling and monitoring for the development of efficiency and quality. The constant and frequent interaction tends to increase the co-creation degree, and alongside this, management control is inclined to be more frequent and intense (Payne et al. 2009). In addition, the performance of customers as co-creators can stop abruptly with the reorganisation of the company, which negatively impacts the process of new product- and service-development.

Social networks have increasingly become significant to marketing departments as well as to consumers as others' recommendations are trusted more than the official marketing message of the brand (Zeng 2014). A social network may be the "most effective way of RM (Reputation Management), since it blurs the link between customers, allies and partners" (Wang et al. 2010). In previous work, social networks are referred to in various ways (e.g. virtual communities, virtual network, online communities). For the purpose of this paper, the term social network is used.

Kirby (2009), whose work is within a hotel's network, suggests that entailing a two-way communication on the network should be active and not purely focused on the hotel itself, but on adjoining topics to provide customers with appropriate information. This is particularly significant within online tourism communities, which have become the connection between individuals in virtual space; they provide user-generated recommendations from their experiences, as well as from those of other members (Chung and Buhalis 2008). The terms 'virtual community' or 'social network' have been a challenge over the years for marketing literature to define. Rheingold (1994) definition was, according to Wang et al. (2010), the most frequently cited definition and still very relevant for this paper: The social aggregations of individuals that emerge online when enough people carry on these public discussions with sufficient human feelings, to form webs of personal relationships in cyberspace. A virtual community is a group of people who may or may not meet one another face to face, and who exchange words and ideas through the mediation of computer bulletin boards and networks.

Wang et al. (2010) also suggested that Online Social Networks (OSN's) are the most cost-effective forms of information dissemination. Yet, cost effectiveness is not the most important research aspect within luxury hospitality. Chung and Buhalis (2008) suggested that information gathering and distribution are key benefits of OSN's. They argued that OSN's can be used extensively for market research, observing customer interaction and increasing customer knowledge. These are the important insights that OSN's can deliver to brands and be incorporated into a marketing strategy. The valuable online information can be used by hotel marketers to enable customers to use and disseminate information online through these OSN's (Wang et al. 2010; Zeng 2014).

Connecting online with the customer is increasingly becoming as important as offline—also described as on location (within the hotel). As the connection with the customers in online communities or brand-owned websites, before or after a customer's trip, strengthens, there is a pressing need to understand why consumers are connecting with brands and what they value is. From a management perspective, functionality should focus on ensuring online presence within OSN's and enabling the user to freely decide to use, share, and/or contribute there. This does relinquish control to the consumer and this is an important element for brands to understand. The spread of opinion-based information for other consumers to read, use and potentially impact on the company's image, are all key elements for practitioners in the new online marketing domain. The company itself has no control of the word-of-mouth process, on which many consumers heavily rely upon to reduce uncertainty and align expectations prior to making a purchasing decision (Buhalis and Law 2008). From another perspective, OSN's provide existing customers the ability to be brand-advocates by re-announcing marketing messages. This can be seen as a way loyal guests can become brand advocates by sharing content like photos, videos and messages on social media platforms such as Facebook, Twitter, and Instagram.

The discussion of how tourist brands can use OSN's to develop and deepen their relationships with customers is the area of interest for reputation management. From a critical point of view, in today's online environment, reputation is developed by both customers and the company. In social media the creation of reputation lies on the customers' experiences. It is the customer who will share a positive review or a negative comment. The sum of all these will shape the reputation of the tourist brand and its ability to manage it. Nonetheless, many aspects of this are beyond the company's control. It is the customer who will shape the reputation and this may pose a great threat for the company itself.

The ability of brands to use and manage relationship-building in OSN's, as a tool of creating reputation and avoiding the creation of a negative reputation, applies to the fundamental use of social networks. Social networks, designed to facilitate communication through a deeper sense of commitment, enable consumers to "obtain information, maintain connections and deepen relationships" (Wang et al. 2010). A wider individual network overcomes any geographic boundaries through OSN's. Along with advances in information and communication technologies, this has significantly changed the way consumers and firms relate and interact with one another. The consumers can now engage directly with suppliers, which in turn reduces the need for intermediaries and provides a transparency of rates for hotels and any third party website selling rooms (O'Connor and Murphy 2004).

## 4 Discussion and Proposals for Future Research

This research attempts to fill a gap in the relevant literature. More specifically, there is little in hospitality research related to the way in which hotels announce their corporate identity through the use of public relations activities. In this sense, this study could be of interest to everyone dealing with corporate identity, business communications hotels and researchers involved in reputation management. Fill (1995) observes that corporate reputation is a valuable asset element for every organisation, and that it requires careful management and communication. The literature has highlighted many indications that professionals are interested on the reputation of their companies, as well as on the advantages of a good corporate identity. On the side of in hospitality and tourism, there is no doubt that today, the business need for present a unique identity is more pertinent than ever. Following the results of this study, one can conclude that in the future hotels will need to place more attention to corporate identity issues. At this point, it is important to note that reputation management is as challenging as it is essential in today's era of digital media. Indeed, social media have a strong impact on reputation management and especially on reputational risk.

Holiday brands are, way more than before, exposed to the individual comments and grievances from their customers. Keeping in mind that tourists are affected from word-of-mouth and that a single one negative comment can lead to several negative comments, then it is fair to say the reputation management is more crucial than ever and that tourists are the ones who pose the main source of reputational risk.

Regarding future research, there is a need to produce a conceptual framework which will help us to understand the factors affecting reputational risk for tourism companies in the digital era; with an emphasis placed on social media. Indeed, digitalisation can play an important role for reputation management, since the customer becomes a reputation co-creator.

## References

Balmer, J. M. T. (1995). Corporate branding and connoisseurship. *Journal of General Management, 21*(1), 24–46.

Banks, J., & Humphreys, S. (2008). The labour of user co-creators emergent social network markets convergence. *The International Journal of Research into New Media Technologies, 14*(4), 401–418.

Bennett, R., & Kottasz, R. (2000). Practitioner perceptions of corporate reputation: An empirical investigation. *Corporate Communications International Journal, 5*(4), 224–235.

Buhalis, D., & Law, R. (2008). Progress in information technology and tourism management: 20 years on and 10 years after the Internet—The state of eTourism research. *Tourism management, 29*(4), 609–623.

Chung, J. Y., & Buhalis, D. (2008). Web 2.0: A study of online travel community. In P. O'Connor, W. Höpken, & U. Gretzel (Eds.), *Information and communication technologies in tourism 2008*. Vienna: Springer.

Cooper, A. (1999). What's in a name. *Admap, 34*(6), 30–32.

Davies, G., & Miles, L. (1998). Reputation management: Theory versus practice. *Corporate Reputation Review, 2*(1), 16–27.

Deloitte & Touche. (2015). *Travel consumer 2015. Engage the empowered holiday maker*. Accessed July 15, 2017, from https://www2.deloitte.com/uk/en/pages/consumerbusiness/articles/travel-consumer-2015.html

Dolphin, R. R. (2004). Corporate reputation: A value creating strategy. *Corporate Governance, 4*(3), 77–92.

Fill, C. (1995). *Marketing communications: Frameworks, theories and applications*. New Jersey: Prentice-Hall.

Fitzpatrick, K. (2000). Toward a professional responsibility theory of public relations ethics. *Journal of Mass Media Ethics, 16*(2/3), 193–212.

Hosany, S., Ekinci, Y., & Uysal, M. (2007). Destination image and destination personality. *International Journal of Culture, Tourism and Hospitality Research, 1*(1), 62–81.

Hoyer, W. D., Chandy, R., Dorotic, M., Krafft, M., & Singh, S. S. (2010). Consumer cocreation in new product development. *Journal of Service Research, 13*(3), 283–296.

Hutton, J. G., Goodman, M. B., Alexander, J. B., & Genest, C. M. (2001). Reputation management: The new face of corporate public relations. *Public Relations Review, 27*, 247–261.

Kirby, J. (2009). Viral marketing. In J. Kirby & P. Marsden (Eds.), *Connected marketing*. Oxford: Butterworth-Heinemann.

Kohler, T., Matzler, K., & Füller, J. (2011). Avatar-based innovation: Using virtualworlds for real-world innovation. *Technovation, 29*, 395–407.

Morgan, N. J., Pritchard, A., & Piggott, R. (2003). Destination branding and the role of stakeholders: The case of New Zealand. *Journal of Vacation Marketing, 9*(3), 285–299.

Mowat, B. (2010). Social media: Is it a friend, or foe? *Canadian Travel Press, 42*(26), 8–22 Retrieved from Hospitality & Tourism Complete database.
Nguyen, N. (2006). The collective impact of service workers service-space on the corporate image formation. *International Journal of Hospitality Management, 25*(2), 227–244.
Nguyen, N., & Leblanc, G. (2001). Corporate image and corporate reputation in customers' retention decisions in services. *Journal of Retailing and Consumer Services, 8*, 227–236.
O'Connor, P., & Murphy, J. (2004). Research on information technology in the hospitality industry. *International Journal of Hospitality Management, 23*(5), 473–484.
Oh, H., Kim, B. Y., & Shin, J. H. (2004). Hospitality and tourism marketing: Recent developments in research and future directions. *Hospital Management, 23*, 425–447.
Payne, A., Strobacka, K., Frow, P., & Knox, S. (2009). Co-creating brands: Diagnosing and designing the relationship experience. *Journal of Business Research, 62*(3), 379–389.
Piller, F., Vossen, A., & Ihl, C. (2012). From social media to social product development: The impact of social media on co-creation of innovation. *Die Unternehmung, 66*(1), 7–27.
Potts, J., Hartley, J., Banks, J., Burgess, J., Cobcroft, R., Cunningham, S., & Montgomery, L. (2008). Consumer co-creation and situated creativity. *Industry and Innovation, 15*, 459–474.
Rheingold, H. (1994). A slice of life in my virtual community. In L. M. Harasim (Ed.), *Global networks: Computers and international communication* (pp. 57–80). Cambridge, MA: MIT Press.
Rose, C., & Thomsen, S. (2004). The impact of corporate reputation on performance: Some Danish evidence. *European Management Journal, 22*, 201–210.
Ruth, J. A., & York, A. (2004). Framing information to enchance corporate reputation: The impact of message source, information type, and reference point. *Journal of Business Research, 57*, 14–20.
Schmallegger, D., & Carson, D. (2008). Blogs in tourism: Changing approaches to information exchange. *Journal of Vacation Marketing, 14*, 99–110.
Van Riel, C. B. M. (1995). *Principles of corporate communication*. Prentice Hall: Hemel Hempstead.
Wang, H., Yang, Z., Chen, L., Yang, J., & Li, R. (2010). Minority community participation in tourism: A case of Kanas Tuva villages in Xinjiang, China. *Tourism Management, 31*(6), 759–764.
Wilson, E., Nielsen, N., & Buultjens, J. (2009). From lessees to partners: exploring tourism public–private partnerships within the New South Wales national parks and wildlife service. *Journal of Sustainable Tourism, 17*(2), 269–285.
Zeng, B. (2014). What do we know about social media in tourism? A review. *Tourism Management Perspectives, 10*, 27–36.

[illegible]

# Responsible Tourism and Maritime Spatial Planning

**Anca Cristina Stanciu**

## 1 Introduction

In the last years, a growing concern for responsible tourism development is noticeable. More specifically, this refers to a development conforming to standards that guarantee the preservation of ecological balance and prevent resource-overuse and negative environmental impacts. Tourism can have a considerable economic contribution and can be decisive for the development of a region; particularly a coastal one.

The ideas of respect and responsibility have been inexorably connected to tourism since 1980, but it was only in 2002 that the Cape Town Declaration outlined priorities to be incorporated in destination management, fostering more respectful and equitable practices for the environment. Within the tourism sector, it is generally agreed that there are increasing overall societal and environmental concerns, and that this will increase the demand for more sustainable destinations and responsible travel preferences.

Unfortunately, until now, CSR (Corporate Social Responsibility) is still at the infancy stage in the tourism industry, focused merely on environmental management, whilst omitting focus on human rights, governance of employees' interests. There are two aspects to be analysed in the case of CSR in sustainable tourism:

- Environmental: Tourism-CSR is only a part of sustainable tourism development and consequently the environmental impact minimisation has received the most attention of CSR activities in tourism;
- Social and ethical: Tourism plays a significant role in poverty alleviation by creating employment opportunities. In this respect, WCTE (World Committee in Tourism Ethics) is working to eliminate discrepancies and settle interest-related disputes (Hamid 2010).

A. C. Stanciu (✉)
Faculty of Economics, "Ovidius" University of Constanta, Constanta, Romania
e-mail: anca.stanciu@univ-ovidius.ro



A. Papathanassis et al. (eds.), *Yellow Tourism*, Tourism, Hospitality & Event Management, https://doi.org/10.1007/978-3-319-94664-1_16

Within the tourism industry it is generally agreed that there are increasing overall societal and environmental concerns, and these will increase pressures to implement corresponding destination management policies. In the meantime, in most cases, (e.g. low income countries), tourism is seen as a viable option for economic growth, even though tourism may have a negative impact on the environment, society, culture, and sometimes even on the economy. Sometimes, currently unsustainable tourism practices, can impair the health and well-being of the local communities, as well as the tourism business itself (Tuan 2011). In this respect, Corporate Social Responsibility (CSR), as part of the 'Europe 2020' strategy for smart, sustainable and inclusive growth, can make a significant contribution towards sustainability.

Regarding coastal and maritime areas, which are usually the most popular tourism destinations, are subjected to considerable environmental pressures. In this context, MSP (Maritime Spatial Planning)—conceptually linked with CSR—is a coastal management program that operates at the international level, in order to plan when and where human activities take place at sea and to ensure these are as efficient and sustainable as possible. Stakeholders are involved in a transparent and inclusive planning of maritime activities.

MSP and sustainable tourism can be considered as a complementary and strongly-interlinked set of processes/initiatives, aimed at adjusting environmental and tourism-related legislation in order to address problems related to pollution and global climate change. Initiated in 2012, MSP supports and facilitates the implementation of the 'Europe 2020 Strategy' for a smarter, sustainable and more inclusive growth, the main objective being to ensure that human activities around all the European seas are being as efficient and sustainable as possible (Zubritckaia 2015).

In order to become sustainable, coastal tourism requires a combination of different measures, such as: proper environmental management, consideration of tourists' and local population needs, a permanent dialogue between stakeholders, and coastal governance based on systematic planning.

Coastal tourism has a long history in the Black Sea basin, and it is internationally recognized as being amongst the major strategic assets of this region and the most promising tourism segment in terms of economic growth and employment. The re-orientation of the local and regional policies towards the ecological aspects of tourism could reverse the deterioration of marine systems and offer opportunities for an improved type of mass tourism in the coastal areas (Nichersu et al. 2016). The increasing pressure on the marine resources of the Black Sea and the greater use of the sea for human activities support the need for developing and implementing of MSP in the Black Sea.

## 2 The Role of MSP

### 2.1 MSP-What Does It Actually Mean?

Maritime Spatial Planning (MSP) is in fact a process by which, state authorities define an appropriate decision-making framework for analyzing and organizing human activities in marine areas; in order to sustainably meet the environmental, economic and social objectives. MSP is a coastal management program that operates at the international level and transparently involves stakeholders in the planning of maritime activities. Mainly MSP is concerned with planning when and where human activities take place at sea and ensuring that these are as done as efficiently and sustainably as possible.

As part of EU's 'Blue Growth strategy', the coastal and maritime tourism sector has been identified as an area with promising potential for fostering a smarter, sustainable and more inclusive Europe. According to the 'Blue Growth Study', coastal and maritime tourism represents the biggest maritime sector in terms of gross value added and employment and is also expected to grow by 2–3% by 2020. "Competition for maritime space—for renewable energy equipment, aquaculture and other uses—has highlighted the need to manage our waters more coherently."[1]

### 2.2 MSP Issues

The area covered by MSP comprises a number of sectors including: Fisheries and aquaculture, energy, maritime tourism, shipping, environment, and transportation. The main general benefits of MSP for a region are the following: conflict reduction, investment facilitation, increased cross-border cooperation, and environmental protection. Moreover, there are also aspects that could be considered advantages of using MSP as a strategic instrument for a certain period of time:

- Bringing together central and local stakeholders into a shared dialogue;
- Elaboration of the legal framework;
- Training activities: organized training courses, seminars, field visits, formation of local committees for specific issues such as water, waste, land-use, tourism, etc.
- Tourism Carrying Capacity (TCA) applied on the tourism sector;
- Research concerning the linkages between cultural heritage and sustainable development;
- Integrated land-use management;
- Establishment of a local agenda of principles reflecting economic, social or environmental topics for both local and governmental authorities;

[1] https://ec.europa.eu/maritimeaffairs/policy/maritime_spatial_planning_en

- Established partnerships in the context of several project proposals submitted to funding agencies.

## 2.3 Funding and Legal Framework

The following EU-funded projects are designed to facilitate cooperation between EU countries for the management of maritime space and, since 2015, for supporting the implementation of the MSP-related legislation[2]:

- Plan Bothnia[3]—Preparatory action on maritime spatial planning in the Baltic Sea (2010–2012)
- Balsa Plan[4]—Baltic Sea region programmer "Introducing Maritime Spatial Planning in the Baltic Sea" (2009–2012)
- TPEA,[5] Trans-boundary Planning in the European Atlantic—Project on maritime spatial planning in the Atlantic, including the Celtic Sea and Bay of Biscay (2012–2014)
- ADRIPLAN[6]—Adriatic Ionian Maritime Spatial Planning (2013–2015)
- SIMCELT[7]—promoting practical cross-border cooperation between EU countries on the implementation of the maritime spatial planning directive in the Celtic Seas (2015–2017)
- Baltic SCOPE[8]—Cross-border solutions in Baltic maritime spatial plans (2015–2017)
- MARSPLAN—MSP in the Black Sea (2015–2017)
- SIMNORAT—Atlantic Sea (2017–2018)
- SIMWESTMED—Western Mediterranean (2017–2018)
- SUPREME—Eastern Mediterranean (2017–2018)

In July 2014, the European Parliament and the Council adopted legislation to create a common framework for maritime spatial planning in Europe.[9] While each EU country is free to plan its own maritime activities, local, regional and national planning in shared seas would be made more compatible through a set of minimum common requirements.[10] The legal framework was subsequently completed as follows:

---

[2]https://ec.europa.eu/maritimeaffairs/policy/maritime_spatial_planning_en

[3]http://www.planbothnia.org/

[4]http://www.baltseaplan.eu/

[5]http://www.tpeamaritime.eu/

[6]http://adriplan.eu/

[7]http://www.simcelt.eu/

[8]http://www.balticscope.eu/

[9]http://eur-lex.europa.eu/legal-content/EN/TXT/?uri=uriserv:OJ.L_.2014.257.01.0135.01.ENG

[10]http://eur-lex.europa.eu/legal-content/EN/TXT/?uri=celex%3A32014L0089

- Directive 2014/89/EU of the European Parliament and of the Council of 23 July 2014 established a framework for maritime spatial planning.
- EU countries were required to transpose the Directive into national legislation and appoint competent authorities by 2016.
- The implementation of MSP in Member States' jurisdictional waters must be achieved by March 2021.
- Together with the Marine Strategy Framework Directive (Directive 2008/56/EC of the European Parliament and of the Council of 17 June 2008), the MSP Directive is a foundation stone for the sustainable development of the EU's seas and oceans.

# 3 Coastal and Maritime Tourism: Responsible and Sustainable Tourism

## *3.1 Coastal and Maritime Tourism*

In geographical terms, coastal areas are defined as those bordering the sea or having at least half of their territory within 10 km of the coast. A delimitation of coastal and maritime terms is required. Coastal tourism includes beach-based tourism and recreation activities (swimming, surfing, etc.), and other recreation activities in coastal areas. Maritime tourism covers water-based activities (e.g. boating, yachting, cruising, nautical sports) and includes operations of landside facilities (manufacturing of equipment and services). As part of EU's Blue Growth strategy, the coastal and maritime tourism sector has been identified as an area with a promising potential for fostering a smarter, sustainable and more inclusive Europe. Employing over 3.2 million people, this sector generates a total of 183 billion euros in gross-value-added, whilst representing over one third of the maritime economy. 51% of the European hotel-bed capacity is concentrated in regions with a sea border. According to the 'Blue Growth Study',[11] not only is coastal and maritime tourism the biggest maritime sector (in terms of gross-value-added and employment), but it also is expected to grow 2–3% by 2020.[12]

Concerning land-sea interactions, in terms of setting-up of maritime spatial plans, EU member states are required to take into consideration relevant interactions of activities and uses (article 8 of the Directive 2014/89/EU), such as tourism. Article 5 of the Directive 2014/89/EU, related to the objectives of MSP, stipulate that through their maritime spatial plans, member states should aim to contribute to sustainable development and may pursue the promotion of sustainable tourism.

[11] https://ec.europa.eu/maritimeaffairs/sites/maritimeaffairs/files/docs/body/study-maritime-and-coastal-tourism_en.pdf

[12] http://ec.europa.eu/maritimeaffairs/policy/coastal_tourism_en

### 3.2 Responsible and Sustainable Tourism

Responsible tourism is concerned with creating a more beautiful and healthy living environment, which also means more beautiful and healthy places to visit, unique in their cultural authenticity (2002, Cape Town Declaration, the World Summit on Sustainable Development). Responsible Tourism requires that operators, hoteliers, governments, local people and tourists assume responsibility and take action to make tourism more sustainable.[13] In a less conventional approach, responsible tourism is said to be: captivating, engaging, emotional, simple, peaceful and natural.[14] More responsible and sustainable tourism requires long-term thinking and focus, and understanding that change is often cumulative, gradual and irreversible. As more regions and countries develop their tourism industries, they experience significant impacts on natural resources, consumption patterns, pollution and social systems. Sustainable tourism is about re-focusing and adapting. The need for sustainable/ responsible planning and management is imperative for the industry to survive as a whole.[15] MSP needs sustainability and responsibility in tourism. But are the two terms really different? In fact:

- Both words have been widely-used in the last years to describe a kind of tourism that is not only environmentally-friendly, but also generates social and economic benefits.
- While 'responsible tourism' requires the participants to be as conscious and gentle as possible, 'sustainable tourism' demands a wider analysis of implications/impacts on the long-term.
- CSR stands for responsible and sustainable tourism business operations. Responsible or sustainable tourism? It is only recently that the tourism industry has begun to ask itself this question. ResponsibleTravel.com defines responsible tourism as: "Holidays that care about local communities and culture as well as wildlife conservation and the environment."[16]

Sustainable tourism "participates in the management of all resources that fulfills economic, social, and aesthetic needs while it maintains cultural integrity and biological diversity, and environmental quality", according to the United States Agency for International Development (USAID).[17] The answer is that sustainable should be in the meantime responsible.

Consequently, CSR (Corporate Social Responsibility) in tourism can make a significant contribution towards sustainability because:

[13]http://responsibletourismpartnership.org/cape-town-declaration-on-responsible-tourism/

[14]http://www.responsibletravel.com/holidays/responsible-tourism/travel-guide

[15]http://www.sustainabletourism.net

[16]http://www.responsibletravel.com/

[17]http://rmportal.net/library/collections/gsta/global-tourism-achieving-sustainable-goals/view

- CSR is a new and challenging concept, considered to be an appropriate tool for enhanced competitiveness, but also as a means of improving community responsibility and availability.
- Following the definition of the European Commission, CSR in tourism can be defined as a guiding business policy whereby tourism companies "integrate social and environmental concerns in their own business mission, strategies and operations and in their interaction with their stakeholders on a voluntary basis."
- CSR in tourism initiatives is an attempt to address the great environmental, social and ethical challenges for the anti-corruption movement and efforts.
- Tourism is an industry strongly linked with global issues which require responsibility

In this respect, there are several challenges for coastal marine tourism to be taken into consideration:

- Environment and Natural Resource Security;
- Climate changes;
- Sea and Coastal Landscapes;
- Land-sea interactions;
- Impact of land infrastructure on maritime space;
- Preservation of anthropogenic resources;
- Valorization of cultural heritage of the region.

Like many other activities taking place in the marine environment, tourism also has an onshore implication and is highly related to the economic impacts of MSP for the development of a region. Karman Vela, the European Commissioner for the Environment, Maritime Affairs and Fisheries, during the opening of the Maritime Spatial Planning and Tourism conference in Venice, 2014, declared:

> Sustainable maritime tourism can inject much needed impetus into the economy of Europe's coastal regions but is dependent on a healthy environment and proper management to do so.

## 4 Coastal and Maritime Tourism and MSP

Coastal and maritime tourism represent one of the largest segments of the maritime economic sectors, as well as the largest component of the tourism industry with environmental impacts and compatibilities with other human activities. As tourism is dependent on both natural and human assets for the promotion of the tourism product, the environment, people, and global partnerships for development are imperative to achieve and maintain a healthy industry.

Maritime Spatial Planning could be considered the key point towards a responsible and sustainable maritime tourism. Acknowledging the economic potential of sustainable coastal and maritime tourism in May 2012 the European Commission launched a public consultation on the challenges and opportunities for maritime and coastal tourism in Europe. As a Blue Growth sector, coastal and maritime tourism has been identified as an area with special potential to foster smart, sustainable and inclusive Europe. The public consultation demonstrates a broad endorsement and support from European stakeholders towards an EU strategy for this touristic sub-sector. Taking into consideration the importance for tourism, MSP is considered to be an appropriate procedure in tackling developmental and management issues related to the maritime areas, including issues related to coastal and maritime tourism. Since 2013, the report of the High-Level Panel of Eminent Persons on the Post-2015 Development Agenda emphasized that, without environmental sustainability, poverty cannot be ended and that the oceans and seas should not be forgotten in the development of a post-2015 development agenda.

## *4.1 Scenarios for Sustainable and Responsible Growth*

Coastal and maritime tourism is one of five focus areas for delivering sustainable growth and jobs in the blue economy (by employment rate and GVA). The European Commission's 'Blue Growth Strategy 3' aims at creating sustainable growth and employment in the marine and maritime economy to help Europe's economic recovery (Final report, Call for tenders No MARE/2010/01, August 2012). The year 2017 could be considered a start towards a more responsible tourism growth and jobs in the blue economy. The 2014–2020 EU research program changed the way that marine and maritime research was done. A total of 800 million euros were allocated to marine/maritime research and innovation projects in the period 2014–2016. The approach was adapted to the specific issues in each sector. For maritime tourism, the challenge was to support regional cooperation in order to create joint products such as nautical or cultural routes and create higher-value jobs without harming the marine environment. In Fig. 1 is shown that coastal tourism sector is by far the largest employer in the blue economy as can be seen in the figure below, where indirect employment includes those companies providing goods and services to the primary sectors.

Baring in mind the ocean research and the potential of coastal tourism, the main goals of the European Commission's current strategy for coastal and marine tourism are:

- Reducing uncertainty and increasing the number of high value jobs;
- Reducing tourism's environmental footprint;
- Adding value to activities with a particular maritime-angle, such as: nautical tourism, cruise shipping or underwater cultural heritage—shipwrecks or settlements.

In the meantime, 'Blue Growth' requires a number of framework-related conditions to be fulfilled. Those require: clarity in maritime spatial planning and spatial development initiatives, adequate infrastructure (including transport), highly-skilled staff with access to low skilled workers, public acceptance, a solid international legal framework regarding the international waters, good governance at local and regional

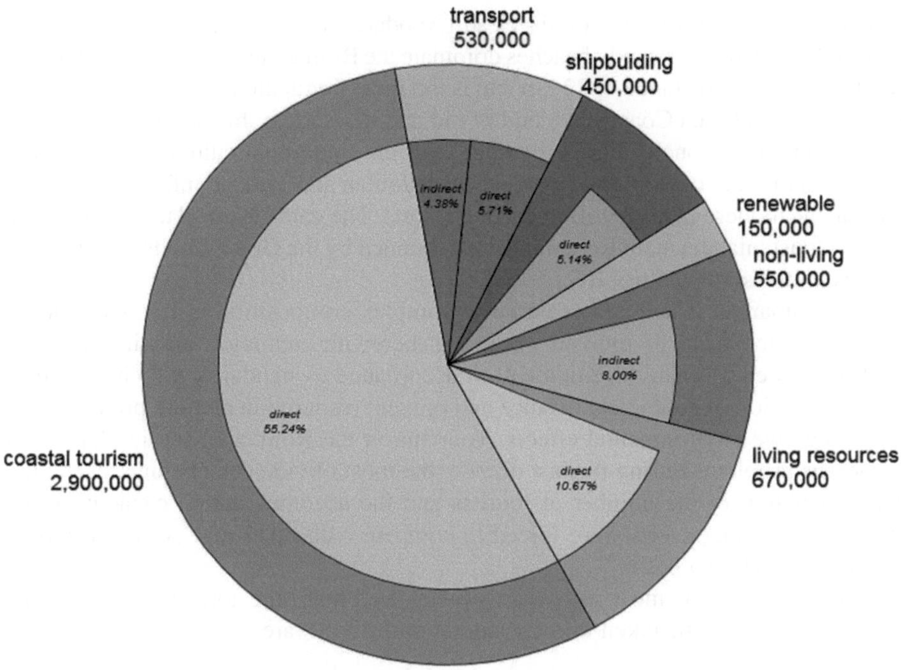


**Fig. 1** Today's trends in the blue economy: employment in blue economy. Source: https://ec.europa.eu/maritimeaffairs/sites/maritimeaffairs/files/swd-2017-128_en.pdf

levels, recognition that choices will need to be made in contexts where space is limited and the combination of all activities is not feasible.[18]

# 5 CSR Approach in the Local Tourism Industry at the Romanian Black Sea Coast

## *5.1 General Presentation of the Romanian Black Sea Coast Tourism's Issues*

The Romanian seaside is among the most spectacular regions of Romania, offering a stunning scenery. With a total length of 245 km, the Romanian seaside stretches from the north, from the border with Ukraine, to the south, to the border with Bulgaria, defining East Dobrogea by the Black Sea. More than half of its stretch (163 km), from the northern-end to Avodart, the Romanian seaside is dominated by the Danube Delta

[18]https://webgate.ec.europa.eu/maritimeforum/sites/maritimeforum/files/Blue%20Growth%20Final%20Report%2013092012.pdf

and coastal lakes. From the Media Head (Avodart) area to Vamp Vice (the border with Bulgaria), the fine sandy beaches dominate the Romanian seaside. This stretch of seashore covers a distance of 82 km and is the most frequented area for tourists. The Romanian Black Sea Coast is a blend of old and new. Many historical sites, ancient monuments, traditional villages together with the traditional culture of the region, which is a mixture of Romanian, Greek, Macedonian and Turkish influences, coexist with all the modern facilities offered in the resorts. The gateway to all the resorts is the city of Constanta, the main Romanian port, founded by the Greeks, under the name of Tomes, in the sixth century BC.

The Romanian Black Sea coast has a complex composition in terms of natural resources, increasing its tourism-value and therewith creating a pressing need for well-monitored tourism development; in accordance to standards, which guarantee the preservation of ecological balance and prevent resource-depletion, pollution and other negative environmental effects. Tourism on the Romanian seaside has faced numerous problems during the last decade, the most obvious one being seasonality. The fluctuation of the number of tourists and the accommodation capacity of the Romanian seaside resorts were forced to compete with other new seaside offers in the entire Black Sea basin.

Summarizing, the most important coastal and maritime tourism issues at the Black Sea Coast to be taken into consideration by MSP are:

- the balance between tourism demand and the environmental carrying capacity
- excessive pressure on the region due to tourism activity and housing along the coast
- mass tourism, concentrated in a belt of resorts along the coast, with a peak season limited to 4–5 months
- cumulative impact on the marine environment by the changes of natural landscape (infrastructure construction, land-filling, destruction of vegetation).
- Seasonality of tourism, with relevant implications for environmental management (waste of resources)
- increased local population during the summer with implications for the environment.
- Over-tourism on the well-preserved natural sites.
- Social impacts of tourism: social-cultural activities, aggressive commerce, noise pollution.

## 5.2 CSR Approach in the Local Tourism Industry

There are certain important reasons for an implementation framework for a CSR approach in the local tourism industry at the Romanian Black Sea Coast:

- accordance with the MSP principles;
- meet the demands of the coastal area responsible tourism;
- building the know-how to develop and implement a corporate social responsibility strategy and commitments;
- enhance tourism companies' responsibility;

- integrate social and ecological objectives into the company's core business activities;
- take into account the interests of various stakeholders, etc.

Starting from these issues, the MARSPLAN-BS Project meets the needs of the stakeholders: customers, employees, owners or shareholders, hoteliers, suppliers in the destinations, local communities, etc. Stakeholder-consultation is a necessary objective in order priorities problems, to identify land-sea interaction, and to minimize conflicts related to use. The purpose is to make professionals, institutions and travellers aware of what is at stake and to underline the necessity of changing behaviors and adjusting regulations for the sake of responsible tourism goals.

One of the previous actions in the MARSPLAN-BS Project was the 'stakeholders meeting', that took place in November 2016 in the Emory resort, in order to meet the demands of the coastal area responsible tourism and to identify the local MSP issues and needs. The purpose of this work-meeting was to bring together the scientific community, authorities and stakeholders, representatives of local communities and the civil society, in order to work together towards identifying common threats and corresponding solutions for territorial development and coastal protection. The key steps for developing a local CSR implementation framework are:

- Meetings with stakeholders, representatives of the tourism industry, owners, in particular hotel and restaurant managers
- Focus groups with representatives of hotels at seaside resorts (two of each resort)
- CSR reporting model for local tourism operators
- Guidelines for travellers
- Guidelines for tourism organizations

Those proposed actions aim at enhancing the accessibility and visibility of responsible tourism offers and at promoting sustainability by reducing the environmental impact of tourism activities, in order to involve coastal and maritime tourism issues into existing MSP's programs and policies. Consequently, a recommended measure could be the implementation of a local, tourism-focused CSR framework, in accordance with the MSP principles, containing information on how to develop and implement a CSR strategy and associated commitments, in order to meet the demands of the coastal area responsible tourism. The main steps in this approach can be the following: decide and plan, workshops & communication, data review, data assessment, developing strategies, developing a program for improvement, CSR report and external audit at the end.[19] The content of a CSR-reporting model should contain information and specific indicators on: company profile, sustainability within the company, responsibility for customers, environment, employees, social responsibility, product responsibility in the supply chain, transport, program for improvement.[20]

[19]https://earthresponsible.files. wordpress.com/2013/03/csr-leitfaden_eng_ger-kate.pdf

[20]https://earthresponsible.files.wordpress.com/2013/03/csr-leitfaden_eng_ger-kate.pdf

Another type of instrument useful in the CSR implementation process is a set of guidelines, for both tourists and hotels. In this respect, guidelines for a 'responsible tourist' should comprise advice on how to:

- conserve resources and avoid waste (water, electricity, etc.),
- demonstrate responsible behavior and act as an example for others, be sensitive to the local culture,
- use local transportation, guides, inns, restaurants and markets,
- remember that they are visitors with different concepts,
- encourage practices to conserve the environment,
- comply with international environmental conventions,
- inform themselves about the environmental guidelines set up to limit and maximize the positive impact of tourism on the local environment and culture,
- continue with your commitment to conservation at home.

Guidelines for hotels, beside environmental aspects, should also address economic and social requirements like:

- suggestions of measures for reducing water consumption at the destination,
- relevant suggestions to reduce damage to the environment, wildlife and marine ecosystems,
- suggestions of ways to minimize negative impacts on local cultures
- suggestions for excursions/visits to local social projects,
- active demonstration that the company is actively seeking to employ locals
- communication of how (and why) the company is encouraging local sourcing of food, drinks, soft furnishing, guiding etc. and requiring suppliers to sign up to this commitment

Procedures should be in place to respond to all these requirements.

## 6 Conclusions

The role of MSP in organizing and planning coastal and marine tourism activities is crucial because it can assure: spatial regulation, good environmental conditions for the tourism sector, quality of landscapes and other important resources for tourism, adaptation to climate change effects, proper allocation of human resources in the coastal zone. Seasonality and sustainability threats (pressure on natural resources and habitats) could be considered the main challenges ahead for maritime and coastal tourism at the Black Sea Coast (for MSP).

Responsible tourism ought to be a 'must' for coastal and marine tourism. A responsible policy that sets achievable and realistic targets will enable tourism companies to continually reduce the negative impacts and increase the positive effects of operational practices on the economic, social and physical environment. In developing an effective Responsible-Policy it is recommended to consult as many relevant stakeholders as possible (own staff, local communities, suppliers, experts in the relevant areas, competitors, NGO's, etc.). It is very important to inform about, and demonstrate commitment towards, economic, social and environmental best practices to one's own staff, suppliers and travellers. It is also important to monitor and record the levels of operational impacts, adherence to guidelines for travellers and operators.

**Acknowledgement** This work has been supported by the European Commission through the European Maritime and Fisheries Fund, grand No. EASME/EMFF/2014/1.2.1.5/2/SI2.707672 MSP LOT 1 /BLACK SEA/MARSPLAN-BS.

## References

Blue Growth Scenarios and drivers for Sustainable Growth from the Oceans, Seas and Coasts Final Report. (Final report, Call for tenders No MARE/2010/01, August 2012). Retrieved from https://webgate.ec.europa.eu/maritimeforum/sites/maritimeforum/files/Blue%20Growth%20Final%20Report%2013092012.pdf

Cape Town Declaration on Responsible Tourism. Retrieved from http://responsibletourismpartnership.org/cape-town-declaration-on-responsible-tourism/

Guidelines CSR-Reporting in Tourism 8 Steps To Sustainability Reporting. Retrieved from https://earthresponsible.files.wordpress.com/2013/03/csr-leitfaden_eng_ger-kate.pdf

Hamid, A. (2010). *CSR in tourism industry*. Retrieved from https://www.slideshare.net/mahamid_biz/csr-in-tourism

Nichersu, I., Nichersu, I., Nanu, C. N., & Bozagievici, R. (2016). Aspects of mass coastal tourism in the Black Sea Romanian coast. *Scientific Annals of the Danube Delta Institute, 22*, 91–100. Retrieved from http://ddniscientificannals.ddni.ro/images//22_11.pdf

Tuan, L. T. (2011). Corporate social responsibility and sustainable tourism. *Business and Economic Research, 1*(1), E4. Retrieved from http://macrothink.org/journal/index.php/ber/article/viewFile/890/1603. ISSN 2162-4860.

Zubritckaia, O. (2015). *Sustainable tourism and coastal management in Mediterranean countries*. Bachelor's Thesis Degree Programme in Sustainable Coastal Management Raseborg 2015. Retrieved from https://theseus.fi/bitstream/handle/10024/93803/Zubritckaia_Olga.pdf?sequence=1

MIX
Papier aus verantwortungsvollen Quellen
Paper from responsible sources
FSC® C105338

If you have any concerns about our products,
you can contact us on
**ProductSafety@springernature.com**

In case Publisher is established outside the EU,
the EU authorized representative is:
**Springer Nature Customer Service Center GmbH**
**Europaplatz 3, 69115 Heidelberg, Germany**

Printed by Libri Plureos GmbH
in Hamburg, Germany